Lordy!

Tutankhamun's Patron As A Young Man

Copyright 2012
William Cross, FSA Scot and Dr Alfred Jones Ph.D(Introduction)

Lordy! Tutankhamun's Patron As A Young Man was first published on
1 September 2012.

Published in the UK only by William P. Cross.
In conjunction with Book Midden Publishing

All rights reserved. Apart from any use permitted under UK copyright law, this publication may not be reproduced, stored, or transmitted, in any form, or by any means without prior permission in writing of the publisher or in the case of reprographic production, in accordance with the terms of the licences issued by the Copyright Licensing Agency.

Every effort has been made to trace and contact the copyright holders of all materials in this book. The authors and publisher will be glad to rectify any omissions at the earliest opportunity.

ISBN 10 1-905914- 05-9
ISBN 13 978-1-905914-05-0

Published by
William P. Cross
Book Midden Publishing
58 Sutton Road
Newport
Gwent
NP19 7JF
United Kingdom

Lady Anne Chesterfield & daughter Evelyn
Lordy's grandmother and mother

Lordy!
Tutankhamun's Patron As A Young Man

William Cross, FSA Scot

With an Introduction by Alfred Jones, Ph.D

INTRODUCTION

A PSYCHOLOGIST TAKES A LOOK AT LORD CARNARVON AND HOWARD CARTER

It will soon be 90 years since the historic discovery of the tomb of Pharaoh Tut-Ankh-Amun. This might be a good time to put to rest some of the bad press and innuendos regarding both Carnarvon and Carter. We fail to realize the enormous impact that this discovery had worldwide. It set in motion a universal interest in both ancient history as well as Egyptology in general. It reinforced the need for scientific methods in location, on site study, removal and ultimate public display. In this instance, Carter made never before contributions to these aspects of Egyptian exploration.

The Bard tells us that "nothing is either good or bad, but thinking makes it so" How the public thinks is often complicated and often has little or nothing to do with the truth of the matter, but what the psychological needs of the public demand. More often than not, we tend to project our own sins on others to divert the focus of our own conscience thus diminishing our feelings of guilt.

The price that we must pay for fame and fortune is "total disclosure." The public demands to know everything about us and the liberty of making up bits and pieces of real or imagined titillation.

Holy Scripture relates, "though your sins are scarlet, they can become white as snow". The public often turns this around to say 'if you are so lily white, there must be something about you that is nefarious.

Taylor, in his book SEX IN HISTORY postulates that our sexual attitudes and orientations are based on our direction of worship. When the sun is the primary deity, then our sexual mores are ridged, authoritarian and often harsh. When we worship the moon, we are far more sexually permissive the point being that we cannot make up our mind regarding our opinion of sexual activity. If any person appears on the scene, we want to know more about their sexual behaviour than their accomplishments.

In Polynesia, there have always been very liberal attitudes regarding sex. There is no marriage as seen in other parts of the world. Youth copulates freely, either heterosexual or homosexual. In this part of the world there is no murder, suicide or anti-social behaviour.

The animal kingdom can't make up its mind either. Many species are bisexual. And so it goes. In this instance, we are asking our readers to view the lives and accomplishments of Lord Carnarvon and Mr. Howard Carter based on their extraordinary contribution to history, archaeology and science. This does not mean that we must close our eyes to some of their alleged activity both anti-social as well as foolish, but to de-emphasize it as we view both men and their respective accomplishments.

Today, psychology with its many years of research and observations, can answer questions that here to fore have been no more than folklore without any scientific basis. There are now valid answers regarding human behaviour warts and all. We are now taught to understand cause and effect without the need to be rejecting, critical or superimposing our own often ill founded personal beliefs. Even now there are those who seek a university education not so much to acquire knowledge, but learn how to rearrange their prejudices.

We have two gentlemen who had backgrounds, which were poles apart, but psychological needs and areas of interest, which were virtually identical. These needs and interests brought them very close together to form one of the most important teams in modern history.

Both men were avid adventurers. Both had a boundless curiosity about life and came to apprehend it with a wonder tempered with awe and excitement. Both were prepared to invest their sum and substance. They were brought together because of their needs and interests in this regard easily transcending social boundaries of the time. Prior to the formation of this team, Carter spent many years with virtually no gain. He had a dedication, a drive and the ability to work tirelessly. "This doesn't matter," says various groups," what we really want to know is whether or not they were queer." See Epilogue to this book.

I gained extremely valuable information regarding both gentlemen in my acquaintanceship with Lady Carnarvon in the 1950s whilst a psychology student in the University of Bristol.

She was ill-treated by his lordship, while at the same time she related many positive behaviours and traits. Howard Carter was her friend who, many times provided her with much needed assistance. Although I personally never knew Lord Carnarvon or Howard Carter, I came to know them through her Ladyship. Utilizing my newly acquired knowledge of psychology, particularly child development, I was able to see a much clearer picture of these men.

There are many reports of the failings of both men and few features of their personal life are exempt from prying eyes. We as a public are seldom concerned with the truth of gossip, but to be carried away with the thought of certain things that they were supposed to have done.

Since the beginning of human history there have been many who have made profound positive contributions who were at the same time accused of all sorts of things. This is the nature of the human mindset. There have been those whose life had absolutely no redeeming features and justified any universal condemnation. This is very far from the truth in this instant.

Without Carnarvon money there would have been no tomb discovery in 1922. Without his support at every juncture, there could have been no strong encouragement and assistance given to Carter. These men developed a keen friendship, an entity seldom found in any day or generation. This was a team effort. Certainly Carnarvon could have accomplished very little on his own. Without Carnarvon's money and support, Carter could not have succeeded Without Carter's determination and his ability to pursue his dreams, nothing would have been discovered.

We need to remember that after the death of Carnarvon, Carter had years of work ahead of him. He had to supervise the removal, the cataloguing, and the safekeeping of all items while at the same time is available to the press and dignitaries worldwide. He was forced to do battle with the power structure of the Egyptian government. Few people could have stood up to this type of continued stress. Ultimately, he learned that there would be absolutely no personal compensation of any kind.

For many years, he served as a world ambassador for the tomb discovery. He travelled to America, he wrote and lectured. He could not take criticism and often behaved badly. One might ask, "Who wouldn't?" Carter was a unique and unusual person and would have gone to his grave as a "no body" if it were not have been his good fortune to meet Lord Carnarvon and make one of the most important discoveries of all times. He did meet Carnarvon and his diligence and determination did result in the tomb discovery. What may or may not have happened between these two men is apropos of nothing .We know that they were straight forward with each other. They were loyal to each other and as a team were worth far more than they might have been worth as individuals.

As we celebrate this anniversary, may we put both of them in the proper perspective, which they deserve?

Alfred Jones, Ph.D
Texas, USA.

Alfred Jones has a Ph.D in psychology, advance studies in law and education. He is an Egyptian scholar having taught in the UK, USA and China. He is also a former consultant to the San Jose California Egyptian Museum. Author of seven books and over twenty articles for professional journals., Mr. Jones delivered speeches to such groups as the World Health Organization, the British Psychological Society, the American Psychological Association, the State of Washington Psychological Association and the State of Texas Psychological Association

Foreword

George Edward Stanhope Molyneux Herbert, the 5th Earl of Carnarvon and husband to the Rothschild heiress, Almina Wombwell[1], was a multi-faceted character. Yachtsman, motoring pioneer, race-goer, horseracing stud establisher, crack shot, big game hunter – his interests were indulgent. Yet all these activities are dwarfed by Carnarvon's finest hour: his unearthing, with archaeologist friend Howard Carter, of the ancient tomb of a boy king in Egypt; a discovery that captured imaginations worldwide.

Tutankhamun's tomb would have remained lost were it not for Lord Carnarvon, the project's patron. "Lordy"[2], as he was named by the natives of the desert who were employed to dig and shift colossal sand dunes and debris, eagerly spent his wife's money on several years of excavations in the Valley of the Kings, led by Carter. How excited he was, then, following the events of 4 November 1922 when the army of diggers uncovered a stone staircase leading down to a lost treasure. The rest is a well-known fable, with Carnarvon dying soon after the opening of the tomb – the victim of an ancient curse, according to many.

Ninety years later, the list of books about Carnarvon and Carter's daring enterprise is long. Lord Carnarvon's sidekick, Howard Carter, is explored in two good biographies[3] and another book includes the period of Carter's life "before Tutankhamun"[4]; but there is no similar treatment for his Lordship. A quaint biographical sketch survives, written after his death in 1923 by his sister, Lady Winifred Burghclere.[5] That work, although elegantly drafted, contains no depth and indeed it deceives the reader, since it portrays Lordy as a saintly figure.

In *The Life and Secrets of Almina Carnarvon*[6], my biography of Carnarvon's widow, I offer a view of the Earl that straddles his birth, marriage and death. I challenge several issues, including the paternity of Almina's son, Henry, later the 6th Earl; and I point out some of his Lordship's darker proclivities besides his love of Egyptian artefacts.

Now, in this retrospective on the 5th Earl, I offer a portrait of his very early days within a family saga, based on a critical review of the content of Lady Winifred's biographical sketch of 1923 alongside the more detailed truths within the diaries and correspondence of the 4th Earl, Lordy's father.[7] Here, I present Lord Carnarvon in a fresh light, one that has hitherto been buried as deep as the entrance to Tutankhamun's tomb. Indeed, Lordy's father and stepmother, Elsie Howard, butchered parts of the diaries, removing scores of pages, and Elsie arranged the publication of a watered-down biography of her husband, so keen were they to bury family secrets.[8] (Such suppression of key facts was repeated in recent years by the Herbert family in their whitewashing of Almina's life.[9]) Thankfully plenty of evidence about Lordy was not erased, and it is through detailed research that I am able to present this account of his early life.

The Epilogue to the book provides an opportunity to confront aspects of Lordy's personal life and relationships. It also aims to correct certain aspects of the historical record in relation to George, Fifth Earl of Carnarvon. This includes previously unpublished disclosures relating to the Earl's exact state of health towards the end of his life.

William Cross, FSA Scot

Chapter One

The lost boy

Lordy cowered in his cubbyhole, as scared as a hunted rabbit. The den was one of several hideaways in the grounds that he would retreat to alone. But the search party of unrelenting hunters, drawn from the estate tenants at Eggesford House[10], were hell-bent on finding him before the evening's darkness fell on this dismal January day. The closeness of the trackers made him shiver: these roughnecks were capable of giving a fellow a clout. He was unnerved further on hearing mention of them bringing out his uncle's fiendish pack of foxhounds to help in the search.

As the pursuers approached the spot where he'd dug in, Lordy heard the cheeky blighters refer to him as "the brat" and call out his family's pet name: "Porchey" (less of a mouthful than his baptised name: George Edward Stanhope Molyneux Herbert). Then the mob bellowed, at least more reverentially, his formal rank of "Your Lordship" and "M'Lord". The boy was indeed an English lord, the son of an Earl, with the courtesy title Viscount Porchester. He was the heir to the Herbert family name, titles and estates, notably Highclere Castle[11] in Hampshire.

Despite suffering from the cold and damp, Lordy was determined to stay hidden. On that freezing day in 1879, the scrawny twelve-year-old was contemplating a fearful act for one so young: suicide through exposure.

He could not give himself up; that would be weak-willed. Even as a fierce snowstorm blew through the Devonshire countryside, he proved his mettle in refusing to obey instructions to come inside.[12] Instead, he stayed outdoors nursing "a maudlin mood", a phrase often applied to his state of mind by Lady Winifred, his "clever-clogs sister"[13] who was aged fourteen.[14]

The grounds in which the Carnarvon heir had sought refuge were adjoining his aunt and uncle's country estate of Eggesford House in England's "Happy Valley"[15], this being a description given to the area around the large "multi-chimney-stacked edifice of Eggesford House, among its surrounding hills, covered with wood... [once deemed a legendry place in which fittingly] to meditate, the world forgetting".[16] Lordy was staying at Eggesford under the care of his aunt, Lady Eveline Wallop, the 5th Countess of Portsmouth and his father's younger sister.[17] Since the death of their mother, Lady Eveyln Stanhope, Eggesford had "become a second home"[18] to Lordy and his three sisters, Ladies Winifred, Margaret and Victoria Herbert.[19]

Lady Eveline Wallop "was a strenuous advocate of open air"[20] and had attempted to convert Lordy from a "white-faced child... into a hardy young sportsman".[21] So when Lordy was eventually found by one of the estate's hard-nosed servants, a wet, shivering mass amid the snowdrifts[22], she was vehement in her condemnation of the boy's stupidity. For Lordy was "a delicate little fellow"[23], "never robust"[24], who had been cautioned to avoid chills and draughts and getting soaked to the skin. He had frail lungs, a congenital Herbert-Stanhope affliction, scarred from an abominable birth and exacerbated by a life-threatening illness as a young child.

With Lady Eveline at the helm death was not an option and Lordy was nursed back from the brink. This was a lady who had brought twelve of her own children into the world and had seen them thorough the ravages of childhood plagues and tantrums; and was an accomplished nurse and attendant to her own three brothers and a fragile sister, Lady Gwendolen Herbert, who, like Lordy, was a slight, sensitive and stubborn soul.[25]

And so Lordy's plot was thwarted. But what had driven a young boy to such an extreme act?

First, there was school to consider. Following the New Year holidays, Lordy was due to return to his preparatory school. Life in the milder climes of the south coast at Brighton, Sussex, was considered better for his chest, for he had diseased lungs. But being a boarder was ghastly because he was frequently ill and homesick. Besides which, he was not a scholar – he did not possess any natural gift for learning – and next term his uncompromising papa would expect him to go up a remove.[26] There was talk of him going to Eton College, following the Herbert family's long tradition for the Carnarvon heir that included his father and grandfather, a prospect that daunted him.

But if school was a nightmare, it was home that had driven Lordy to the brink. The reason for the latest rush of wretchedness was of the matrimonial kind. His absent parent, Henry Herbert, had taken a new wife: in fact he was on his honeymoon, at Pixton Park, Dulverton, another family residence in the West Country of England.[27]

Henry Herbert, the 4th Lord Carnarvon, was a man of substance, a noble lord, a peer of the realm and an established Tory politician who'd served in the Cabinets of two of Queen Victoria's prime ministers.[28] Now, after barely four years as a grieving widower, Henry had taken a new wife: Miss Howard of Greystoke Castle, Cumbria had been transformed overnight into Elizabeth, 4th Countess of Carnarvon of Highclere Castle, Hampshire.

Now, Lordy must contend with a stepmother whom he did not like. She was in fact closer to Lordy in age than his father – at twenty-two years to the 4th Earl's forty-seven. And they were all uncomfortably close blood relations, as the bride and groom were first cousins.[29] But worst of all, she was not his mother – his lost mother whom he ached for.

Chapter Two

A loss too much to bear

It was on Saturday 30 January 1875 that Lordy's happy, innocent childhood ended.

It had been raining constantly throughout the morning's comings and goings, and a harsh winter wind blew the Union flag floating at half-mast on the tall tower of Highclere Castle. This imposing Carnarvon home, five miles south of the town of Newbury, Berkshire, had been built from a design (for Lordy's grandfather, the 3rd Earl) by Sir Charles Barry, the architect who later went on to create the Houses of Parliament. But today its grandeur was marred by closed blinds at every window and an air of mourning. For the lady of the house, Evelyn Georgina Katherine Stanhope, 4th Countess of Carnarvon and the only daughter of the 6th Earl and Countess of Chesterfield of Bretby Park, Derbyshire,[30] was dead, and today she would be laid to rest.

Evelyn's lingering final illness had played out over several weeks, resulted ultimately in her passing on five days before. The cause was puerperal fever that had set in after the birth of her fourth surviving child, a daughter, Victoria, on 31 December 1874.[31]

Now, the dead Countess's gleaming silver coronet lay on top of the coffin lid together with a number of wreaths and crosses made of white winter flowers. Gazing at her coffin, Lady Evelyn's only son, eight-year-old Lordy, was told to keep his head up, to act with dignity and to show that he possessed a manly backbone in the face of such great tragedy. But for the sensitive, lonely child, the loss was too much to bear. He simply could not conceive that his beautiful, adorable mother had left him. Tears streamed down his cheeks and his slight frame was wracked with sobs. He stood, transfixed by the sight of the heavy leaden shell that contained his mother's remains. He imagined himself a stag being gunned down. He felt himself fall, stunned and lifeless. Then he saw himself inanimate, standing upright like one of the stone pillars in the castle foyer.

The warmth of his eleven-year-old sister clutching his frozen hand stirred Lordy back to harsh reality. Lordy soon realised he was not alone; his family were equally heartbroken. Winifred was braver than Lordy could ever be. At her direction, he pulled himself up and stood tall alongside her and their other sister, Margaret, aged four. All eyes rested upon the small, scared children; all except their father's, who was unable to speak to them, consumed as he was by an aching guilt and dread, imagining the pain to follow for himself and his children without his wife, their mother. He was in shock, standing silent and lonely like one of the marble statues in the castle grounds. It was at Winifred's command that Evelyn and Henry's three oldest children became a united consolation for each other and closed in to join their distraught father. At least their sister, Victoria (Baby), who was only a few weeks old, was spared the ordeal. They would tell her about their pretty, loving mother who shone with such grace and dignity, if their father allowed them to say anything in the years ahead.

As one, the family gazed at what was left of their beloved – this most precious daughter, sister, wife and most of all, parent. She had being lying in state within the library at Highclere for two days. Eight wax candles burning brightly on pedestals covered in black cloth surrounded the catafalque, arranged on each side of the coffin. Around the walls candelabra threw out a dim light. The gleaming brass plate bearing Lady Evelyn's name, birth date and date of passing brought further distress; for at just forty-one, that final date was painful to behold.

The suffering widower Earl, Henry Howard Molyneux Herbert, had given instructions for the body of his wife of fourteen years to lie in state until midday. The funeral to Highclere Churchyard was due to take place at half past one. The proceedings were to be kept simple. Evelyn, who it was said "was wholly averse from anything like ostentation"[32], had wished that all pomp and show be avoided. The Countess had chosen the spot for her grave at the northwest corner of the chapel precincts of Highclere Cemetery. She wished to be laid in the open cemetery (rather than inside a church tomb), beside the graves of those who had been devoted and faithful in the service of the Highclere family.[33]

The rain did not deter family and friends, who arrived to pay their last respects to a gifted and remarkable woman. Finally, the sun emerged, but even this improvement and the natural beauty of the location could do nothing to lift the mood. No sign of life was visible within the grounds, save when from time to time another carriage halted before the doorway of the house over which the Herbert griffin (holding a bloody hand in its mouth) grinned in stone.

It was a walking funeral. The Earl had not issued a formal invitation to his tenants and tradesmen to attend, but a long line of worthy gentlemen congregated on the lawn in front of Highclere to pay their respects to the 4th Countess of Carnarvon. The funeral knell tolled at Highclere and church bells pealed in the adjoining town of Newbury, Berkshire, as well as in neighbouring parishes.

> At about a quarter to two the coffin was borne from the library, and the procession slowly wound its weary way from the castle down the hill to the little local cemetery. As the procession moved onwards, every sign of respect was shown by the groups of bystanders, whose moistened eyes and sad countenances bore evidence of the grief which filled their hearts... many beyond the [family] circle who by Lady Carnarvon's death had lost a near and dear friend.[34]

In the midst of the mourning, a most touching scene was observed. The Earl of Carnarvon was handed a wreath of white camellias, sent by Lady Evelyn's widowed mother, Lady Anne, the Dowager Countess of Chesterfield. Lady Anne had been at her daughter's bedside throughout the last weeks but, overcome with sorrow, had retreated to her home of Bretby Park in Derbyshire. Her thoughts were subsumed by the knowledge that *both* her children had perished before her own life was over.[35] One commentator remarked that the flowers from Lady Anne were "for the coffin of the last of her beloved children... [The Earl tenderly] kissed the pure white flowers, and gently placed them upon the coffin."[36] Others flowers from relatives and friends who held Evelyn in loving remembrance were then placed on the coffin. Despite being pressed earlier to demonstrate to others that his courage was resolute, Lordy was unable to hold back streaming tears and bouts of sobbing as he witnessed his mother's passing into the grave.

In the aftermath of her death, tributes flooded in. Among them were many personal anecdotes about the Countess of Carnarvon's acts of kindness, for she genuinely gave to one and all, to her family and friends and to her tenants and their families living near and far.

Newspapers captured the essence of the woman, as in this tribute that appeared in the *Daily Telegraph* the day after her death:

> [Lady Evelyn was] a devoted wife, a tender mother, a careful and an indulgent mistress to the Carnarvon's various households, indeed she was an example to all. To the poor she was a sympathetic friend. To her friends and acquaintances she was always the kind and graceful hostess...

But who was this great lady who was so grieved? What made Lordy's mother so special that her loss would forever cast a shadow in his heart?

Bretby Park, Seat of the Chesterfield Earls

Eggesford House, Seat of the Portsmouth Earls

Pixton Park, one of the Carnarvon Seats

Chapter Three

Lady Evelyn Stanhope

Evelyn Stanhope was an exceptional pioneer, and a woman admired for her natural gifts and cultivated tastes. In her short life she worked to make an impact, knowing perhaps that she was a doomed aristocrat given her poor genes that made her susceptible to illness. As each new illness hit her harder, she grew more uncertain about whether she would survive beyond early middle age. So she thrust herself into the centre of a large political, social and Court circle, and was among the first of her generation to be a classed as a notable Tory *grande dame* and country house hostess away from the London scene.

If the truth had been confronted, Evelyn was never of a strong enough constitution for marriage. She was far from fit to serve *any* man as a full wife, not least one expected to produce children. If she had wavered on the role she might have lived longer and been happier as a spinster or the wife of an older man, or one of the era's dilettantes who have avoiding consummation of the marriage.[37] That said, in choosing the life of a duty-bound married woman, as many of her generation did, she has left a mark as one of the great Countesses of Carnarvon.

Lady Evelyn Georgina Catherine née Stanhope was the only daughter of George Stanhope, the 6th Earl of Chesterfield, and his wife Anne Forester, who married in 1831. The family of Stanhope drew its name from the town of Stanhope near Durham, although their ancestral home and seat was later at Shelford, Nottinghamshire, and subsequently at Bretby Park, Derbyshire.[38] The peerage of Stanhope was created in 1616, and twelve years later the title was advanced to an Earldom. Philip, the first Earl of Chesterfield, was succeeded in the titles by his grandson Philip Dormer, and the 4th Earl, Philip Dormer Stanhope, was the celebrated Lord Chesterfield, who became well known as a wit and politician and the author of a famous series of letters to his son and godson.[39]

Lady Evelyn was born on 3 November 1834 at the family's palatial townhouse, Chesterfield House[40] in London's Mayfair.[41] Her public life began with a very grand christening for the House of Chesterfield, which took place at Bretby Park in January of 1836. Evelyn's only brother, George[42], heir to the family titles, shared the special service of baptism and blessing. Arthur Wellesley, Duke of Wellington and the hero of Waterloo, stood as one of the godfathers of the two infants of the 6th Earl and Countess of Chesterfield.[43] Also in attendance at this grand social event was Sir Robert Peel, who had been prime minister just the preceding year and would be again a few years later. Whilst many ordinary people in Britain starved under the effects of the passing of the notorious Corn Laws (which controlled the price of bread), unelected, self-centred aristocrats like Wellington and Peel ruled the country. The Chesterfields were a part of this elite, privileged class.

Lordy's mother and his namesake, Uncle George, were cherished, spoilt, socially aloof children who were educated as befit children of the gentry. Her mother was Evelyn's first teacher, but it was her French governess who taught her to speak a number of Continental languages, with French being her favourite. Even as toddlers Evelyn was out and about in Society circles; she and George regularly appeared on the promenade in London's Hyde Park alongside their mother, which was the fashion for prominent Society children.[44] Once she was older, Lady Evelyn learnt the importance of poise and style attending parties and balls chaperoned by her mother at London's best parlours during the "season" – the Capital's social jamboree that ran each year from January through to July.

There were times, however, when life was less glamorous. Lord Chesterfield, Evelyn's father, was often liberal and sometimes rash in his spending, and had a heavy gambling habit. His passions for horse racing and gaming led to him suffering substantial debts. For a time – and this is reflected in some remarks by Evelyn's daughter Winifred years later – economies had to be made which restricted Evelyn's (and her mother's) living standards. Winifred describes part of her mother's childhood as being "isolated"[45], but this blip (which was as much about her fragile health as a shortage of funds) was of short duration. It was Evelyn's mother who found ways of controlling and curbing her husband's excesses, and she took direct charge of some estate matters; a skill for good housekeeping she passed on to her daughter.

Evelyn shared her father's passion for horses, and the Chesterfield stud at Bretby Park was large and well regarded. One visitor to Bretby remarks: "went to Bretby... to see Lord Chesterfield's racing stud, consisting of nineteen brood mares, three first-rate stallions, besides twenty brood mares taken in from strangers to be put to the stallions. The arrangements most princely, and the expense unbounded."[46]

But it was in performance, not horse riding, that Evelyn most excelled. At the age of just ten she was entertaining her parents guests at Bretby. Evelyn's theatrical shows, with their colourful and convincing character portrayals[47], were always one of the highlights for visitors to Bretby Park, who came for the shooting and horse racing. Visitors were encouraged to participate; indeed, one memoir writer from the mid-1840s records: "On my second visit to Bretby I remember we acted De Musset's play, *Le Caprice*. Lady Chesterfield's daughter, Evelyn Stanhope... and Miss Anson... took the girls' parts."[48] By the age of thirteen, Evelyn was already known in wider Society circles for her fine skills as a performer. She acted in French plays with Mademoiselle Rachel, a notable tragedienne of the time.[49] Then, during the festive period and into the New Year of 1851, Evelyn presented her *tour de force* – the performance of various plays over the course of several nights, including one French one and two English comedies. Even the production was professionally handled: Evelyn set up a stage and had scenery built for her specially by a local carpenter that was laid out in the dining rooms at Bretby Hall. The delighted audience demanded encores galore, and one reviewer remarked of a publicly presented piece that Lady Evelyn Stanhope acted "with peculiar grace and artistic force".[50]

Her grace was in evidence in all appearances in Society, not least her most important. All Society ladies had to be presented at Court, and Evelyn was first presented to Queen Victoria by her mother at Her Majesty's drawing room on Thursday 29 April 1852.[51] This was a magical moment for the eighteen-year-old Chesterfield heiress, better than *all* the many French plays she had taken part in put together. Her dress was of "white lace, with three petticoats of tulle, chatelaine of white verbena, a train of rich white lace with a garniture composed of tulle and white verbena and a corsage trimmed with pearls and lappets of blond"[52], and she added feathers and pearls to create a stunning look that made her the talk of the hour.

Lordy's mother, then, was a charismatic creature. She loved life and found, despite her privileged upbringing, a commanding empathy with people, a way of touching folk from all walks of life. She was a celebrated beauty, taking after her mother and aunts. The latter were dubbed "the cynosure of every eye"[53], known as the "beautiful Forester sisters – Lady Chesterfield, Mrs Anson and Lady Bradford"[54]: all of them admired for their looks, intelligence and ability to manage their men folk.[55] Among those tamed by the sisters was Benjamin Disraeli, who was smitten by them: although "Mrs Anson died comparatively young [it was said she took poison by mistake[56]]... the other two sisters reigned as goddesses [in Dizzy's] Olympus so long as he lived".[57] Disraeli and another prime minister, Lord Derby (the 14th Earl), both offered Lady Chesterfield marriage.[58] After his death, she raised a memorial to Disraeli in Bretby Church (in the name of his later title of Lord Beaconsfield) to record "a much-prized friendship and a lasting regret".[59]

Anne Chesterfield's only daughter, Evelyn, was marked out early as being a clever woman, but at her height in Society she was canny, heady and manipulative.[60] And although such qualities of strong, independent womanhood were less demanded or admired by husbands seeking a show wife, these gifts made Evelyn a good candidate for "a short let" to any ambitious, rising politician or nobleman with an estate that required a sharp-witted, assertive businesswoman at the helm. Yet Evelyn's mix of beauty, brain and cunning could also be viewed as off-putting by potential suitors, which explains in part why she languished unclaimed until the age of twenty-seven: any prospective husband had to see through the armour. But another factor was kept silent: Evelyn Stanhope was an incurable consumptive and riddled with a range of crippling health problems.

**Lady Evelyn Stanhope
as a child**

THE EARL OF CHESTERFIELD.

THE COUNTESS OF CHESTERFIELD

Chapter Four

The 3rd Earl of Carnarvon

The Earldom of Carnarvon descended from the family of the Earls of Pembroke and Montgomery, associated today with Wilton House, Salisbury. The second son, Henry (1741–1811), of the Honourable William Herbert, a major-general in the army, fifth son of Thomas, 8th Earl of Pembroke and Montgomery as first created Baron Porchester of Highclere in 1780 and Earl of Carnarvon in 1793.[61] That said, of more recent times, the histories record that the family dates "back to Charlemagne, the great Duke of Brabant, King of France and Emperor of the Romans".[62]

Lordy's father, Henry Howard Molyneux Herbert, later the 4th Earl, was born on 24 June 1831 in London to mother Henrietta[63] and father Henry George Herbert, the 3rd Earl of Carnarvon from 1833. There were two younger brothers, Alan and Auberon, and two sisters, Eveline and Gwendolen.[64] These Herbert uncles and aunts played a significant part in Lordy's life as a young child, especially after the death of his mother.

The Herbert children from the generation that included Henry were reared with a quaint combination of processing by old nurses, wet nurses and new-style (mostly French, but some German) governesses. Their mother was much less of a social butterfly than most rich heiresses. She was most interested in promoting local education at Pixton and Tetton, in Somerset, where the family lived when not at Highclere.

It was commented that with "all the auguries, the fourth Lord Carnarvon ought to have been a very great man... the offspring of the two historic and gifted houses of Herbert and Howard".[65] The 4th Earl's childhood was, by all accounts, a privileged one. Henry was brought up by his mama and papa to believe in God and to show mercy and kindness to God's creatures, including dumb animals.[66] Even many years later, when asked about the wholesale slaughter of thousands of birds on the gentry's estates, in a sport he loved, Henry remarked "whilst I cannot help thinking the excessive preservation of game a mistake... a mere promiscuous slaughter of pheasants is perhaps a little vulgar".[67]

Lordy's grandfather, the 3rd Earl, was something of a dreamer and romantic, a minor poet and dramatist. He was also a seasoned traveller, and Henrietta and the children usually travelled with him, even when the children were very small. Family anecdotes abound of Lordy's father being taken for the winter to Italy when aged just two and a half. Further tales relate to the children being dragged on a succession of mini-grand tours, of being ill and stranded, and of the deaths of a nurse and a governess whilst in several remote corners of the globe.[68]

The 3rd Earl fell seriously ill at the age of thirty-three and was barely aged fifty when he died of "a spinal affliction"[69] at Highclere Castle on 10 December 1849. He was poignantly described by his son, the 4th Earl, thus: "enthusiastic in temper, cultivated in mind, a good linguist, he had but one drawback – indifferent health".[70] On Lordy's paternal side it is of note that several of the Earls of Carnarvon died before reaching old bones. Henry (a favourite family Christian name), the second Earl – "in private life... singularly kind, amiable, gentle and unassuming"[71] – was only sixty when he died in 1833. Poor health also plagued the 4th and 5th Earls of Carnarvon.

The 4th Earl had been to Eton College, where Rev. Edward Coleridge[72] tutored him alongside his second cousin and lifelong friend, Robert G.W. Herbert.[73] Now, with the early death of the 3rd Earl, the 4th Earl was barely eighteen and only just settling in at Oxford University when he inherited all the family titles and properties and collateral responsibilities. Henrietta saw to it that her son was not disadvantaged by his father's early death and assigned help and guidance for his tasks in life to a collection of men of substance who acted as guardian and private tutor.[74]

Henry completed his education at Christ Church, Oxford University (his father's college) in 1852. He had impressed his contemporaries at Oxford by taking the degree of Bachelor of Arts with a first in Greats after just over two years of study. Several of his fellow graduates were his beloved friends for life, many in the world of politics and the diplomatic service.[75] With one such friend, Dudley Ryder, Lord Sandon[76], the 4th Earl took a trip to Syria and the Lebanon, visiting

Babylon and Damascus on his "way towards the more eastern parts of Asia Minor".[77] Such a trip is evidence of the 4th Earl's eagerness to be more than a gentleman of the time who "for the most part of the class... take pride in describing themselves as "Conservatives and Sportsmen"; in other words, "pleasant English gentlemen of the Eton and Oxford type of education, who had never vexed the brain with great efforts of thought".[78] The 4th Earl, like several Carnarvon men, was more than that: he was cultured and travelled wider than the Grand Tour circuit; he had an appreciation for Latin and Greek verse and the treasures of the east; he had a good command of foreign languages like German, French, Italian and Spanish.

The 4th Earl was growing into a handsome match for of woman of Society. Naturally, given his father's early death, the strong, perpetual force in the 4th Earl's life was his mother, and Henrietta acted out a principal role as her son's marital scout. Since Henrietta had herself once been a blooming heiress (to the wealthy Molyneux titles and lands, a patron of churches[79], hospitals[80] and especially of schools), she knew the ropes around London Society's portals, and the family maintained a prominent London mansion in the heart of the capital.[81] The daughter of the Right Honourable Lord Henry Thomas Howard Molyneux Howard (1766–1824), deputy earl marshall of England, and a niece of Bernard Edward, the 12th Duke of Norfolk, she had a commanding knowledge of the great estates of the country. Henrietta socialised little, but amid her well-chosen network of other peeresses she aimed to find herself an exceptional daughter-in-law.

Chapter Five

First Meetings of Lordy's Parents

All gentlemen in Society had to be presented at Court. The 3rd Earl was presented as Lord Porchester by his own father in 1831[82], but the 4th Earl was too young when he inherited the Earldom to have had his father do the honours before his death. Thus, Lordy's father was presented at the first levee of the 1854 season. His formidable statesman cousin, the Right Honourable Sidney Herbert[83], introduced him to Queen Victoria on Wednesday 22 February in St James's Palace.[84] In the same year Henry also took his seat in the House of Lords.

Twenty-two-year-old Henry Herbert's social life at Court began in earnest in March 1854 when he was invited by Queen Victoria to a dinner party at Buckingham Palace. He remedied his lack of wife by taking as companion his quiet, but highly respected, mother.[85] No doubt his mother spent the evening contemplating which special women were in his range and whom he might pursue and, in time, marry.

Evelyn's name and that of Henry, Earl of Carnarvon, appear together in the company assembled for several events from 1854 onwards, but it seems neither of them was very much worried about rushing into marriage. That is not to say each didn't know or notice the other as contemporaries, and as time passed, as being unattached. However, according to Lady Winifred, her parents were formally introduced the two to each other at "one of Lord Stanhope's literary breakfasts".[86]

Another occasion at which Evelyn and Henry crossed paths was the Society even of the 1854 season: when Queen Victoria paid a visit to the mansion of the French Embassy. The attendance sheet reads like a who's who of the Royal Family and the British houses of Lords and Commons. Included in the grand, excessive, lavish entertainment was a costume ball. Lord Carnarvon dressed as "A Nobleman of the time of Charles II. Blue silk velvet jacket and trunks, trimmed with gold. Hat, sword, boots etc."[87] Lady Evelyn:

> appeared as *Ninon de L' Enclos*, in a very handsome tunic of tissue of blue and silver, trimmed with blush roses; body and sleeves

trimmed with very rich Brussels point; skirt of rich blue silk, trimmed all round with silver, and a wreath of roses, and bouquets of blue and pink silver ribbon.[88]

Perhaps they saw each other and nodded with customary courtesy, perhaps they even dancing together – but nothing in the way of romance is recorded at this particular time.

One of the next events at which the Earl and his future Countess met was at Lady Ashburton's ball at the Ball House, Piccadilly, in 1854.[89]

But neither party seemed interested in marriage at this point. It was said that once a girl had "come out" she had about three years to appraise the availability of a husband, whether for love or not, before she was deemed as "passed over". The marriage matter was often decided along business lines, as an arranged union between the families (love was a bonus, not a necessity).[90] But Evelyn's numerous further appearances in the following seasons (with still no sign of engagement or marriage) indicate she was enjoying her public life season upon season without commitment to any one man. And the 4th Earl could be obstinate and pig-headed, and he was not ready to sweep any woman off her feet. He was far more interested in politics.

When the 4th Earl entered the House of Lords, the prime minister was Lord Aberdeen.[91] The Earl's maiden speech was the Address in Answer to the Queen's Speech made when the bloody Crimean War was still in full progress.[92] But the young Carnarvon's speech did not impress one American visiting England:

> I heard the young Earl of Carnarvon, of whom great things were expected, make his maiden speech, and although at its close Lord Derby [14th Earl, soon to be prime minister] complimented him, as in duty bound (he is a Tory), it appeared to me both in manner and in matter an effort that would have been unworthy of an American school-boy of fifteen.[93]

At times Carnarvon was given to flights of fancy, not unlike, decades later, his son, Lordy. One adventures took place after the Crimean War, when Henry went gallivanting off on an extraordinary battlefield tour. On 9 May 1856, in front of 13,000 spectators, "her Majesty and the Prince Consort... went down to the Crystal Palace for the inauguration and unveiling of a monument in honour of the heroes of the Crimea and of the restoration of peace".[94] At the same time, Carnarvon accompanied the commander of the Mediterranean station, Admiral Lyons, on his outward trip to take up duty, to see the scenes from the past war.[95]

During the period 1857–59 a political career of promising dimensions was anticipated for the fourth Lord Carnarvon. In 1858, aged just twenty-seven, he first held the post of under-secretary to the colonies, under Lord Derby's second term as prime minister. Carnarvon shone in the role.[96] He travelled abroad, contributing greatly to the colonial department beyond his brief and acting as proxy to senior civil servants and a lifeline of support to secretaries of state. In 1859, as well as being named high steward of Oxford University, Lord Derby cited Carnarvon as being the calibre of a future party leader.[97] But Henry was not the ideal politician, because he could also be a shy and awkward man (exactly like Lordy), with social skills not nearly as fine-tuned as his ability in the arena of scholarly debate and argument. He was also already a prominent freemason and a leading light in the Church of England.

In May of 1860 the Earl and Evelyn took part in the Countess of Derby's assembly at her mansion in St James's Square, by which time each of them had ceased to shine in Society's regard and their mothers were losing hope of securing a good match.[98] As late as November 1860 Evelyn was still doing the "tour of visits"[99] with her mother as her enduring chaperone. Tongues were wagging that Evelyn was heading for the spinster's shelf. She was among the last unplaced of her debutante year. Perhaps suitors were put off by her chequered health, which cast into doubt her ability to continue the lineage, or dominant personality. Or perhaps Evelyn was just waiting to fall in love, much as the Earl was waiting for the right Countess who would be up to the arduous job of being mistress of Highclere Castle and Pixton Park.

Finally, Anne Stanhope and Henrietta Carnarvon found common ground: their respective offspring urgently needed a spouse, and the time to allow the parties to find a partner of their own choosing had passed. The Earl's mother, Henrietta, had often observed Lady Evelyn Stanhope and her brother, and of course their ubiquitous mama and colourful papa, on the Derbyshire and Nottinghamshire landowning scene. Similarly, Anne Chesterfield knew Henrietta, who had occasionally attended functions at Chesterfield House in London.

Lady Carnarvon's judgement was that Evelyn was not going to be a placid show wife, and she detected something of herself in Evelyn's style. She decided that the young woman's bolder personality would balance her son's awkwardness and shyness. On paper Evelyn was a high risk match given her health – would she produce the required male heir? – but a fair placed investment money wise. And of course money was at the heart of all aristocratic marriages.

The match would have to be orchestrated. The season's balls in London were often matched by grand reception parties on the great estates of England. The Dukedoms of the land, such as Devonshire and Marlborough, and the Marquesses, like Salisbury, opened up their palatial homes and gardens for throngs of guests to visit them at regular intervals. Concerts were a favourite of Evelyn's. She adored attending those held at Hatfield House, the home of the Salisbury (Cecil) family. Henry Herbert was also a constant visitor at Hatfield House, Hertfordshire, although he was more often engaged in political discussions there with the Salisbury men. But Hatfield House is cited as being where Evelyn and Henry first sensed that a touch of romance lay between them. And there was a further matchmaker at work in the process: Lady Salisbury, who years later told the Carnarvons' daughter, Lady Winifred, that she "distinctly recalled the exact spot in the 'Plantation' at Hatfield where [Lord Carnarvon] confided to her that he had fallen in love with Lady Evelyn Stanhope".[100]

The news of a romantic spark between Henry and Evelyn propelled the families into action. The Houses of Carnarvon and Chesterfield, of Herbert and Stanhope, examined portfolios and worked to arrange a marriage settlement behind the scenes. The match would bring considerable additional lands in Derbyshire and Nottinghamshire (including several good coal fields and collieries around Bretby) into the possession of the Carnarvon family beyond what Henrietta had horded from her antecedents. The 4th Earl and Evelyn were barely involved in these business arrangements; such was Society matchmaking in these times.

And it was once again in the gardens at Hatfield House, the home of mutual friends the Salisburys, that Henry proposed marriage to Evelyn and she graciously accepted.

Henry Herbert, Fourth Earl of Carnarvon

TITLES.—Earl of Chesterfield and Baron Stanhope, of Shelford.

TITLES – Earl of Carnarvon

Chapter Six

An Arranged Marriage

News of the happy engagement between two aristocrats, two equal oddments of sorts, was announced to the world in August 1861. Lordy's match to Almina Wombwell was for money and prestige, not love. Almina brought the money, in the form of backing by Baron Alfred de Rothschild, and Lordy offered Almina the chance to join the ranks of aristocracy and become an instant Countess. But such was not the case for Lordy's parents; at the very least, the two liked each other; and there were indications that this was a love match. Plus, as fairly mature parties – she was aged twenty-seven, and he was thirty – there was a sense that they were ready to settle down.

Anxious to delight Evelyn, Henry asked his mother to make representations in writing to the dean of Westminster Abbey to help secure the Abbey Chapel for the wedding ceremony. There had been few weddings sanctioned there, but a precedent set thirty years before gave him hope it would be possible.[101] Henrietta did so, and worked steadfastly to ensure her prospective daughter-in-law's personal needs received appropriate attention in the Herbert homesteads, with the acquisition of new wallpaper and linen.[102]

On 5 September 1861 the couple were married in style at Westminster Abbey. The wedding was predominately a family affair, "without any unnecessary parade"[103]. The Earl's brother, the Honourable Alan Percy Herbert, was the best man, a newly qualified doctor on home leave from Paris. Evelyn's chief bridesmaids were Lady Mary Stanhope, Lady Catherine Henrietta Wallop and the Anson sisters, all relations of the bride or groom. The "fair bride"[104] was given away by her proud father, George, the 6th Earl of Chesterfield.

After the signing of the register in the Jerusalem Chamber of the Abbey, the company proceeded, while the Abbey bells rang out merrily, in a number of carriages to the reception. Evelyn's mother, Lady Chesterfield, hosted the wedding feast for about twenty guests at the Chesterfield mansion in Grosvenor Square.[105] There were no speeches, but the first of the champagne toasts (moved by Henry

Howard, Carnarvon's uncle[106]) was to the bride and bridegroom, and the second to Henrietta, the Dowager Countess of Carnarvon.

The first part of the honeymoon was spent at Milford Park, Highclere, a small house beside the lake (the old fishpond of the late monks of Winchester Abbey, once resident at Highclere). The Earl wrote to his mother every day of the honeymoon; in one letter he told her "the place looks very well and Evelyn is I think really pleased with it".[107]

Though the 4th Earl and his mother were aware that Evelyn's health was not robust, it had been kept something of a secret quite how delicate she was. In the very first days of her marriage she was plunged straight into illness – a prelude to the doom to come. A dreadfully bad cold threatened plans at the very start of a honeymoon trip through Germany. But during the next weekend the Earl and his new Countess left Highclere, staying over in Dover for a couple of days to rest before making for the Continent and a long tour of Europe.[108]

When the newlyweds eventually returned to Highclere Castle in November,[109] Evelyn was still suffering from ill health, but she was cheered by opening up her orders for new ball gowns. The Dowager, Henrietta, had been busy recruiting (based on criteria laid down by Henry in letters to his mother) for key staff to serve at Highclere, in particular a butler and a cook.[110] And lest the Earl's dotty, doting sister, Lady Gwendolen, should have one of her uncontrollable mood swings – since she was almost certainly jealous of Evelyn and it was feared that the nuptials would leave her feeling she had no longer had a place at Highclere – she was made busy with some parish work.

To mark their return to home turf, a celebration dinner was given by the Earl and Countess at Highclere for the Highclere Yeomanry Cavalry (of which Lord Carnarvon was a captain) and the Highclere tenantry. The Earl reflected on his key role of local squire, remarking that in the period of just over a decade since succeeding his father he had tried "his best to put the [estate] farmhouses into a satisfactory state of comfort, and to convert the cottages into abodes compatible with decency and good morals".[111] The "health of the new Lady Carnarvon" was drunk publically for the first time, with many other toasts.[112]

Chapter Seven

Lady Evelyn, Mistress of Highclere Castle

Lady Evelyn's new home had a long history. Highclere was one of the many country residences of the bishops of Winchester, but by a corrupt arrangement with one Bishop Poynet it passed to the Crown in the time of Edward VI, and hence to the Fitzwilliams and other families. It was purchased by Sir Robert Sawyer, and passed to the Herberts by the marriage of his only daughter to Thomas, Earl of Pembroke, whose great nephew became the 1st Earl of Carnarvon.[113]

Henrietta, Evelyn's mother-in-law, had great plans to improve the house during her time as mistress. In 1840, the 3rd Earl created something of a stir when it was announced he was "causing considerable alterations to be made to his principal dwelling, Highclere House. The front is to be pulled down, and to be rebuilt in the gothic style of architecture…"[114] Such renovations were an investment in the most comfortable of the Carnarvon family homes, modelled on the 3rd Earl's interpretation of the Jacobean style of mansion, copied from the time of James I with impressive brickwork made from grey Bath stone by Thomas Jackson of Pimlico. [115]

Now, Highclere had a new mistress. Evelyn had grown up on a large estate at Bretby Park, Derbyshire, and had watched her mother perfect the challenging role of chief house manager. The Victorian country house was like a giant machine.[116] In addition to managing the house, and fulfilling duties to the estate's tenants, Evelyn was responsible for the hiring and firing of house servants, for planning the entertainment to be done, and for making and receiving calls on her husband's behalf.

The new mistress of Highclere was an incurably romantic girl, a twisted mix of Brontë heroines, and she loved being close to nature, walking regularly about the grounds. Highclere Castle is set in a magnificent park, thirteen miles in circumference, with woods[117] and a lake. There are several hills, and from the highest, Beacon Hill (where the last remains of Lordy lie buried), one can gaze over several neighbouring counties. Highclere is described in 1831 as having by way of its chief glory "the park and pleasure grounds, of which, it may be truly observed, that few places of similar extent in the inland parts of the kingdom can boast of surface more varied, or scenery more interesting".[118]

Neither the house nor its surrounds daunted Evelyn. She was ready to be the 4th Countess in every way, and was esteemed all the way up to the Royal Court.[119] The Earl knew the Herbert home needed an energetic wife and the Castle a hostess, a chatelaine, and Evelyn's mother had groomed her for these multiple tasks. Despite losing the newly appointed butler – who was headhunted by another peeress – Evelyn immediately resolved the hiring of key servants and set about acting to receive her husband's friends and political associates. Carnarvon comments in his diaries on how quickly she achieved these goals, especially endearing herself to his beloved confidante and mentor, Sir William Heathcote, and his wife.[120] It was a good start for the new Countess.

Marriage Beginnings

The new Countess of Carnarvon's parents, Lord and Lady Chesterfield, and her brother, Lord Stanhope, spent the first Christmas at Highclere with her and Lord Carnarvon, and they returned to Bretby Park (via London) for the New Year celebrations.[121]

Carnarvon was known at this time for his accomplishments riding with hounds and shooting birds and game. House guests, such as his father-in-law and brother-in-law, were thrilled at the horse breeding in Hampshire, and the quality of the gentlemanly sport offered to them during visits to Highclere. It fostered enthusiasm towards the 4th Earl, and they were happy to reciprocate with invitations to their own estate.

The first of the New Year political visitors at Highclere was Carnarvon's friend Lord Dufferin,[122] a man destined to distinguish himself in colonial government. Evelyn wisely targeted her husband's inner circle first, but she was keen to prove herself beyond them. As January and February unfolded, the new incumbents at Highclere announced that they intended "to receive a succession of visitors".[123]

But in her first months as Countess Evelyn had done too much and, now pregnant, she fell ill with exhaustion. Carnarvon was left to attend several (largely political) dinners throughout the year alone. Finally, Lady Evelyn travelled to London for the season, occupying rooms at Fenton's Hotel, St James's Street, before the Earl took a lease on "a good house" [124] at 17 Bruton Street, Mayfair.[125]

One of the first appearances by the Earl and Countess in London together was at the midway point of the London season at an annual reception given by the Duchess of Northumberland at Northumberland House. Many titled members of the British aristocracy and several foreign ambassadors were present.[126]

Evelyn knew that competition among the ladies parlours of Mayfair was stiff, and she had fallen behind by missing so many social occasions. The Northumberlands' showpiece was closely followed by a reception hosted by a keen rival, the Countess of Derby, at her family mansion in St James's Square.[127] Then a golden opportunity arose that Evelyn seized. On 21 June the Carnarvons attended an assembly at Cambridge House, Piccadilly, hosted by the prime minister's wife, Lady Emily Palmerston.[128] This was a grand full dress dinner, with a wide circle of notable guests from home and abroad.[129] Evelyn wisely endeared herself to Lady Palmerston, who was seen as the equal of any of the country's grand Duchesses and had invited "everyone who was anyone".[130] Both women liked each other and Evelyn learned much in the next few years from this principal mentor. One of her main social activities became supporting a long list of charitable causes – especially those connected to the arts.

With a first baby on its way, there was no let up for Evelyn, but she was growing increasingly concerned for her health, which remained erratic. An invitation was made to Lord Carnarvon's sister, Lady Eveline Portsmouth, to visit Highclere and support Evelyn through the initial months of carrying her child. Carnarvon was pleased to write to his mother that "the two Es" were getting on well together. To show his own support for his wife, the 4th Earl gave her "a nice diamond", albeit he sought advice of the precise type to purchase from his mother.[131] When Evelyn transferred to London to observe the last throes of the year's season and await her confinement, she was full of joy.

But all the hope and happiness was to end in tragedy.

Days of anxiety and pain

The Carnarvons were dinner guests of Lady Molesworth on Monday 14 July[132] when Evelyn was taken ill and reported she could not feel the baby moving. They hurried back to 17 Bruton Street. Evelyn's mother Lady Chesterfield came immediately from a dinner party (being hosted by her friend, Benjamin Disraeli) to help her daughter through her labour, only to be presented with a stillborn grandchild.[133] Mercifully, the Countess's labour only lasted an hour. She was attended by Dr George Thompson Gream[134], a Royal physician and an opponent of the routine use of giving chloroform to assist child delivery (in any case Evelyn's lungs and heart were not strong enough to inhale chloroform) who was careful to ensure Evelyn's anaemia did not worsen given the blood loss.[135]

The Earl was moved to comment on the whole event of his wife's ordeal: "but alas – alas – the child did not live. It is a trial – but it must be borne." [136] In his diary the Earl further recorded these were "days of anxiety and pain".[137] He let off steam stag hunting at Pixton Park, and left the restoration of his wife's health and spirits in female hands.

Evelyn was forced to stay in bed to regain her strength, and the Countess of Chesterfield attended to her every need. Evelyn's mother-in-law, Henrietta (who was returning to England from Germany when Evelyn went into labour), graciously offered to provide her son's wife with guidance in her grief over the loss of her child. Since Henrietta had herself lost a child, a daughter who lived only a few hours, she knew too well the pain.[138] The Earl also implored his sister, Eveline, to also spend time with his wife to help restore her spirits.

Later, in September, Henry somewhat reluctantly accompanied his wife on a remedial trip to Weymouth. They were able to be alone at last and both benefited from the time there. The following month they spent time shooting at the Chesterfield residence at Gedling, and this time with each other secured the future of the marriage.[139] Whilst the Earl attended to some political matters and other London affairs, including seeing his mother, Evelyn travelled to Eggesford to stay with Lady Eveline.

It was November before Evelyn was completely recovered and able to welcome a regular retinue of guests streaming through Highclere's portals.[140] The cast list was impressive: John Murray, the publisher; and the economist and journalist Walter Bagehot, whose close friendship Carnarvon cherished, despite the political differences between them.[141] Bagehot was asked by the Earl to "keep [Highclere] more decently reasonable while the fast people were there".[142] One of the latter guests (recruited by Evelyn) was Lady Dorothy Nevill, whom Bagehot described as "a pretty woman with an old husband, and several young men".[143] The Carnarvons impressed Bagehot. In a letter he writes: "Lady Carnarvon is very clever and literary – at least with *snaps* of Literature. They will be *people* for some years to come, for they are both clever, very ambitious and have a beautiful place near London to entertain."[144] Another observer who thought Evelyn a most lovely and winning woman was John T. Delane, editor of *The Times*, who said that he believed there could be no successor to Lady Palmerston until he saw her.[145]

Pleasing feedback from her husband, who was proud of Evelyn as hostess, gave the Countess a renewed sense of purpose, and she was cheerful once more as she busily prepared for house guests. But Evelyn was reluctant to consent to lovemaking; she begged for more time and patience from her husband. The Earl's libido could be insatiable.[146] Meanwhile he was kept busy by a heavy workload of commitments at the Hampshire Quarter Sessions (where he sat on the bench), including seeing and staying with the Heathcotes.[147]

In early December the Carnarvons went to Bretby Park to visit Evelyn's parents. A large house party there ensued.[148] The Earl's attentions and sympathy, coupled with her mother's dictate to put the events of the past year behind her, gave the Countess a further boost in morale, after a feeling of being incapable of doing her essential duty to Lord Carnarvon by producing a live son and heir.

As Christmas loomed, the Earl and Countess came back through London en route to Highclere for Christmas. The capital was sombre, following the first anniversary of the death of Prince Albert, on 14 December 1861. The removal of the prince consort's remains from the royal vault in St George's Chapel, Windsor, to a new royal mausoleum at Frogmore dominated the talk in London's high society drawing rooms.[149] It was hoped the gloom would be lifted further as in the following year the Prince of Wales was to marry, to great excitement across the country. The amorous Prince was cited as actually being in love with this wife to be, who was a Danish princess.[150] And excitingly, the Countess was being considered at Court for a position in the Royal Household. Such a busy role for Evelyn, living away from her husband for stretches, would give her more time to manage Carnarvon's expectations of becoming a father.

Chapter Eight

A Lady in Waiting

In February 1863 the Countess of Carnarvon was appointed a lady of the bedchamber to Princess Alexandra.[151] The Princess was Alexandra of Denmark, who on 10 March became Princess of Wales, the wife of Albert (Bertie) Edward, Prince of Wales, and from 1901, Queen Alexandra. Evelyn was present in support of the Princess at her wedding.[152]

Evelyn was in attendance at many of the wider appearances by the Princess of Wales, and was required to be presented at Court again, this time by her father's relative, Lady Stanhope. She hugely enjoyed her role at Court, especially being seen out and about with the fashion setters of the era. Making important visits alongside the Princess was like being in a play.[153]

The new lady in waiting at Court in London was required to rebalance her life: she had to remain, concurrently, a wife and country house hostess in Hampshire. But then Evelyn was brought down to earth. In the autumn she discovered that she was carrying another child, which brought her position at Court to an abrupt end.

Despite impending motherhood, it was business as usual for the busy politician's wife. At Highclere, she greeted another wave of fashionable visitors passing through, including a long stay by the Marquis and Marchioness of Salisbury.[154] During the time the Salisbury's graced the Carnarvon household, numerous personalities of the era came and went through its doors.[155] The guests were a combination of family collaterals and people with wide social circles of friends, like the gossipy Lady Dorothy Nevill[156], who could be relied upon to efficiently broadcast the latest news from Highclere so as to reach all the important London ears. Such gatherings gave the ladies an opportunity to show off their latest high-fashion dresses, hairstyles and accessories. Playing cards was a popular activity in the morning and evening, mainly for the ladies, whilst riding and hunting was a shared pastime, although the men also enjoyed shooting and playing billiards. But Society gossip always pipped these activities.

Birth of Lady Winifred Herbert

A large-scale New Year's party was given at Highclere to welcome in 1864. Perhaps the year ahead would finally see a Carnarvon heir. So far Evelyn had felt more optimistic about her own physical constitution and the baby's welfare.

Carnarvon visited his sagacious sister, Eveline, and her husband at Hurstbourne Park in May.[157] Eveline always spoke frankly and honestly, and Carnarvon appreciated her candour. Throughout his life the Earl turned to his Eveline to help him better understand the intricacies of domestic life with women. Eveline also held strong views on political issues. As a Liberal (as was the Wallop family political stance), her opinions ran quite contrary to her brother's Toryism. The two of them enjoyed debating with one another. One subject they agreed on, though, was giving women more of a say in politics. [158]

Concurrently, the Earl, noted by one newspaper as being "the rising statesman"[159], was engaged in political warfare in Parliament.

Meanwhile preparations were underway for Evelyn's pregnancy to reach a happier conclusion than two years before. A birth in London was favoured, where a specialist physician could be on site. Lady Winifred Anne Henrietta Christiana Herbert was born on Saturday 2 July 1864 at the family's new townhouse in Lower Grosvenor Street, London.[160] Despite the child being female, there were widespread celebrations to mark Winifred's birth throughout the Carnarvon and Chesterfield seats among family and estate tenants.

In early August the Carnarvons, with their newly baptised daughter, left London to travel to Highclere.[161] Evelyn's parents had been on hand at Chesterfield House in the weeks following the delivery of their granddaughter, and they now returned to Bretby Park. Both mother and baby were, it was hoped, well placed to survive.

At Highclere, Evelyn resumed her tasks as chatelaine. She threw herself into large-scale entertaining during September and October, mixing political guests and family members.[162] But Evelyn was in dire need of a change of scene, so it was announced in October that the

Carnarvons were to spend time away on the Continent. An announcement on the 19 November states: "The Earl and Countess of Carnarvon have left Folkstone for Paris, on their way to Italy."[163] A few days later they were reported as "sojourning at Nice, on their way to Italy, where they propose to remain during the winter months".[164] From the account of this trip in the Earl's diary it is clear that they socialised with British expatriates, foreign diplomats, French and Italian nobles and members of the Rothschild family.[165] They spent Christmas in Rome and attended the service in St Peter's Square. The Earl is full of praise for Roman antiquities.

Lady Evelyn In Extremis

In the middle of January 1865, still in Rome, Evelyn fell violently ill with a fever. Yet she rallied sufficiently, perhaps under pressure from the Earl, by 26 January to continue their sightseeing, including joining the Earl for some horse riding. However, Evelyn's health deteriorated again on 7 February.[166] Malaria was diagnosed, with complications involving her liver function. The Countess was near death, and was only saved by the Earl's prompt actions in getting her maid to put the Countess immediately to bed and promptly seeking medical aid, coupled with the early attention of her doctor, Pantaleoni.[167] The Earl loudly sang the latter's praises, whilst including a prayer to God too; both savours were equally held in his gratitude. He records in his diary "it makes me shudder, how very near we have been treading to the precipice..."[168] The fever continued for several weeks and only completely abated in late March. The situation was helped by the arrival of Dr Alan Herbert (the Earl's younger brother) from Paris to assist with the medical treatment.[169] From that time onwards, on the incitement of his brother, Alan Herbert became devoted to Evelyn's wellbeing.

That the Countess was *in extremis* was not divulged outside of the family circle.[170] The official record issued to the inhabitants of the town of Newbury and neighbourhood was that, with much satisfaction, the sojourn of the Earl and Countess of Carnarvon in the sunny climes of the South of Europe had been attended with gratifying results, the noble pair having derived considerable benefit. But their return home was not to take place until after the Easter holidays.[171] A further announcement said:

The Earl and Countess of Carnarvon are expected at Pixton House, Dulverton, on their return from the Continent during next month... Our readers will be glad to learn that the winter's sojourn in a warm climate has materially improved his Lordship's health.[172]

The Carnarvons arrived back in London on Wednesday 26 April, and the press indicated that fact that the Countess had "quite recovered from her indisposition".[173]

The Earl was appointed back to the Hampshire Quarter Sessions bench in April and addressed the House of Lords in May on the subject of the Metropolitan homeless poor.[174]

Evelyn and her husband first re-appeared in public together on Wednesday 14 June, at a dinner at York House, Twickenham, given by the Count and Countess de Paris.[175] The success of this evening ensured that the Carnarvons were ready to present themselves to Queen Victoria at the sixth Court of the year at Buckingham Palace on Saturday 17 June.[176] As a result of London hostesses seeing Evelyn in full bloom again, invitations to receptions, balls and dinners flooded in.

To celebrate her survival, Evelyn hosted a grand gathering at Highclere attended by her parents, aunts, uncles and close friends, as well as the man who had saved her life in Rome, Dr Pantaleoni, who came with his wife.[177]

The Earl attended Parliament throughout June and he spoke on various subjects. In opposition, the strain from his parliamentary load was relatively light, although he spoke away from Parliament on prison reform, education and the Church of England. He was back at Highclere in July to receive guests Lord and Lady Derby who were en route to the races at Goodwood, an event that traditionally brought the London season to a close.[178]

Agriculture was hit hard in 1865 by a large-scale cattle plague, which brought concerns for the Earl as a politician and a landowner. He fell on a tool that he often used to speak out, sending a letter to *The Times* newspaper with suggestions on how to quell the situation.[179]

Meanwhile, in September, Evelyn first went alone to stay with her parents, who were holding a house party at Bretby Park for the races at nearby Derby.[180] Later, Evelyn was joined by the Earl and together they celebrated (with a flood of further guests) the 34th birthday of Evelyn's brother, Lord Stanhope, which a game of cricket, Stanhope's favourite sport of which he was an accomplished player.[181] On the home journey the Earl and Countess were lucky to escape injury when a train they were on was involved in an accident. The Countess's maid sustained a cut on the forehead.[182]

As Christmas 1865 drew close Evelyn travelled down to Pixton Park as a guest of the Dowager Countess.[183] To great cheer, and after much renewed pressure to now produce an heir, Evelyn declared she was expecting again.

Sir Charles Barry

HIGHCLERE HOUSE, HAMPSHIRE.
GENERAL VIEW OF THE HOUSE PREVIOUS TO THE ALTERATIONS

HIGHCLERE HOUSE, HAMPSHIRE.
GENERAL VIEW OF THE HOUSE AS ALTERED

Highclere Before And After Changes by Charles Barry

**Lady Evelyn Stanhope
Fourth Countess of Carnarvon**
[Leadbetter Collection]

Chapter Nine

1866

On Tuesday 6 February 1866, Queen Victoria opened the seventh Parliament of her reign. Evelyn watched the proceedings from the peeress' gallery.[184] She then took part in a stream of engagements in London between February and March, including attending a dinner hosted by the Salisburys, a dance at Marlborough House and Lady Stanhope's assembly, and in turn she hosted a small party at the Carnarvon townhouse at 66 Grosvenor Street.[185]

The Earl was busy too, but far away from season's social trifles. The cattle plague raged through the early months of 1866, and the cause continued to baffle veterinary surgeons, farmers and science. Lord Carnarvon also became embroiled in a campaign – led by the Archbishop of Canterbury – for a symbolic day of national fasting. The government refused the request. In addition, the Earl was sucked into several social issues, including the welfare of inmates of prisons, workhouses and infirmaries. This year was a controversial one for Carnarvon in opposing the Reform Act – an issue that his mentor, Lord Salisbury, had resigned over the year before. Memories surfaced of the 3rd Earl's memorable stand in Parliament, when he was still Lord Porchester, in the white heat caused by the Great Reform act of 1832, before his political career was subsumed by illness.[186]

A sudden attack of ill health caused Evelyn to postpone a reception she was planning to hold in London on Saturday 28 April, but she was well enough to resume attending social functions and did so in mid-May. However, a family member's descent into serious ill health was to be a shattering blow to the Countess's wellbeing, especially in her pregnant state.

Death of Lord Chesterfield

On Saturday 26 May 1866, with Evelyn almost at the end of her third pregnancy, her father, the sixty-year-old 6th Earl of Chesterfield (who had enjoyed the day in question at the races), was found unconscious on his sitting room floor of his London home in Grosvenor Street. He had suffered a massive stroke, which left him paralysed. Although he briefly rallied in the days that followed, he was not expected to survive for long. He died in the evening of the following Friday, his wife, his son and his son-in-law, Lord Carnarvon, at his bedside.[187] Evelyn's only brother, Lord Stanhope (who sat in the House of Commons as MP for South Nottinghamshire), immediately inherited the earldom.[188]

Chesterfield's illness and subsequent death cast a tremendous gloom in London Society and Highclere, but more especially at the Chesterfield seat of Bretby Park, where he was regarded as a fair landowner. His obituaries map out an immensely colourful life. He is described as possessing "a genial English face and... a natty, manly figure, dressed in that peculiarly quiet but unmistakable Chesterfield style as he passed by on his way to Tattershall's in his faultless male phaeton".[189] A contemporary, the Earl of Malmesbury records in his memoirs: "June 1st. Lord Chesterfield died of a paralytic stroke. A very amiable man, and had led the fashion in his day."[190]

Born in 1805, George Chesterfield lived life to the full. He was a man who enjoyed a long association with the sport of kings, the turf, and had expensive links with exclusive horse studs, with a mix of great wins and great losses in horse races and sometimes rakish gambling schemes.[191]

Orphaned by the age of ten (both his parents died within a few years of each other, his mother in 1813, his father in 1815[192]), he was brought up at Court, his father being a knight of the garter, sometime an ambassador to Spain and long time postmaster general and master of the horse, and his mother (a daughter of the first Marquess of Bath) a lady of the bedchamber to the queen consort. A half-sister died before his birth in 1803; his other sister, Lady Georgina, died in 1824, the first wife of Frederick Richard West, of Ruthin Castle, Co. Denbigh.

After Eton and Christ Church, Oxford, George enjoyed a largely leisurely life. He played no active part in politics but instead became a sporting man of legend, especially in his conquests as a bold and good rider, as a master of buckhounds as well as riding with local packs of hounds, a passion he shared with his own son and daughter.

The Earl had a remarkable array of racing accolades, with his horses winning the great English races from the Derby to the Grand National, and these were woven into stories told to her grandchildren by Lady Chesterfield and by her daughter to the same children.

Although he did not live to meet his grandson, Lordy, or see his efforts on the English turf, Lordy often reflected on the glory days of his accomplished Chesterfield grandfather. The 5th Earl modelled himself as a follower of the turf in part based on the legends of his Chesterfield grandfather.

Birth of Lordy

Lord Porchester (Lordy), the Carnarvon heir, was born on Tuesday 26 June 1866 at 66 Grosvenor Street, London. Lordy was named after Lady Evelyn's father George. His mother chose this name, resisting the name Henry which had, in any case, been that chosen for the first son who was stillborn in 1862.

Given Evelyn's track record on births and health, a detailed bulletin was issued early on Wednesday 27 June regarding mother and child: "The Countess of Carnarvon gave birth to a son and heir yesterday morning. Up to an advanced hour last night her ladyship and infant were progressing favourably."[193]

The Earl wrote immediately to his mother, who was on retreat at Harrogate:

> [It was] a very bad confinement and more than a question at one moment whether the child could have been saved but thank God all has gone well and I hope and trust that E. [Evelyn] though very much exhausted will do well. She has not yet been able to get much sleep but I hope this will come. Dear Pal[194] most kind and useful as ever he administered the chloroform. The child... certainly has abominable lungs and makes more noise than Winifred." [195]

A further letter next day declared:

E. had a really good night and is now dozing or lying quiet whilst Lord Porchester seems extremely well and comfortable in all respects. He enters the world oddly enough as I entered it, in the midst of a considerable storm in the political world on the subject of Reform. Meanwhile he is taking everything very quietly, in which he shows a greater philosophy than most of the wise men who are about. For my own part I am so well content with home matters...[196]

The Earl and his mother both mused at the echoes going back to the 1830s and the controversy of the reform of the franchise. The Dowager Countess's husband, when Lord Porchester, had been one of the politicians who was strongly against extending the right to vote to the masses in the Reform Bill of 1831-2. While that debate ensued the Countess had given birth to the 4th Earl in 1831. Lordy's birth had now taken place whilst another Reform Bill was before Parliament in 1866, and to which his father – the 4th Earl – was opposed. Hence her remark: "so thankful for the good news. The same thing had struck me of the curious coincidence of the dear little lad being born at a very similarly exciting Reform period as yourself 34 years ago..."[197]

Shortly after his son's birth, the 4th Earl father was appointed secretary to the colonies by prime minister, Lord Derby.[198] And on 6 July, less than two weeks after giving birth but motivated more as a Cabinet minister's wife than the Carnarvon heir's mother, Evelyn was up on her feet for attendance at a royal banquet (with the Prince and Princess of Wales and in honour of the King and Queen of the Belgians) at the Mansion House, hosted by the Lord Mayor and Lady Mayoress of London.[199]

In August 1866 Lordy accompanied his sister, Winifred, his parents and his grandmother, Lady Chesterfield, on his first trip from London, to be shown off at Bretby Park, his mother's old homestead, with its "castellated mansion"[200] and well wooded park.[201] The child's next excursion was with his parents, sister and Chesterfield grandmother to Buxton, Derbyshire, by way of partaking a spa break for the benefit of both Countesses' recovery from childbirth and bereavement.[202] Then, when only a few months old, Lordy was given "hearty cheers" by the children of the various schools in the Newbury on their annual excursion to Highclere Park.[203]

Chapter Ten

A new style of political hosting

In October 1866, when Lordy was four months old, Highclere received a visit from Benjamin Disraeli[204] and his devoted wife, the witty Welsh woman Mary Anne Evans.[205] Disraeli was the newly appointed chancellor of the exchequer in Lord Derby's Conservative government, and Lordy's father was colonial secretary. As for Mrs Disraeli (who had previously been married to an MP, Wyndham Lewis, who died in 1838, the year before she married Disraeli) and Evelyn, two of the country's leading political hostesses, it was clear that instead of doting on the newly born Carnarvon heir they had much more serious business to attend to. Evelyn wanted to learn from Mary, forty years her senior, how to be the best hostess in England. The game was a clear enough one: to promote the worth and calibre of her husband, whom she saw (as Lord Derby had seen) as a future prime minister, and she a prime minister's wife. Both the woman folk were more keen to keep an ear on the political gossip than the workings of the nursery wing at Highclere Castle.[206]

As a young girl, Evelyn had always enjoyed the limelight when performing her ambitious entertainment shows at Bretby. She knew what delighted important visitors, and her long experience at countless receptions, dinners and balls and the Court had taught her the art of polite conversation. She had acquired a flair for small talk, for casually flirting, relating amusing anecdotes whilst paying full and proper attention to being religiously faithfully to her spouse. She was determined to thrive off her husband's opinions, but it was not an easy duty. With an often shy and sluggish-willed husband Evelyn frequently had to push him. But she was undeterred in her ambition of seeing Carnarvon achieve high office and she, in turn, enjoying the status of one of the leading political hostesses of the era.

Lordy and his sister paid a price for their mother's social manoeuvring in the little attention she was usually able to pay her growing family. The lady of the house was frequently busy, and sometimes away from home, presenting prizes, opening fêtes and exhibitions and travelling with her husband. But absent parenting was an established tradition for the gentry; the daily chores in the nursery (and later the school room) were left to nursemaids and governesses.

In her time Evelyn was looked upon as a strong-minded, highly intelligent and accomplished wife of a politician and notable Cabinet minister who seemed to have found in overseeing the colonies his own particular niche. According to the writer and hostess Lady Dorothy Nevill, Evelyn also a hand in some of her husband's speeches.[207]

After the New Year festivities in 1867 the Carnarvons left Highclere for London for the start of the season.[208] Almost immediately Evelyn broke new social ground by arranging a "small and early" gathering on Saturday nights. There were larger dinner parties too. The invitations were kept politically neutral, and one of Evelyn's first guests was the Liberal party leader, William Gladstone[209], which astonished some of her Tory guests.[210] Evelyn also led her fellow peeresses by holding several select parties for all comers at Grosvenor Street. The Countess had broken a social taboo, that such gatherings should be strictly partisan, and she had done it with such style that mixed parties soon caught on across London.

The Earl's steps down

Towards the end of January the Earl's state of health plummeted. This point marks his first major medical crisis, and he would never be the same man again. His condition was crippling gout (probably a misdiagnosis that covered up a progressive cerebral or nervous condition[211]). In agony, Henry forced himself to the House of Lords on 19 February to move the second reading of the Bill for the Confederation of Canada. The result of this Bill was one of his great life achievements.[212]

Before resuming further activity, and now in deep physical and mental distress, he sought a period of rest at Buxton's spa. In a letter he confided the serious extent of his illness to his mother:

> My dear Mother: You will have heard from Evelyn of all our recent troubles and difficulties. It has been a painful affair and I am sorry to say that the anxieties are not likely to diminish. I doubt whether

the wound is curable. It is some probable that the irritation will grow until the difficulties become irreconcilable...[213]

But aside from his health, which the Earl constantly risked for the sake of staying at the forefront of the game of politics, he was irked by some policies afoot. Particular trouble was brewing, as he was far from happy about the government's moves on voting reform. On 2nd March he resigned from this position as secretary to the colonies; not on a colonial issue, but on the issue of the extension of the franchise.[214] His resignation caused a rift with Lord Derby, the prime minister. Carnarvon relied on his friendship with old university chums like Lord Cranborne (the heir to Lord Salisbury[215]) and his guardian, Sir William Heathcote, to see him through the crisis.

Frederic Blanchford, Carnarvon's under-secretary at the Colonial Office, said he found the Earl's failing was having "too much self-consciousness, and a disposition to be caught by showy schemes".[216] But he added that Carnarvon "was friendly to everybody... as a chief [and he had] a wish to shine before the public and to distinguish himself in the ordinary sense of the word".[217] One other diarist, however, observed that "Carnarvon made a poor nervous speech"[218] in the Lords by way of explanation for his actions in resigning. But the Earl later made what the same commentator called an "admirable" speech when the Reform Bill (which became law in August 1867) was debated.[219]

Carnarvon remained ill off and on throughout 1867.[220] Since both he and the Countess were suffering from strain from the weeks of political conflict, they retreated to Pixton Park in late April en route to spending a few days at Torquay with the children.[221] Whilst all the commotion caused by Carnarvon's resignation was going on, the Dowager Countess[222] and her daughters, Gwendolen and Eveline, had been enjoying a stay to Veale's Royal Hotel at Teignmouth.[223] A grand reunion followed, which gave everyone renewed inner strength. This was a family who pulled together.

Suitably refreshed, the Carnarvons were at 10 Downing Street on 8 May at a grand event given by Lord Stanley, secretary of state for foreign affairs.[224] And despite Carnarvon being out in the political wilderness, he made frequent speeches throughout the remainder of the parliamentary session.

Evelyn was determined to be loyal to Carnarvon always. She could best do this by focusing on her fellow wives, her political counterparts, and she continued to attend the various ladies' assemblies. The Carnarvons also appeared together as a couple at the season's usual social and Court events. But in an effort to allow a breathing space from mounting controversies in Parliament, and for some further relaxation, the Carnarvons travelled to Paris on 7 June to spend the Whitsun recess there, returning to London on 19 June.[225]

Having shown great solidarity to her husband, and fulfilled her line-up of London engagements, including an appearance at the Queen's Drawing Room on 27 June[226] at Buckingham Palace, Evelyn was ready to leave town. In late July returned to Highclere, to prepare for several guests expected to stay there in the height of the summer months, leaving Lord Carnarvon in the city.[227]

In late September, the Carnarvons went to their beloved Hatfield House to stay with the Salisburys, where they were certain of a friendly welcome, and then returned to Highclere where they were reunited with their children.[228]

1868

After the New Year festivities, the Carnarvons left Highclere. They planned to spend some weeks away together in the South of France.[229]

On 27 February, Lord Derby resigned as prime minister and was succeeded by Benjamin Disraeli. In the weeks that followed Derby snubbed Carnarvon's attempt at reconciliation.[230]

Carnarvon's mentor, Lord Salisbury (the 2nd Marquess), died on the 12 April 1868. Robert Cecil, Lord Cranborne, who had resigned with Carnarvon the previous year over the franchise and was a close ally, became the new Marquis of Salisbury. Lord Salisbury's death was a terrible blow for Lord Carnarvon, but also Evelyn. Carnarvon wrote in his diary that he was "overwhelmed by the news".[231] The Earl's daughter, Lady Winifred, later a notable literary figure, reflected on this years later when she edited some Salisbury letters.[232] From this work we learn that when Lord Salisbury died, Lord and Lady Carnarvon's sympathy was a great support to Lady Salisbury in her widowhood. And as we shall see, it was sympathy which she remembered and repaid some years later.

On 25 April the Carnarvons hosted a dinner party at Grosvenor Street, with the Countess holding her own "small and early reception afterwards".[233] Other dinners and the Countess's popular, much-talked about receptions followed in later months. By August entertaining had moved to Highclere, and a steady stream of guests arrived. Among those was Lord Carnarvon's cousin, Edward Herbert, who was to meet his death in terrible circumstances at the hands of kidnappers less than two years later, an event that would result in Carnarvon suffering a nervous breakdown. Another regular guest, Cyril Graham, was Carnarvon's private secretary. He was already a seasoned explorer and traveller, and destined for even greater glory in colonial service.[234]

That year Evelyn made a point of involving three-year-old Lady Winifred in the annual treat for the waifs and strays of Kingsclere Union on 13 August. The workhouse children were driven to Highclere and on arrival were warmly received by Evelyn and the Earl. Following games, tea was laid on, Winifred being the one to serve the guests with a delicious slice of plum cake.[235] Lordy was too young yet to participate in these rituals, but his time would soon come.

Disraeli's Tory government fell in 1868 and the Liberal William Gladstone resumed the premiership. Evelyn was on good terms with both these men, and their wives. She was relieved that the change in power meant her husband might be persuaded to relax away from the centre of politics. Evelyn's political ambitions for her husband (as well as for herself) had not diminished. But she worried for Carnarvon's wellbeing, with periods of work stress causing him bodily pain and mental fatigue. Whilst the Tories were in opposition there would be a quieter period, since Carnarvon would not hold office, and she was determined to seize this chance to see him recover fully his health.

1869

As the year broke, Highclere was the scene for several days of shooting, combined with a meeting of the Craven hounds across the Earl's extensive grounds and parkland.[236] The sport was fine, and several of the shooters and riders joined the Earl for breakfast, prior to the "throw-off".[237]

Meanwhile, the Dowager Countess, Henrietta was at Osborne, Isle of Wight, to stay with Queen Victoria.[238] The Queen wished to know at first hand of Henrietta's take on education, especially of her work in kindergartens. The Carnarvons were in London for a few days in mid-February before returning to Highclere.[239]

A visit to Highclere on Sunday 21 February is recorded in the memoirs of the Marquis of Lorne (later the 9th Duke of Argyll).[240] He records a "pleasant little party"[241] of house guests[242], and the passage is noteworthy as it demonstrates that part of Evelyn's enormous charm as a hostess was in the recounting of amusing anecdotes about her husband's contemporaries; in this instance, Lord Mayo (a few years later, an ill-fated viceroy of India, he was assassinated).[243]

Before leaving on a continental tour with her husband, Lady Evelyn laid the foundation stone of a new church at Highclere, paid for entirely by Lord Carnarvon, on Monday 26 February.

During the summer months Evelyn hosted several Saturday evening dinners at Grosvenor Street, with a notable one being held on 19 June.[244] The Carnarvons returned briefly to Highclere at the end of July.[245] They later passed through London en route to a continental tour.[246] On 6 August a letter writer at Wildbad, one of the German spa town, records that the Prince and Princess of Wales had taken up residence there for peace and quiet. The Carnarvons were also in retreat[247] at another part of the same resort. Wildbad was a haven for the British gentry to meet up socially (after taking the waters and resting); the town boasted some fine restaurants and a casino. Even those in retreat wished to learn the latest news and gossip from England.

The Carnarvons were back at Highclere for the autumn. In the run-up to Christmas, Evelyn received the Earl and Countess Stanhope, on holiday from their estate at Chevening, near Sevenoaks.[248] Engaging the company of the Stanhopes was crucial to Evelyn's plans to increase her foothold in London's best social and political circles. They were branch of her own Chesterfield family, widely connected and important go-betweens at Court, and they also hosted lavish summer garden parties at Chenening.[249] With Carnarvon's health back on track, all this planned socialising suited Evelyn's continuing plans to raise their ranking in Society; some were already calling her hospitality grander than that of any duchess.

Lordy's birth

The Cedar Tree, Bretby Park : Another Curse

Chapter Eleven

A political shift

After celebrating Christmas and New Year at Highclere, the Carnarvons travelled to London and then spent the first weeks of 1870 at Pixton Park.[250] Evelyn spent a short time in London with her brother, Lord Stanhope, and Carnarvon also left the Capital at the same time to return to Bretby to hold a shooting party.[251] One of Chesterfield's guests at Bretby was Lord Londesborough, who was to be at the centre of a drama that was to lead to Chesterfield's death in 1871.

With the resumption of Parliament (the Tories were in opposition and Gladstone was prime minister) Carnarvon went up to London on 3rd February. Evelyn joined him on the 4th and they travelled down to Hatfield House together for the weekend before the children were due to join them in London on the 7th. The talk with Salisbury (3rd Marquess) was of a new Tory leader in the House of Lords, probably Stanley (15th Earl of Derby).[252] Carnarvon was politically active once again, with a period better health. He recorded in his diary a feeling that he might again play a role in active party politics.[253] In the end Stanley refused to be the leader in the Lords, as did Salisbury. A rank outsider, the Duke of Richmond,[254] became the new leader, with Carnarvon (who had been in the political wilderness, operating independently outside the Tory Party, since his resignation over the Reform Bill, three years before) one of the new leader's key lieutenants.

The family were scattered to enable Evelyn to prepare for the season and spruce up their London townhouse at Grosvenor Street. On 23 February, the Carnarvons were at a dinner given by the Earl and Countess Beauchamp at their home in Belgrave Square.[255] They also attended a dance party given by the Prince and Princess of Wales at Marlborough House on 10 March,[256] then a dinner with Lord and Lady Dufferin at their house in Grosvenor Square.[257]

Life and death

The Carnarvon marriage was among the most successful of mid-nineteenth-century unions in the aristocracy. It was customary when

Parliament was sitting for Carnarvon to go up to town and the Countess to follow him (but only occasionally with the children). The round trip of Highclere–London–Bretby Park–Pixton with various configurations formed the normal pattern for the year. The children were raised by others: occasionally farmed out to relatives at Bretby, Pixton and Eggesford, or simply left at Highclere or in the London townhouse in the care of governesses and nursemaids and a retinue of other servants.

Although they were distant parents who did not see their children regularly, the Earl wanted another son. Lordy was such a miserably weak child, and there was a shadow of doubt over him surviving to take his place as the next Earl. The staff of the nursery wing at Highclere reported details of the boy's welfare to the housekeeper. No one with hands-on duties was informed of what Lordy's parents were actually told, but they were almost certainly given any news (when/if they asked of their son's condition) and were alerted about any serious concern for his health. As he was frequently sick, Lordy's early years were spent separated from other children, even at times his siblings, with usually a few adult females attending his needs. Doctors made calls as necessary and saw Evelyn if she was at home. A local physician was summoned at once if Lordy (or his siblings) was suffering from any alarming symptoms, but with him it was mostly chronic colds and sickness after feeding. The child was able to travel, but he cried a good deal. Lady Evelyn's news of a new baby offered a prospect of there being a healthier son than Lordy to inherit, so naturally the Earl was delighted by the news. Evelyn was more anxious – on account of her own health and strength – than pleased, but hoped the Earl's wishes would be granted.

On 25 March, the Carnarvons left London for a short stay on the Isle of Wight.[258] They later escaped there again when terrible news was received from Greece concerning the Earl's close cousin, Edward Herbert.[259] Edward had been "murdered by Greek banditti, near Athens"[260] on 21 April 1870. He had been seized near Marathon, held for ransom and murdered with three others after a botched rescue attempt by the Greek authorities.[261]

Evelyn attended the funeral and internment in the Carnarvon vault at Burghclere Church, near Highclere, on 16 May, alongside the other grieving members of the clan.[262] The Countess arranged for several wreaths of pure white flowers to be provided for the ladies of the family to place on Edward's coffin. A service of dedication to Edward and his companions was also given at Westminster Abbey.[263]

Lord Carnarvon had looked upon Edward Herbert as a brother. This loss was a devastating blow that affected him very deeply for many years thereafter.[264] Evelyn was also far from well from carrying her next child, but the season, and the Earl's deep depression, induced her to keep her own concerns hidden, despite a busy few months of social engagements.

Whilst the Earl attended to his parliamentary and Masonic commitments, Evelyn gave attention to more feminine pastimes, including her ever-changing wardrobe. Despite Evelyn being six months pregnant, on 21 June the Carnarvons attended a State Ball at Buckingham Palace, followed by the Queen's garden party at Windsor Castle the same week. On 6 July they were at Chiswick for a garden party given by the Prince and Princess of Wales. Their social activity continued throughout July, with Carnarvon involved. They returned to Highclere in August to welcome the American diplomat the Honourbale John Lothrop Motley[265] and his family, and later, Lady Chesterfield.

On 18 September Evelyn gave birth to a daughter, Margaret, at Grosvenor Street, London. Mother and baby were reported to be well.[266] Evelyn's mother, Lady Chesterfield, was present throughout the confinement. Over the ensuing weeks the remainder of the family came to view the new Carnarvon addition. By the end of October, Lady Chesterfield was able to return to Bretby Park whilst the Carnarvons took their older children for a short trip to the seaside before returning to spend the autumn at Highclere.[267]

The consecration of St Michael and All Angels, the new parish church serving Highclere, took place on Saturday 19 November. The ceremony was conducted by the Bishop of Winchester assisted by several local clergy, including Carnarvon's celebrated friend, Dr Mansell, the dean of St Paul's Cathedral, London. A reception for over a hundred guests was held at the castle, as well as a dinner for one hundred and sixty estate employees and tenants. During the weekend of events marking all things Christian and spiritual, Lady Margaret

Herbert, the latest addition to the Highclere family, was christened in the presence of a large congregation.[268]

Deteriorating Health

Evelyn's health was in decline following the birth of Margaret, and she was not herself. The Earl was also depressed; he had not been physically well, and the death of his cousin had been difficult to come to terms with. The Earl and his wife did their best to put on a brave face, but grief and failing health haunted the family.[269]

On 26 January, disaster was averted when a chimney caught fire at Highclere but fortunately burned itself out after an hour, "leaving only a fright and a nasty smell in the house".[270] But the Countess's sensitive lungs took in such smoke as did escape.

On Lordy 2 February 1871 it was time to open Highclere to the children of Kingsclere Workhouse once more. Lordy was occasionally soon well enough to leave the nursery behind, and from the age of five until seven he enjoyed respite, in particular at events staged at the castle for the workhouse children. He proudly associated his mother with a passion for serving the wider community around Highclere, and the first of these fond early memories, when he was barely five years old, was of watching her in action at this event. With his mother and Winifred, he distributed presents to the children. A sumptuous dinner was given to the guests in the castle's dining salon, which had been decorated with a Christmas tree, fully lit and laden with toys and bon-bons, and before the workhouse children left they were given a further treat of tea and plum cake. Comment was made of the youthful Lordy and Lady Winifred handling their parts in these proceedings successfully.[271]

Whilst making preparations for the season in London, Evelyn fell ill again on 12 February, this time with a severe cold. The virus spread through the entire house, affecting Ladies Winifred and Gwendolen (who was visiting from Pixton Park) and the Earl himself. Evelyn was bed-bound for two weeks as her weak lungs struggled to recover.[272]

Accepting the advice of several of her friends in Torquay (a favourite retreat for invalids because there the winter was usually milder), the

Countess agreed, with her husband's consent, to be treated by a Dr James Averst[273], a naval doctor who offered homeopathic remedies and had once treated the naturalist Charles Darwin. Lord Carnarvon administered aconite on the instructions of Dr Averst, and his wife responded favourably within twenty-four hours.[274] Still, Averst doubted that Lady Carnarvon would ever be "entirely and absolutely" healed, because diagnosis pointed to pulmonary tuberculosis, which was considered incurable. The treatment would only provide temporary relief. Indeed, within days Evelyn suffered a relapse. The Earl wrote in his diary: "She is much better than she was but she does not gather strength as I could desire. She seems subject to relapses with any change of weather or circumstances."[275]

Evelyn's health continued to be erratic over the next few weeks, and under Dr Averst's supervision, the treatment was changed to a series of vaccinations. The Countess was well enough in May to resume some social engagements again and to see the Carnarvon children, including Lordy, who passed through London from Highclere en route to Pixton Park to stay with their Herbert grandmother.

As well as worries about his wife, Lord Carnarvon received grave news from Paris, which was in chaos as a result of the infamous siege.[276] This was an event that Dr Alan Herbert was swept into. Indeed through the efforts of Herbert and others, the English expatriates in the city and surrounds were kept alive with an elaborate supply line of food and medicines. At least one diarist recorded Dr Alan as "of Parisian celebrity".[277]

The London Season of 1871

Lady Carnarvon was obliged, through being a busy politician's wife and herself a leading hostess, to balance her increasingly desperate state of health. This is described in numerous entries in the Earl's diary for the year, but it must have been a particularly grim period of high drama – more so than can be ascertained – as many pages were severed.[278] Evelyn's life was a regime of relentless receptions and lavish entertaining. Newspaper reports are heavy and varied, providing only one conclusion: that in participating in such an exhausting programme during the 1871 London season, she was putting her life on the line to further her husband's causes, with his extensive collection of society, parliamentary and foreign contacts at both public and private level. The line-up of appearances was among the most demanding she had ever staged or experienced. Her assembly was a great towering success, and she also held several receptions at the family house in Grosvenor Street and attended at many other functions with the Earl.[279]

Occasionally there is evidence of Carnarvon wishing to amuse and please his wife. In May of 1871 he bought her a horse.[280] From the time of riding at Bretby she had greatly loved the sport, a gene she passed on to her only son, Lordy. The couple spent some time together in the country air at Pixton, with the children shunted off to Highclere, and then on 22 July the family were reunited at Highclere. A family wedding followed: the Earl's radical brother, Auberon Herbert, a newly elected MP[281], married Lady Florence (Dolly) Couper (Cowper) on 9 August.[282] The happy couple spent their honeymoon on the Carnarvon estate at Milford, the picturesque residence near the lake at Highclere.[283] Evelyn was determined that everything should be done to ensure both wedding and honeymoon went perfectly for her husband's brother and his most likeable wife.

Lady Carnarvon, though, was still feeling unwell. A trip to the spa towns of Germany was prescribed, taking in a visit to a homeopathic specialist, Professor N. Friedrich of Heidelberg, who had a good record in tuberculosis cases and whom it was considered might provide a better treatment programme for Evelyn's crippling illness. The Earl was determined to leave no stone unturned in seeking a cure, not least because he still wanted Evelyn to produce another son. Accordingly, the Carnarvons announced they were leaving Britain for two months.[284]

It proved an extraordinary long and trying trip, first with a ferry crossing to Ostend and then travelling by rail to Brussels and through to Cologne, where Evelyn was just "too tired to go out".[285] By 7 August they had reached Wildbad where a succession of hot and cold baths were taken. It was only on 22 August (at the time of the twelfth bath taken) that the Earl was able to record: "I cannot help hoping that the baths are beginning at last to agree with E., apparently little discomfort – little of the neuralgia remaining – only fatigue which is natural..."[286] At the time of the eighteenth bath, Evelyn had been examined by the local guru, a Dr Hauffmann[287], whose advice was that the Countess would feel the benefit of the rigours of the hot/cold bath treatment in about a month. He said this would reduce her susceptibility to bronchitis and rheumatism and give her more general strength. Hauffmann cautioned about exposing Evelyn to "the salt baths at Ischl".[288]

The trip continued, with the taking of even more baths, and the Carnarvons finally removed themselves to Baden Baden on 1 September. The whistle-stop tour included a day at Strasbourg and Freiborg, setting down in other towns en route by 10 September to Neuhaven, where Evelyn's health slumped. She developed a severe throat infection and swallowing problems, requiring the administering of "a poultice and aconite"[289] and the services of a local doctor. The Earl's health was also affected. Carnarvon had improved by the 17 September, but Evelyn was in a deep depression.

The next phase of their tour was through Switzerland, to Zurich and Lakes Lucerne and Como. Evelyn was very ill and caused Carnarvon much anxiety, but we shall never know the details for certain, since the key pages of his diaries covering 24 and 25 September and 28 September – 1 October 1871 were removed. Only one small clue survives from the entry for 27 September, which reveals the Earl's "state of continual anxiety about E".[290]

On the 3 October 1871, they reached Heidelberg, their destination to consult with the leading homeopathic specialist Dr Friedrich.[291] The latter was away and not expected to be back for several days. They didn't want to leave without seeing him, so they waited, which gave Evelyn a chance, at last, to rest. Friedrich was consulted on 7 October, and since the pages of the Earl's diary are removed for 7–11 October 1871, the news could not have brought any comfort whatsoever.

The Carnarvons planned their return to England and on 12 October 1871 they arrived via Ostend. They went immediately to Tunbridge Wells to see the Dowager Carnarvon and their children, who were being well enough looked after by their grandmother and Lady Gwendolen.

Carnarvon was not keeping well either; he was experiencing chronic throat pain. On 18 October he went up to London and called on a "[Dr] MacKenzie of 13 Weymouth St, Portland Place" who examined his throat "with a laryngoscope and prescribed – in some respects satisfactory, in some an unsatisfactory opinion".[292] At the same time the Earl lost no time in consulting a Dr Cotton, an English lung specialist about Evelyn.[293] Cotton "stethascoped her carefully"[294] and made several recommendations to ease her condition.[295]

Death of the Earl of Chesterfield

Lordy first experienced death in the family when his mother's only brother died of a very severe form of typhoid fever at his home at Bretby Park on 1 December 1871. George Philip Cecil Arthur, aged only forty, the 7th Earl of Chesterfield, was "a popular landlord, and a quietly estimable member of the aristocracy".[296] He had been in company of Bertie, Prince of Wales, on a visit to Lord Londesborough, at Londesborough Lodge, Scarborough in November 1871, to shoot game. The Prince contracted the same disease and was at one point seen to be in peril of his life, but treatment at Sandringham in the following days by the highest medical authorities in the land saved his life. Lord Chesterfield was not so lucky and suffered a desperate death. Lord Carnarvon vividly describes the full horror in his diaries.[297]

As a result of George's death, much of the Chesterfield estates passed to Lady Evelyn, Countess of Carnarvon, save for her own mother's life interest, with these lands being eventually passed to Lordy.[298]

Lordy was now deprived of his *only* maternal uncle, and as his maternal grandfather had no brothers, there was no male figure on that side of his family to guide the boy's path in boyhood and in life. The Chesterfield title itself had to revert to the "parent tree"[299]; the new Lord Chesterfield was deemed to be an obscure Ulster squire.

Lady Chesterfield was shaken with grief; she had lost a husband and a son in the space of just a few years. She still had a surviving sister (Selina, Lady Bradford, whose husband, the Earl, was a political colleague of Lordy's father) and her brothers, Lordy's great uncles, survived. [300]

As Christmas loomed, Evelyn went alone to stay with her mother at Bretby, to share their sorrow together. The Earl spent the festive period at Highclere, and in the aftermath of his brother-in-law's horrific death, which he had witnessed at very close quarters, it was his Lordship, not Evelyn, who had a complete breakdown.[301]

Edward Herbert : Adored cousin of Henry Herbert who was killed by bandits in Greece in 1870

**Henry, Fourth Earl of Carnarvon
Lordy's father**

Chapter Twelve

The 4th Earl's Breakdown

Carnarvon was suffering from a deep depression. Charged with sorting out the Chesterfield family's financial obligations to the new Earl (on behalf of Evelyn's mother), in his melancholy he also turned to rewriting his own will.[302] The first few pages of the 1872 diary are cut out, suggesting he was in despair. A fragment of a sentence on one page survives in which he records "How gloomily the New Year opens".[303] Evelyn was equally as touched by the events at Bretby a few weeks before. Carnarvon records "E very low".[304]

By mid-January, whilst a national day of thanksgiving was being planned to welcome the restoration to health of the Prince of Wales, the official record was that Carnarvon was "seriously indisposed"[305], but the full extent of the Earl's incapacity was naturally played down to a state of "fatigue and anxiety". At the beginning of the year. Queen Victoria sent a telegram, from Osborne, to Lady Evelyn saying she was distressed at hearing of Lord Carnarvon's illness. Evelyn thanked the Queen, remarking that "there was a gratifying improvement in her husband's health during the past two days"[306]. As well as Carnarvon's usual medical attendant, a Dr Joseph Bunny of Newbury, a London physician, Dr George Burrowes, was called in for expert supervision.[307]

The diary entry for 21 January 1872 reveals more details of the Earl's serious condition:

> Highclere – I have been very ill and this is the first day that I have been able to come downstairs. I am very weak but thank God infinitely better and mending every day. The attack came upon Friday 5th and had clearly brewing for some time previously. I felt very ill, what I found was fever. On Monday night I had a sort of collapse – my pulse being down I imagine. It had been 54 a great part of Saturday and Sunday and I almost thought that I was going but brandy and beef tea in the space of a few hours brought up the pulse to 68 or 70 but at the time everyone was most alarmed and I thought myself going. E telegraphed and Bunny arrived, Burrowes

who came on Friday and who argued with him that it was due to overwork – the anxieties and troubles of last month a complete break down of the normality of the nervous system.[308]

In a later passage in the diary he records :

> [The doctors] gave me but little medicine but prescribed absolute rest and so I have vegetated and regained my strength though I am still very feeble, Alan [the Earl's brother, and a doctor], dear fellow arrived on Thursday morning from Paris as he heard how ill I am. The Queen telegraphed to know the facts and altogether I have given much alarm and trouble as I could well do – but I am very thankful when I look back on the course of events and see how I have been spared.[309]

It had been a very close call.

In February, the Carnarvons left Highclere for London, but the Earl was still too weak to attend to his parliamentary duties.[310] An update in the diary records:

> Saw Gull and Burrows [doctors] who are satisfied with me but insist on great prudence and abstinence from all briefings, They think that I may be able to come [again] to London after Easter, but I expect for the best part of summer I must be most careful...[311]

Two weeks later, back at Highclere the Earl says: "I... do a good deal of business of one kind or another but cannot work long – above all cannot write – I find that dictating is far easier."[312] A relapse followed: "very poorly [again] it began with a headache, violent retching and a chill. Dr Bunny called, I spent most of the day in bed."[313]

Five-year-old Lordy was also most unwell at the same time. His father records in his diary for 14 March :

> I was called upstairs by a sudden and serious [report]... of Porchey. He was shivering from heard to foot as if in an ague, his colour gone, except a sort of purple spot on his face. His feet and hands very cold, I got him confined, hot flannels and blankets and called for Dr Bunny and gave him a dose of brandy and hot water. Bunny on his arrival thought it was a chill... at dinner time, Porchey much

better, Bunny slept at Highclere.[314]

The Earl's withdrawal from society continued until mid-April, when Evelyn accompanied the Earl to London from Highclere with the children in tow (it was only then that the Countess felt confident that the children could see their father at close range; before she had taken them away to Bretby Park to stay with Lady Chesterfield).[315] Lordy had recovered well from his earlier illness.

Carnarvon is mentioned in Lord Derby's diaries for 16 April, when they were both at a political meeting. Carnarvon's mind was on money matters:

> Walked with Carnarvon... he has been living in the country... He talks at length of his (or rather Lady Carnarvon's) recent accession of fortune [from her late brother] which is for a long time to come more nominal than real, for the Chesterfield estates are encumbered almost to their full value.[316]

The Earl did make scattered appearances in the House of Lords, making only slight comments on the issues of the day.[317] Evelyn, meanwhile, kept herself busy in these dark days. As a member of the organising committee at the South Kensington Museum, together with other titled ladies she prepared for an exhibition of ancient jewellery.[318]

The couple made the effort to appear together publically at a Herbert family wedding at St Paul's Church, Knightbridge, on 25 June.[319] A further appearance followed at a garden party at Chiswick hosted by the Prince and Princess of Wales on 2 July.[320] But after a series of commitments, including speaking engagements involving his work on prison reform (he chaired the International Prison Congress[321]), the pressure became too great for Carnarvon and Evelyn's health was wavering too.

In August, they took a long holiday with the children on the Isle of Wight, and the plan was to remain there until mid-September.[322] One newspaper report gave further details:

> The Countess of Carnarvon and family are residing at a villa in the vicinity of Ryde. The noble earl is yachting, and has greatly

benefited in health during the last few months through abstaining for a time from his parliamentary and magisterial duties.[323]

The villa at Ryde was Spring Vale, Oak Hill. One of the cruises by the Earl was on his yacht, the *Mercia*, out to Land's End and back from Cowes.[324]

The Carnarvons left their sojourn on the Isle of Wight earlier than expected, and travelled with the children to Bretby Park via London. News reports said that the Earl's health "appears quite re-established"[325] and that "he had recovered from his late severe illness".[326]

The Earl made his first public address in the second half of the year on 16 September at Carlton, near Nottingham, at the laying of the foundation stone of a new mechanics institute (with an adjoining bowling green) to serve as a memorial to his brother-in-law, the late 7th Earl of Chesterfield.[327] Evelyn was present to witness a highly emotionally charged ceremony. This was followed with a speech about the labour market at the Highclere Agricultural Association gathering on Wednesday 25 September. Evelyn was on hand in case of unforeseen difficulties, and she presented the prizes.[328]

Visitors arrived once more at Highclere.[329] On the Earl's return from a shooting trip with his friend (and collateral) Lord Ducie, there were several days of shooting among Highclere coverts.[330] In November, after resuming activities in the public arena and having friends and family passing through Highclere, the building was cleared of all guests. The Dowager Countess left Highclere with Lady Gwendolen for London and later they returned to Pixton Park. Lord Carnarvon went up to London, leaving Eveline, Lady Portsmouth, only at Highclere.[331] On his return, Eveline returned to Eggesford House.[332]

In December the Earl was at Sandringham visiting the Prince of Wales.[333] The Prince was anxious to let Carnarvon know that he painfully mourned Lady Carnarvon's brother, one of his best friends, and wanted to ensure this grief was conveyed to her. He recognised that he was lucky to survive whilst the Earl of Chesterfield had died.

The Carnarvon children spent the winter of 1872 with Anne at Bretby Park.[334] Lordy, had adjusted to the long spells when his parents were either dreadfully ill or flitting around the social scene, and his grandmother was his surrogate parent. Socialising during December took Lord and Lady Carnarvon to Sandringham and Knowsley,[335] but they were back in time to spend Christmas at Bretby with the children.[336]

Business as Usual in 1873

At the beginning of the year the Carnarvons left Lordy and his sisters in the care of their grandmother, Lady Chesterfield, at Bretby Park, to travel to London en route to the South of France.[337] By the tail end of January the Carnarvons were expected to return and come via London to Bretby to see the children. The Earl intended to remain in Derbyshire, until Parliament resumed.[338] But the plan was thwarted when the Earl was caught up in London, and Evelyn left him there and went on to Bretby alone with her maid.[339]

The Carnarvons were back together in London in mid-February to fulfil a number of social engagements. The Earl was planning a lengthy yachting trip to the Mediterranean, along with some male companions. Meanwhile Evelyn was due to go to stay at Bretby Park.[340] In April it was reported that the Earl "was yachting off the coast of Spain"[341], whilst Evelyn had spent the period of the separation from her husband at Bretby Park, Highclere and London.

On his arrival in England the Earl returned to Highclere and a storm of protests over his decision to give notice to a number of his estate labourers. Carnarvon was sensitive to local Hampshire and Berkshire critics, sometimes even more so than the London hacks who hounded him or the taunts from his political enemies. It was asserted in a local newspaper (the *Reading Mercury*) that some of the people to be evicted had left their jobs on the Highclere and surrounding estates to go to work on the railways – with the lure of better wages – and that the Earl was punishing them. The Earl's defence was a limp one, but he was determined to dig in to stop the loss of his agricultural workers to the railways. He said he had given notices to occupiers, over the confiscation of their cottages, because the buildings were unfit to live in and, because of the unsanitary conditions prevailing in some of the dwellings, the buildings had to be rebuilt.[342] Despite harsh comments continuing for several weeks, he would not back down.

Since the family's home at 66 Grosvenor Street was sold[343] the Earl and Countess installed themselves in London at Pulteney Hotel, Albermarle Street, awaiting a new London residence to come ready.[344] On 14 May they were at Buckingham Palace for a state concert attended by over 800 guests, and the next day the Countess gave a dinner party at Bruton Street.[345] They went on to attend a number of dinners and receptions during the second half of May.

As Whitsun approached the Carnarvons travelled down to Pixton Park.[346] Lordy was with his siblings at Pixton to greet his parents, and he later travelled back with them to London. Lordy was rewarded for the good reports on his behaviour from his grandmother at Pixton with a trip with his father down to West Cowes, Isle of Wight, to share in some sailing.[347] Even at this early age Lordy adored messing around in boats.

Evelyn's handling of her husband's illness and a period of stability in her own health were nothing short of miraculous. She revelled as hostess supreme, giving an assembly at Bruton Street. This was followed by staging a grand dinner there on Saturday 14 June with many distinguished guests.[348] Other such dinners and evening parties followed. The Carnarvons were also present as guests at dinners, balls and receptions across London in June and July, including a garden party in Chiswick for the Shah of Persia.[349]

News of Evelyn's supreme and dazzling skills as a hostess was in constant circulation. Carnarvon often entertained many colonial leaders and magnates. With Evelyn's abilities not only did Carnarvon make himself available in London to personally acquaint himself with visiting representatives, but, with Evelyn, he ever extended the hospitality of Highclere to them and accordingly brought relations to a head where there had been previously little dialogue, stalemate and suspicion. Reverand Egerton Ryerson DD, LLD, a man who spent sixty years in the public service in Canada, is one such individual who records in his memoirs of being warmly greeted by Carnarvon whilst on a visit to London.[350]

Evelyn's close friends at Court included the Princess of Wales and Princess Mary Adelaide, who had known Evelyn for close on twenty years[351] and was the mother of Princess Mary of Teck (later Queen

Mary). At a dinner at the Austrian Embassy, Belgrave Square, on Monday 7 July[352] Princess Mary Adelaide found time to enquire about Evelyn's state of health and morale. It was an ideal occasion as the Earl was busy elsewhere.[353]

Meanwhile the Countess gave her name to a new project to establish a national training school of cookery.[354] This campaign reunited Evelyn with Henry Cole, who had stayed at Highclere in 1871. "King Cole" (he was so named by the Princess of Wales) had first won support from Evelyn, her mother, Lady Chesterfield, and the Dowager Countess, Henrietta, for his efforts to raise funds for a national training school for music.[355]

The lull in Lord Carnarvon's depression was shaken when his mother was taken ill in the summer of 1873. The Dowager Countess, Henrietta, a widow for over twenty years who lived mostly at her preferred residence at Pixton Park, Dulverton, Somerset, developed congestion of the lungs, a medical condition that haunted her grandson Lordy all his life. Lord Carnarvon and his brother Dr Alan Herbert were at hand in case of any rapid decline.[356] But Henrietta recovered sufficiently to be out of danger, and Carnarvon and Evelyn took some time out at Cowes, sailing, before returning to Highclere at the end of August.[357]

In August and again in September of 1873, Lordy and Lady Winifred were on holiday with minders, staying at the Granville Hotel, St Lawrence on Sea, near Ramsgate.[358] By this point Lordy was missing his mother on such outings, and resenting her absence. Although sister Winifred was an ally and protective, she was precocious. Lordy was not one to seek attention, and inevitably he became more withdrawn than his siblings.

When at home, Evelyn did spend time with Lordy – albeit less than he would have liked. She saw her children in the afternoon, by arrangement with the nursery staff. As one commentator states of country-house life: "It was considered undesirable for children, servants and parents to see, smell or hear each other except at certain recognised times and places."[359] Evelyn read to her children in French, her favourite language; she especially wished them to know and learn languages. She also wanted to ensure they were given an appreciation of poetry, music and dance. These short sessions with his darling mother were cherished. Lordy's proficiency in French was praised by his mama, which made him glow. He almost never received any praise from his father.

Nursemaids and governesses were otherwise charged with firm undertakings over the rearing of Lordy and his sisters, and it was these employees who exercised a stream of rules for the minding and upbringing of the Herbert children. Closeness, love and tenderness were in short supply from these third parties, with more correction than attention and even less kindness sometimes than the scant parental warmth. The cold regime administered by parents and minders with its absence of affection was a component that resulted in difficulties for Lordy forging close and loving relationships as an adult.[360]

On 17 September the Earl and Evelyn left Highclere for Bretby Park to see their children.[361] They later travelled to Gedling Lodge, their place in Nottinghamshire, for a few days shooting with several guests.[362] Evelyn travelled back to London alone and on to Highclere to fulfil a local engagement, presenting the prizes at the Highclere Agricultural Association's annual ploughing match and show.[363] The Earl and Evelyn were reunited at Bretby Park and travelled back together to Highclere in the middle of October.[364]

Another autumn of house parties and shooting was lined up.[365] On 8 November the Carnarvons returned to Highclere after a visit to Lord Cowper at Panshanger.[366] Count Beust from the Austrian Embassy (whom Evelyn had charmed during the London season and invited to the countryside[367]) was a guest at Highclere, along with others, in mid-November.[368] In one fortnight in November the succession of visitors reached a high, with an assortment of personalities, including Meredith Townsend, the editor of *The Spectator*,[369] the Nevills, the Northcotes, the Charles Russells, several members of the Forester family, Henry Cole, the Portals, and the writer Augustus Hare.[370]

Hare had met the Carnarvons at Chevening[371] in the summer of that year. On first seeing Evelyn's accomplishment at staging entertainment and dramatic shows for Highclere's guests he was immediately besotted by her: "Lord Carnarvon is agreeable and his wife most lovely and piquant."[372] He records a visit to Highclere in his autobiography, quoting a letter to a lady friend dated 12 November:

This is a beautiful park, with every variety of scenery, hill, valley, woods, with an undergrowth of rhododendron, a poetical lake! And [it] is so immense – thirteen miles round – that one never goes out of it, and rather feels the isolation of the great house in the centre, which, though very handsome, is not equal to the place.[373]

Hare also makes a further flattering reference to Evelyn as being "very lovely and winning, and boundlessly interesting to listen to... She says that she has hitherto been too exclusive; that henceforth she shall wish to fill her house more with people of every shade."[374] He says of Lady Winifred: "The little daughter of the house – Winifred – is the most delightful and unspoilt of children."[375]

Evelyn's circle, and hence her guest list, included all sorts of people. She could charm politicians and diplomats easily, and with her love of literature she sought the enrichment for her guests by cultivating the popular writers of the day. Hare was not the only one who passed through Highclere that autumn. The next wave of guests on 18 November included the poet Robert Browning, who is recalled by fellow guest Lady Knightley of Fawsley[376] as being, "different from his poems as anything one can imagine – a loud-voiced, sturdy little man who says nothing in the least obscure or difficult to understand!"[377]

Another visitor at this same time was Lord Carnarvon's cousin, Elizabeth Howard of Greystoke Castle, Cumberland, who was later to become the Earl's second wife.[378]

Evelyn's clever combination of house guests often stirred sparring, but the atmosphere remained friendly. In the main the pace was leisurely, with walks organised to Beacon Hill to see the fine views and luncheon taken at Milford House beside the lake. Dinner was grander and more formal, with entertainment and card games. The Countess delighted in showing off the house, with its many pictures and furniture, whilst the Earl was the principal custodian of the contents of the library. But it was the witty anecdotes and accurate gossip, gleaned from Evelyn's connections, that were most enjoyed. Lady Knightley remarks of the experience: "I wish I had the pen of a Boswell, to put down one-half of the things which I have heard here."[379]

As the year drew to a close, the family were in good form. On 18 December, Carnarvon opened the new cattle market at Newbury.[380] He was constantly conscious of his duties among local organisations, and as a major English landowner was at the forefront of promoting agriculture and local commerce.

By Christmas the whole family were together to celebrate. Evelyn provided a Christmas tree for the children attending Woodcote School. On 10 January the Countess and her children distributed presents to the little ones from that school, joining them at excellent tea party.[381] On such occasions Lordy was firmly attached to his mother's side. It was often as near to her as he was allowed for months at a time.

A new position, and a new child

Evelyn moved her children to Bretby Park in the middle of January. Meanwhile the Earl, who had travelled to Pixton Park to see his mother, joined Evelyn at Bretby Park.[382]

Gladstone had been prime minister of a Liberal government since 1868. The Tory Benjamin Disraeli succeeded him on 18 February 1874. It was Disraeli's second term as prime minister, having been in office previously for 281 days in 1868. He announced the members of his new ministry to Queen Victoria at Windsor on 20 February. There had been a shadow over the Earl of Carnarvon resuming a Cabinet post due to his health problems of the preceding year. Pundits had tipped Carnarvon for education, as lord president of the council, and Lord John Manners for the colonies.[383] But Carnarvon's refined and cultivated mind and his thorough conscientiousness, as well as his past government experience, made him ideal choice for the Colonial Office. He accepted Disraeli's offer of the colonies and travelled to Windsor to shake the Queen's hand on Saturday 21 February. In the following week, Carnarvon took up his post as colonial secretary. As the townhouse at Bruton Street was undergoing alterations, he was living at Lady Chesterfield's house at Hill Street.[384]

The Carnarvons, with Lady Chesterfield, returned to Highclere on 7 March, at which point Evelyn fell ill with a chest infection. She was therefore unable to accompany her husband to Windsor Castle for the state banquet on Monday 9 March, a grand dinner traditionally given by Queen Victoria to her outgoing and new incoming ministers.[385]

The doctors suggested the sea air might help Evelyn's breathing, and rooms at a Brighton hotel were obtained. By the 24 March the Countess was fit enough to travel to London, to Thomas' Hotel, where the Earl was already in residence and had reserved additional rooms.[386] The Countess attended the Queen's drawing room at Buckingham Palace on Wednesday 25 March, and was presented to Her Majesty.[387]

The writer Augustus Hare was a supreme admirer of Evelyn. He attended a dinner party in London given on 14 July by the Dowager Countess of Carnarvon, who had promised him the renewal of his acquaintance with Lord Stanhope.[388] Evelyn, her mother and the Earl were also in the company. Augustus Hare noted:

> Dined at Lady Carnarvon's to meet Lord Stanhope. Only two mothers of the house, Lady Chesterfield and Lady Carnarvon – a charming good-humoured old lady. Lord Carnarvon talked much of his interests, of regular work and the unutterable weariness of interruptions. Lord Stanhope was very agreeable at dinner, but fell asleep afterwards. The younger Lady Carnarvon, with her hair sprinkled with diamonds, looked unspeakably lovely.[389]

In August, Benjamin Disraeli was expected to spend a few days with the Carnarvons at Highclere.[390] Disraeli was by this time a widower, his wife Mary having died in 1872, and was in regular correspondence with Evelyn's mother and aunt.[391]

The Earl and Countess were at Bretby Park visiting Lady Evelyn's mother in early October, and returned to Highclere on Monday 5 October.[392] Evelyn was carrying another child; it was going to be a Christmas baby.

By the Christmas week Evelyn's pregnancy had reached its crucial nine-month stage. Carnarvon visited his mother at Pixton Park with Lordy and his sisters, who were left there to spend Christmas with their grandmother.[393] As all four previous confinements had been terrifying, with each experience all the more painful and distressing, Evelyn knew she faced a daunting birth ahead.[394] This time she felt less confident of her survival, and she changed her will on 24 December 1874, with an emphasis on leaving her son Lordy in no doubt about his duty to preserve Bretby at all costs.

Evelyn's last child, a daughter, was born on 31 December. It was a difficult birth that occurred amid tragic circumstances prevailing in the Highclere household: the death of Mrs Laverick, the Countess's faithful housekeeper-maid, in a railway accident. Lord Carnarvon was pleased that Evelyn's unpleasant ordeal lasted only a few hours. She went into labour at one thirty in the morning and the baby was born at four o'clock. But the little girl was in a critical state, and was only saved by the expertise of Dr Arthur Farre, a leading figure of the time in childbirth. Evelyn's mother, Lady Chesterfield, was disappointed that the child was not a boy.[395] So was the Earl, despite recording in his diary that such things were, of course, out of his control. But the fact remained that the heir in waiting, Lordy, was a sickly child. And so was his mother. Evelyn, Countess of Carnarvon, was dying.

The loss of a Countess

Evelyn was exhausted, with a fever and a racing pulse. She was delighted to learn that Queen Victoria wanted to be the godmother of the newest Herbert daughter, and after this news she was able to eat a little and sleep better.[396] But her state of calm was not to last, and her condition weakened.

Lord Carnarvon continued to work in Cabinet as normal. Benjamin Disraeli, writing from 10 Downing Street to Evelyn's aunt, Lady Bradford, on 15 January, remained hopeful after dining with Lord Carnarvon:

> Instead of dining yesterday with the gay revellers [this refers to an invitation from a number of society ladies to dine] I partook of a Bretby turkey in Bruton Street – rather a melancholy repast, for Lady Carnarvon had a relapse in the morning and Lord C. was very nervous and depressed. Gull [the physician] came in the evening and was not discouraging, and C. told me at the Cabinet today that her pulse had again subsided.[397]

On 23 January Lordy's mother had a further relapse. The bulletins were grim and terrifying: "At Midnight the Countess of Carnarvon was stated to be in a most critical condition. Sir William Gull and Dr Farre were both in attendance."[398] The 4th Earl's biographer records: "It was a shattering blow; the sudden ending of the happy companionship of 13 years, and the loss of one so singularly gifted... seemed to bring life to a standstill..."[399]

Lord Carnarvon was present, along with Lady Chesterfield, when Evelyn's life slipped away.[400] The Earl's sister, Lady Portsmouth, took control of supporting him in his darkest hour. He was devastated, but as much for himself as for his dead wife. He later recorded that in the immediate aftermath of Evelyn's funeral his sister had been "everything to me".[401]

Others who were greatly saddened by Evelyn's death included Walter Bagehot, whose friendship with the Countess had "given him much pleasure for many years".[402] Bagehot immediately offered support to the Earl with genuine compassion for his grief.[403]

Lord Derby records in his diary for the 25 January 1875: "Lady Carnarvon, who had been dangerously ill for a fortnight, died this morning: a great loss to the party... She will be regretted by many, being hospitable and social in disposition."[404]

A letter from Lord Derby's wife, Mary (widow of the 2nd Marquis of Salisbury) to Lord Carnarvon reveals how she had mentioned Carnarvon's grief over losing Evelyn to Queen Victoria. The Queen remarked that she admired his courage and self-control, but added that he had been made to do too much.[405] In reality, it was Carnarvon's own decision to work till he dropped from fatigue and grief.[406]

Of the many Evelyn admirers, Augustus Hare, in his memoirs of 1900, gave the most touching of tributes:

> The news of dear Lady Carnarvon's death came... as a shadow over everything. Surely never was there a more open, lovable, unselfish, charming, and truly noble character... Apparently radiant with happiness, and shedding happiness on all around her, she yet had often said latterly that she did not feel that the compensations made up for the anxieties of life, and that she longed to be at rest.[407]

Lady Dorothy Nevill's tribute was also moving:

> I felt the death of poor Lady Carnarvon very much, for I was very fond of her, and used to spend a good deal of time at Highclere. She was woman of excellent judgment, and the influence which she exercised over her husband in political matters was invariably good, and this he thoroughly appreciated.[408]

Evelyn's mother, Lady Chesterfield, returned to Bretby soon after her daughter's death to perform the painful task of expunging from Evelyn's correspondence and personal items any secrets lying therein. This was a ritual act amongst the aristocracy. In the case of a woman it was usually performed by a close female friend or relative; the husband was totally excluded and was never informed of what was discovered.

A grieving father

Carnarvon could not rest. In February 1875, after a short stay with his children at Bretby Park, he returned to his work in government service, staying at his London home at 16 Bruton Street. Henrietta, the Dowager Countess Carnarvon, and Lady Gwendolen joined him there, as did Lordy and Lady Winifred.[409] It was agreed at a family summit that in the short term the children would spend time with Lady Portsmouth at Eggesford House and as well as with their Herbert grandmother and Lady Gwendolen at Pixton. At Highclere, rooms and nursery staff would also be available to relieve the aunts of the routine labours and tedium of child rearing.[410]

But before he could pass the burden of the children onto others' shoulders, Carnarvon had one more daunting task to perform: the christening of "Baby". The event took place at the Savoy Chapel (or Royal Chapel Savoy)[411]. Being the Queen's goddaughter, the child was named Victoria Alexandrina Mary Cecil Herbert.[412] The little baby girl was blessed with a full set of illustrious godparents; besides the Queen, she had Lady Derby as godmother and Lord Salisbury as godfather.[413] Lordy, Winifred and Margaret were present to share the moment with their grieving father. The Reverend Henry White conducted the service and the font was tastefully decorated with flowers. No doubt Carnarvon was lost in memories of the last occasion he had been inside this ancient church, taking communion alongside Evelyn.[414]

To add to Carnarvon's worries, which were affecting him greatly,[415] his mother suffered another alarming health scare which rippled on for several uneasy months, caused by her recurring respiratory problems from weak lungs which were the bane of her existence. Keeping a watchful eye for reports of any change from his sisters, the Earl (who described himself as "so poorly") finally gave in to pressure and sought a few days of rest away,[416] taking Winifred with him to visit Eveline at Eggesford. Winifred's array of Wallop cousins [417]subsumed her into their company, allowing the Earl some quiet contemplation and one-to-one conversations with his sister, whose husband was absent. Excursions to the cliffs at Northam where he could gaze out to the sea gently eased Henry's state of mind.

Carnarvon later escaped from London to spend the Easter holidays of 1875 at Eggesford with the Portsmouths, taking the chance to see his children who had travelled there.[418] Nine-year-old Lordy was singled out for grave attention by his papa, to discuss a subject about which both father and son fretted: namely, the heir's education, including his religious knowledge. Canon John Troutbeck, DD, MA, who commanded fees of a guinea for three lessons, was coaching the boy.[419] A reasonable report was received from Troutbeck, who judged that the Carnarvon heir had a "very good head and is fairly advanced: but has been pushed on too fast and too far in his Latin".[420]

Henry called on horseback at his wayward brother Auberon's farm at Ashley Arnwood and received a warm welcome from Auberon and his wife, Dolly. He took a peculiar interest in asking after his nephew, Rolf, a little boy of three whose health was as troubled as Lordy's.[421] Afterwards, a trip to Cowes proved a quiet diversion for Henry.

But none of these activities stopped the nightmares and sleeplessness he was suffering. Pages from the Earl's diaries throughout this period have been savagely cut out, at his hand or that of his second wife, Elsie.[422] The pain of Evelyn's loss remained overwhelming. Support from family was augmented in London by Lady Derby's close affections. Henry found himself attempting a visit to the Royal Academy, but turned himself back as he felt he was not yet ready to engage with a wider spread of society folk.[423]

On 7 May Henry applied for probate on his late wife's last will and testament. He was named as sole executor. Evelyn's personal estate was sworn at under £18,000. *The Times* reported:

> The testatrix charges the estates in the counties of Derby and Notts, which she became entitled to on the death of her brother, the Earl of Chesterfield, with the payment of £40,000 in favour of her younger children, and she begs her son, Lord Porchester, to look upon the said estates, which he would thereafter succeed to, as a solemn trust, to be used not for his own gratification or pleasure, but for the glory of God and the honour of those who have gone before him...[424]

Evelyn also made provision for some "annuities and legacies, pecuniary and specific; and the residue she gives to her husband for life, and after his death to her younger children, in such manner as he may appoint..."[425]

On the Whitsun holidays Henry took the children to sail at Cowes. Sailing on his father's new yacht was a tremendous thrill for Lordy, and cemented in him a lifelong love of sailing. However, such close contact with his demanding papa inevitably meant there would be a direct discussion about his academic progress (or rather, the lack of it), particularly in the study of Latin. Lordy was very afraid, and his father often made him cry. Once again the boy was reduced to tears at his father's taunts at being "very indolent and without any persistency or industry".[426]

As summer approached some respite from Lord Carnarvon's grief was achieved with the commission of a portrait of his late wife Evelyn, by Frederick Percy Graves.[427] He also made a trip to his adored old school Eton College on 27 June, whilst he was at Windsor, to see Queen Victoria on official business. The monarch offered her minister every sympathy for his family burden and commanded him to bring *all* the Herbert children to see her, which the Earl did on 2 July, storming Windsor with his offspring and their domestic entourage.[428] Another healing excursion was taken to Hatfield, where Henry had proposed marriage to Evelyn. Less formal than at Court, the children were "happy racing about the house and dragging each other up and down the Gallery on a bear skin".[429]

Henry found more time to engage with the children in the second half of the year. He particularly focused his attention on Winifred, whom he saw as being, in time, a helping hand. He endlessly worried about any cold or infection she might be exposed to, with one major incident arising over an outbreak of scarlet fever that affected one of the servants.

Besides these domestic challenges, Henry was also bogged down with Masonic commitments, and worries over his mother's state of health and his sister Gwendolen's morale in taking care of his mother, plus a range of political questions. Henry plunged himself into an exhausting work routine for much of the remainder of 1875. This grim year saw him at loggerheads with his Cabinet colleagues over his proposal for a confederation of states in South Africa. The rejection of Carnarvon's idea (which had worked well in Canada) ultimately led to great instability and economic trouble in that corner of the world between the British and Dutch settlers and culminated in the Boer War(s) a few years later.[430]

Entries from Lord Derby's diaries provide a glimpse into the troubled state of Carnarvon's mind. Some entries refer to Carnarvon's short fuse: "Carnarvon came: in a fidget..." and "Carnarvon, inclined to be too hasty in his action". Another concerns his declining state of health: "Carnarvon... seemed very ill, coughing incessantly...".[431] The most telling is the entry for 14 November 1875, which reflects how much Carnarvon had changed since his wife's death:

> Carnarvon dined with us, alone: I was struck with a change in him which I can scarcely describe. He talked incessantly, in a rapid excited way, which is new with him, except that he has done the same in cabinet. Lady Derby was impressed as I was by his manner, it seems as if since his loss he had thrown himself into work with a feverish activity, not quite healthy or natural.[432]

Whilst attending the House of Lords, Carnarvon found it easier to take rooms in London at Brown's Hotel, staying only occasionally at his townhouse in Bruton Street. Meantime, the Dowager Countesss and Lady Gwendolen were installed in a house in Green Street, with plenty of space for the children to live there on visits and where Carnarvon could also call to see them.

A collateral death on 17 December shocked the surviving dynasty. It was that of Lady Chesterfield (the wife of the Evelyn's "Irish" cousin who had inherited the title from her late brother in 1871), who shockingly took her own life.[433]

The Chesterfield family seemed cursed. There was a old superstition at Bretby Park involving one of the cedar trees in the grounds, known as "the Cedar of Lebanon", reputed to be the oldest of its kind in England, that said a branch of the tree always fell before the death of a member of the reigning family. It seems this superstition was taken sufficiently seriously for the tree to be supported by chains to prevent the branches ever falling.[434]

A Distracted Father and Surrogate Mothers

In the capital the Earl's job in the government required him to be on almost continuous call. His workload at the Colonial Office was heavy and constant, as he had a personal hand in all the strategic matters of running his department, home and abroad, as well as a say in virtually all administrative and legal postings to the colonies. His ear was frequently bent by job seekers and people seeking favours by recommending their offspring or the offspring of friends to plum posts supporting established post holders. Many young men began their careers by first securing (through the right word in the appropriate ear) a job as a private secretary. Carnarvon was required to frequently clear colonial appointments with George, Duke of Cambridge, the commander in chief of the British Army.[435]

With Carnarvon so busy, his children were farmed out, and often the older and younger Carnarvon children were separated from each other for long spells. Lordy was usually paired with Winifred, which suited him: Winifred led and he followed. In April 1876, he and Winifred stayed with their paternal grandmother, Henrietta, at Pixton Park, whilst the Ladies Margaret and Victoria were cared for by their maternal grandmother, the Countess of Chesterfield, at Bretby Park.[436] The children missed their father, but they enjoyed the travelling circuit with their barrage of heady governesses, maids, nursemaids and articulated luggage.

From the 4th Earl's diaries it's plain that he thought (at least on paper) often about his children's health and welfare, whilst leaving the actual upbringing to others. He was guided by the input of his mother and sisters, and occasionally by his unmarried brother Alan, who had treated children in his hospital in Paris. The Earl's eccentric brother, Auberon, only contributed from the sidelines; he was often abroad in the early days, and later he had his own family worries, with a needy wife and a clutch of needy children.

The Earl's children were drilled about their father's important role in the nation's life and hence his routine absence from their everyday lives, and that even when he was at home with them he must not be disturbed in his study. The children came to know their place, and also the importance of God, the Royal family, truth, charity and such events as the London season and of raising funds for good causes. As the children grew up, the Earl accompanied them to church and to London each June, for the start of the capital's main society summer events.[437]

The children were encouraged to write to their father, especially when he was abroad on the business of the Queen. Subsequently, the children would receive a reply, always encouraging learning and obedience. Family messages and requests were passed on that way. One letter from Gwendolen to the Earl mentions Winifred's great wish to go to an art gallery in London and a hope that her father would also be interested in a visit.

While Carnarvon was immersed in his work, his sisters Lady Gwendolen Herbert[438] and Lady Eveline Portsmouth played the role of surrogate mother. A mostly kind, loving friendship, which lasted into later life, formed between Lordy's sisters Winifred, Margaret and Victoria and Ladies Gwendolen and Eveline. Even when Winifred was happily married to her second husband, Lord Burghclere, she and Gwendolen took their holidays together.[439]

Lady Gwendolen stayed regularly at Highclere, but also maintained her own property at Faircroft, 375 Upper Richmond Road, Putney, where she lived with an older female companion.[440] She had an element of the innocent child about her. One diarist of the period described her as "a little sickly, gentle, faded old maid".[441] Yet there is no doubt she was a kind, popular aunt, and was great fun, especially for the Herbert girls. On Highclere headed notepaper Gwendolen wrote whimsically to her brother:

Dearest Carnarvon

Your family are all well only desiring to see you again shortly. W. still feels her knee in going up or down stairs but otherwise is well. She has been out in the carriage twice a day. Dear Margaret has been to her garden but greatly desires mice chocolate fingers.

W. hopes you will remember her Autograph book and the baby heaves deep sighs for a jack in the box. Such are the various wants of your family. We shall all rejoice greatly to see you again.

Yours most affectionately

Gwendolen Herbert

PS: W. says you are left no peace but she would much like chocolate mice for luncheon also. They say you promised...[442]

Lordy was a more troublesome specimen to his aunts than any of his sisters. He was thought lazy, untidy and brash – and Aunt Gwendolen had little time for boys.[443] On the other hand, Gwendolen adored her brothers, especially Dr Alan (Pal) whom she kept him informed, by letters to his home in Paris, of all kinds of gossip and family business.[444]

In later years, Gwendolen Herbert was a leading spirit in the Vegetarian Society, an active committee figure who contributed papers and made speeches for the promotion and advancement of food and health reform.[445] She also supported (not least because it was her brother, Lord Carnarvon's, first social calling) "Our Dumb Friend's League".[446] In society circles the two oddball spinsters, Gwendolen and her niece Lady Victoria, were regular sights during the London season, and especially at the Countess of Jersey's annual garden party at Osterley Park.[447] Lady Margaret Herbert (later Mrs George Duckworth) was much less of a participant in London haunts once she had married and begun to raise her family.[448]

From 1878 onwards, after her marriage to Carnarvon, Elsie Howard took over much of the responsibility for rearing the children. Whilst Lordy never warmed to his stepmother, she made some effort to appeal to him. She enthralled his sisters, and it was Elsie who guided her three stepdaughters through the crucial stages of womanhood and, in the case of Winifred and Margaret, into their married life. The youngest child, Victoria, never knew any mother except Elsie.[449]

Highclere Castle c1890
[Leadbetter Collection]

Henry, Fourth Earl of Carnarvon

Henrietta Howard, 3rd Countess of Carnarvon
[Leadbetter Collection]

Chapter Thirteen

The Death of the Dowager Countess, Henrietta

On Friday 26 May seventy-one-year-old Henrietta, the Dowager Countess of Carnarvon, widow of the 3rd Earl, died at Pixton Park after an illness lasting several weeks. [450] The Countess had been very ill before, but this time she quickly deteriorated with severe jaundice. A Central News telegram in her last hours reported that, although conscious, she was sinking fast.[451]

Whilst the rest of the clan were summoned, Lord Carnarvon rushed down to Pixton Park from London, accompanied by royal physician, Sir William Gull. Sadly, Gull pronounced Her Ladyship as having "no hope of a recovery".[452] Flanked by her three sons and two daughters, "Muddy" (as she called by her daughters[453]) slipped away. She had held their lives together, not as a tyrant, but as the family's astute ruler. She would be remembered for her sharpness, shrewdness and commanding attitude over all the family issues, possessing with age great strength and wisdom.

Henrietta's large collection of grandchildren, Wallop and Herbert alike, had seen loved their grandmother, whom they called "Gran-Mammy", and gained much from her guidance.[454] Winifred records: "The Dowager Countess of Carnarvon's death in 1876 was an unspeakable grief".[455] Eveline gave this affectionate retrospective:

> Although singularly unworldly, the natural cheerfulness of Lady Carnarvon's mind asserted itself in many ways, and she took pleasure in seeing the young dance; she accompanied them on the piano while they sang songs and choruses of the day, and sometimes of her own composition...[456]

The Dowager's son Dr Alan Herbert, who had taken a long sabbatical from his medical work in Paris, accompanied the body of his darling mother by train to Newbury for the funeral and burial in the Carnarvon family's vault at Burghclere Old Church. The Earl was distraught – but had to briefly return to London to complete a number of Colonial Office and parliamentary obligations. He soon reappeared at Highclere to join his siblings to see their beloved mother laid to rest.

Although many years had elapsed since she was chatelaine of Highclere, many members of Newbury Corporation and the town's folk turned out for the funeral. The coffin, draped in a black cloth and placed on a bier, was placed in the chancel at Burghclere and people were allowed time to come forward and pay their respects. Later, Reverand G.R. Portal, Carnarvon's own chaplain and close Masonic friend, conducted the service. Then, "Amidst the tear-shedding of relatives and friends, the corpse was lifted from the bier and borne to the vault, and the remains of the lamented Countess were deposited in their last resting place, close to those of her husband."[457]

The 4th Earl's grief over losing his mother was on a par with his son's feelings over Evelyn's death. The loss plunged the statesman, then in his second term as colonial secretary, into deep despair. The family united behind him once more, and by mid-June it was reported that the Earl's "indisposition [was] somewhat better".[458] He returned with Lordy and Lady Winifred to Highclere on Saturday 5th August, from London, ready to resume being a parent and squire. The Earl's colonial colleagues had also proved supportive.[459]

A Wedding

For the Herbert children some of the gloom caused by the death of their mother and grandmother, and also their father's prolonged absence from their lives, was at last lifted by a family wedding just before Christmas of 1876 at which Lady Winifred was a bridesmaid.

As the year closed, the Earl's children at last received their father's close attention. All but the baby, Lady Victoria, accompanied him to visit the Portsmouths (Wallops) at Eggesford House, a home from home since Lady Portsmouth had become such a big part of their upbringing. Lady Catherine Wallop[460], their cousin, married Milnes Gaskell[461] on 7 December 1876 in the Arcadian village of Wembworthy. This was where the Wallop family church was situated, in "a most unassuming place, consisting of a few score houses... but the centre of the parish being Eggesford House, the seat of the Portsmouth Earls".[462] Lord Carnarvon made Pixton Park available to the newly married couple for their honeymoon.

Lordy was overwhelmed by the Eggesford event. The constant encroachment of the female members of the Wallop family suffocated him. He was not comfortable with girls, and any female older than his sisters was viewed with suspicion (except his grandmother, Lady Anne Chesterfield, at Bretby Park). As if it was not enough to have these three demanding sisters constantly badgering him, added to that were five Wallop cousins who, like Winifred, were obsessed with being bridesmaids to Lady Catherine. These creatures fawned over their cute, motherless relation who would one day be an earl. Several of them told him they wanted to be his countess, which horrified Lordy. Poor Lordy had to endure spending Christmas here too.[463]

1877

Judging by the severe cuts in the diaries for 1877, it was a difficult year for Carnarvon. His daughter Margaret was unwell and was being treated by Sir James Paget.[464] Eleven-year-old Lordy was at a prep school in Brighton – the Sussex location was a proven centre for several schools for the sons of the rich, and being on the coast it was also therapeutic for Lordy's health.[465] He was back at Highclere before Easter but soon, his pleas of being homesick ignored (although private coaching was under consideration), he returned to Brighton to continue his education.

The Easter recess of Parliament of 1877 was an opportunity for the Earl to unwind. He had experienced an uneasy time inside the Cabinet over the policy on Russia and Turkey, where there was a fear of war (on a par with the early Crimean War) in the Dardanelles, with Russia being the aggressor. The issue rumbled on throughout the year.[466] Determined to find refuge, the Earl returned to Highclere and was reacquainted with his young family.

A fashionable political wedding at Westminster Abbey on Tuesday 17 April served as an opportunity for Lady Winifred to accompany her father. Reginald MacLeod married Miss Agnes Northcote, the eldest daughter of Lord Northcote, the chancellor of the exchequer.[467] As the daughter of a politician and Cabinet minister, other invitations, often novel ones, presented themselves to the thirteen-year-old Lady Winifred. She was even invited to launch a ship by Napiers of Glasgow.[468] Winifred was growing up to be a fine young woman with inner confidence and good prospects. Carnarvon took great comfort from his daughter's bloom. His friend Lord Dufferin had written him after Lady Evelyn's loss:

> I only wish that your little daughter Lady Winifred and your other children with every day become a greater source of comfort and happiness to you. I know from my own experience what fresh delight one derives from the expansions of one's daughter, and the growth of her affections.[469]

Lordy, meanwhile, was still receiving private coaching on his Latin verse from Reverand Troutbeck in London and Highclere. On 7 April, Troutbeck had "a long talk" with the Earl about a tutor for Lordy's general education.[470]

In May of 1877 the Earl took his family to visit the Portsmouths at the Wallops' other country seat of Hurstbourne Park.[471] They then travelled to Pixton Park, but Lordy headed to Bretby to stay with his grandmother. At Pixton it was the first anniversary of the death of the Dowager Countess, which for the Earl was "all the day through [his] mind".[472]

The Earl also spent some time at the end of September at Bretby Park and then in early October returned to Highclere to relax with some shooting.[473] The Christmas holiday period was spent at Highclere with the children.[474]

Chapter Fourteen

A Man of Principle

In January of 1878 Carnarvon was confined to bed, very ill for much of the time, and although improving, "was sometimes scarcely able to crawl from one room to another".[475] Lord Derby records in his diary that was in a "fidget"[476] and was "excited... agitated and a rather lachrymose strain, entreating his colleagues to believe in his good will etc.".[477]

On 23 January, the Earl offered his resignation to Queen Victoria over the matter of the government sending the British fleet to the Dardanelles to maintain the peace between the Turks and Russia. With memories of the Crimean War in the 1850s still lingering, Carnarvon thought it insanity to go to war and risk a repeat of the slaughter there twenty years previously. He objected to the Government's policy and felt that this was "a departure from the policy of neutrality which the Government had pledged themselves to preserve".[478]

In the days before his resignation Carnarvon had been criticised in Cabinet.[479] The Queen had spoken to Carnarvon at length at Osborne on 4 January about war being inevitable, and she declared that the whole matter required fighting spirit and that Carnarvon's approach was wrong and cowardly. Now, Prime Minister Disraeli (now Lord Beaconsfield) accepted the Earl's resignation but condemned it. The Queen was similarly incensed, especially when Lord Derby also resigned. She considered Carnarvon and Derby weak willed and it is said that when they returned their emblems of office she refused to shake their hands.

Carnarvon was isolated. He had angered some close allies and made himself unpopular with contemporaries. Despite being in the political wilderness, he continued to play out his sometime erratic role as a critic of the government's Eastern policy. There was also much political trouble at this time in South Africa, with a war on that front. But he decided to concentrate, so far as possible, on family and estate matters away from London.

When the Earl was required to act as a host at Highclere, his sister Eveline, Lady Portsmouth, generally stood in as the castle's chatelaine. As the mother of six daughters, she saw to it that her fourteen-year-old niece, Winifred, was groomed for the role of earl's daughter and the responsibilities entailed for any woman running a large house. Increasingly, as she grew from child to woman, Lady Winifred was the choice of her father's female companion for public functions. This is evidenced in September 1878 by her presence (facilitated by Aunt Eveline [480]) at the inauguration of the Falkland Memorial on the site of the Battle of Newbury, 20 September 1643, when Viscount Falkland fell on the side of King Charles I.[481] Lordy, meanwhile, was largely ignored, his father making little effort to groom him for the role of Earl, perhaps due to the boy's ill health, listlessness and great stubbornness. The boy was in fact on holiday from prep school, under the supervision of a minder, a Mr Rawson (or Rawston). [482]

A new wife

Although they were bumbling along adequately, Carnarvon knew that he needed to find someone to manage his family's domestic scene, act as his hostess and guide the children with consistency unachievable by aging aunts, nursemaids and governesses. He also craved companionship from the fairer sex. And since Lordy was such a disappointment, he was also looking for a male heir. In short, he needed a wife.

Carnarvon's solution to his predicament was his cousin, Elizabeth Catherine Howard, of Greystoke, Cumberland.[483] Following in the footsteps of his father, who had married a Howard, he would reunite the Houses of Herbert and Howard. The Earl wrote to his sister, Lady Portsmouth:

> My dear Eveline: I do not think you will be as much surprised as most of our friends and relations when I give you the news that once more a great change in life is at hand for me and that I am engaged to be married to dear Elsie. Many things will, I think, have prepared you for this – my conversation visits to Greystoke, admiration as you know for her charming character...[484]

It fell upon the Eveline and Gwendolen to tell the Earl's children of his plans to marry Elsie. Letters survive from Winifred and Margaret to their father saying how happy they were for him. There is no surviving letter to this effect from Lordy.[485] Concurrently, his father had the boy's longer term future education to decide. [486]

Lordy was in a state of utter desperation. A twenty-two-year-old stepmother to rule over him? The thought was abhorrent. He travelled up to Cumberland with Lady Winifred to witness the snowy wedding at St Andrew's Church, Greystoke, on Boxing Day of 1878. But the twelve-year old boy longed to be home again at Highclere, or better still, in safe seclusion with his grandmother at Bretby Park. [487]

After the wedding the Earl and his new Countess headed back to London to honeymoon at their townhouse at 16 Bruton Street, whilst Lordy and Lady Winifred took a detour to Highclere and were then shunted off to Eggesford with Alan Herbert (who had been their father's best man) and dotty Aunt Gwendolen. [488]

Lordy was ill-prepared for the consequences of having a new mother take over the reins at Highclere Castle and Pixton Park. While the Earl and Elsie spent their honeymoon at Pixton Park and then Highclere, Lordy spent a miserable period at Eggesford, and only just recovered from the chill brought on by staying out in the snow drifts. He then moved on to Highclere, where he anxiously awaited his return to prep school in Brighton and stayed out of Elsie's way as far as possible.

His baby sister, Victoria, was besotted by Elsie,[489] and the new Countess already commanded influence over staff and tenants. But Lordy was resolute in his rejection of his new mother, and in early February he found it difficult when she took over his late mother's role of distributing the prizes at the school at Burghclere.[490] He wanted to like this woman, but he was just not convinced about her taking over being his mother. He missed his own mother too much to accept a replacement.

Lordy was even more unsettled when his father informed him that he would have to make a little speech of thanks when the local Masonic lodge (Loyal Berkshire Lodge of Hope, No. 574) paid a visit to the castle to offer a congratulatory address to his father and the new Countess. The speech came after the toasts at the subsequent luncheon, one "to the health of Lord Porchester and Lady Winifred

Herbert" which the twelve-year-old successfully, albeit painfully, "returned with thanks".[491]

The Earl, meanwhile, could only see good in Elsie and was convinced all his children loving her from the word go. In a letter to his sister, Eveline, he contemplates the future:

> Winifred sees the future painted in the most beautiful colours with dearest Elsie as the central figure and Porchey is evidently captivated by her. A great change has come over him – a great desire to be at Highclere as home and an appreciation of everything there. I think the thought of Elsie is fixing all their other thoughts... you need not think years of time are needed to create any feeling – it is there and only needs the years to grow to full strength and power.
>
> I will do anything about the children going to Highclere to facilitate any wish of yours or dearest Elsie's.[492]

There was a worry of history repeating itself over how Lady Gwendolen (Gee) would see her brother's new wife. Gee had been jealous of the first Lady Carnarvon, Lady Evelyn, how would she accept Elsie, without some supreme effort being made? Lady Portsmouth cautioned her brother about Gee [493] and gave feedback to Elise about her making a wonderful impact as the new Countess. Eveline also agreed to present Elsie at Court as the new Countess.

" I shall be delighted to present Elsie and very proud...." [494]

Lordy's younger sister, Lady Margaret, had been left behind at Eggesford, suffering from measles. Now, sister Winifred went down with the illness. Fearful of contracting the disease, the Earl and the new Countess escaped to London, where, naturally, everyone in society wanted to meet Elsie. Lordy was dispatched to school once more.[495] Stuck between a rock (school) and a hard place (home), Lordy was by now relieved to leave the pressure of being a good son to his new stepmother behind.

Chapter Fifteen

Sibthorpe's School, Brighton

Winifred Burghclere insinuates in her 1923 retrospective on Lordy that Gordon House School, Brighton, had its faults, recording that: "His private school was not happily chosen. It subsisted on its former reputation, and neither diet nor instruction was up to the mark..."[496] Still, the 4th Earl took the opinion of the school's headmaster, Mr Sibthorpe, seriously.

Lordy's school report in early 1879 from Mr Sibthorpe was "satisfactory".[497] One remark in a letter from Sibthorpe refers to certain worries about Lordy's health; another of him being bilious from "eating too many sweets, after dining".[498] Sibthorpe assured the Earl that his son had promised not to repeat the matter. In a letter home to his father, Lordy said he longed to see him and invited his Papa to a firework display at the school.[499]

Lordy had gained a reprieve from what he anticipated would be his father's wrath over his mediocre school performance. The boy knew that satisfactory was definitely *not* the standard his papa would be content to see continue as the year unfolded. Indeed, when the Earl visited the school on 7 May and saw Lordy's headmaster, he demanded a long talk about the boy, and despite hearing once again that everything was satisfactory and Lordy was working well, he wanted his son's education pushed further; the Earl had fears that Lordy would otherwise struggle to be taken into the remove.[500]

At Brighton, Lordy was schooled alongside two of his younger Wallop cousins, the sons of Lord and Lady Portsmouth. These boys were the Honourable Frederick Wallop (Freddy)[501] and the Honourable Edward Wallop (Teddy).[502] The friendship between the male cousins was more obligatory than close, but on one visit the Earl and his new wife took Lordy, Freddy and Teddy to a Brighton hotel for a slap-up tea.[503]

By the time of the holidays, Lordy was back home at Highclere. There was to be no let up in his studies: a private tutor[504] was assigned to coach him hard throughout the summer months as a forerunner to his enrolment exams for Eton College. However Lordy won a short respite when ill [505] and when he appeared at the children's party at Highclere, given each year to those from the local workhouses, where he displayed his skill at performing conjuring tricks to an audience of 300.[506]

Elsie was putting every effort into the task of being a wife, stepmother, sister-in-law, chatelaine and Countess. She revelled most in the latter. [507] Public invitations flowed in for the new Lady Carnarvon. On 26 August 1879 she cut the "first sod [on the construction of] the Didcot to Newbury section"[508] of the Great Western Railway, later officially opened on 13 April 1882.[509] Lordy was present to support his stepmother, and offered thanks to the ladies. He much impressed his father with a loud speech; the Earl had been "horribly nervous"[510] about Lordy's ability to carry out the task.

Attendance at Eton College

By September Lordy was due to leave the safe surroundings of his school life at Brighton and even safer home life at Highclere for a giant leap in his life: attendance at Eton College. In a dramatic scene between the Earl and his son, each spoke of their hopes and fears for Lordy entering this brave new world. The Earl recorded in his diary:

> Porchey's last day at home. Tomorrow he begins his Eton life – and walks alone… he goes in good heart hoping and expecting for more than he fears… and a sense of emancipation probably greater than he will ever again know…"[511]

His father and stepmother accompanied Lordy to Eton. The Earl saw the boy's housemaster, G.E. Marindin,[512] for a long chat about Lordy's strengths and weaknesses, his erratic state of health and the gaping holes in his knowledge of the classics, especially Latin grammar. The Earl truly believed that "parents could do nothing so good for their children as to give them a good practical Christian education".[513]

But to his father's horror, Lordy fluffed his entrance exams and was placed in the lower middle forth. It was a very dark day for the Earl. He recorded in his diary: "It is a disappointment… so great a mess… I was prepared for a certain amount of failure but nothing like this…"[514]

Lordy's Aunt Eveline, who was the one voice that the Earl would listen to (and be persuaded by), rose in a letter to the boy's defence:

I am very sorry that dear Porchey has not taken so high a place as was expected but I don't think this need in any way lead you to form an unfavourable opinion of his future... [He] is only 13 and a quarter...

He may have been very nervous and he may do much better... [than being] too high up at first...

On no account I hope will he be discouraged. His own greater readiness to work is worth everything. You took so high a place at Eton that you may judge a little unusually of the generalities of boys and Porchey is specially uncertain. What he will be able to do I am positive if you takes pains with him is to peak well when he prepares – I think his nerve will not if you cultivate and encourage him...

... some of my boys have not taken high places who have or are taking interest in works of literature that I think I judge of the common run of boys better than you...[515]

The Earl felt ashamed for himself, not as much for his son. This had an immediate effect on his health en route with Elsie to Greystoke Castle, Cumberland. He records being "poorly" and "keeping quiet"[516] for several days. On return to London, the Earl was laid up with crippling gout.

The storm over Lordy's dreadful showing in his exams and the Earl's health scare had almost blown over by the end of October. A social trip to Reading to visit close confidantes Sir Robert and Lady Phillimore[517] at The Coppice (a rambling gothic house), at Shiplake, Henley on Thames, was combined with a visit to Lordy.

Lordy's Eton Schooldays

Lordy was placed in a small house in the school, with his own room. He was told he must be self-reliant. This required that he organise himself, making his own bed and so on, which was a big step up from prep school and home where almost everything of a domestic nature was laid on for him by maids. The rigorous regime at Eton was a shock, with its chapel, prep, prefects, faggings, beatings, cold water baths and compulsorily dress, including the wearing of toppers (top hats), stick-up collars (instead of turn-down ones) and great tail coats. Masters also wore a cap and gown and boys traditionally "capped" (touched their toppers) in deference to the school's line-up of headmaster, housemasters, tutors and any school visitors.

Lordy was dubbed a shy, skimpy boy and allowed privileges, with confinements to sick bay (on account of his health) and medical exemption especially regarding taking part in the school's obsession with the field sports of rugby and soccer.[518] All the public schools were equally as proud of their sporting feats as they were of academic achievement, so games were compulsory. The Eton College Archives show that Lordy "played cricket for the house Lower Boy team and indeed got his choices (i.e. colours)[519] but [he] does not seem to have otherwise distinguished himself"[520] in *any* sport. Lordy always loathed the physical games of rugby and soccer in particular. These hard-fought combat playoffs on the school pitches shaped other boys (some of them later Britain's greatest fighting soldiers) who relished the battles against opposing public schools on the playing fields of Eton. Lordy did enjoy watching the Eton crews preparing for Henley, however, for his father's interest in sailing had given him a love for messing about in boats.

The Earl expressed hope that Lordy would improve his form position at Eton, and Lordy, in return, told his father he enjoyed being there. From the Earl's diary entries one can deduce a feeling of optimism for the future. The Earl extended his wishful thinking to Lordy also ultimately accepting Elsie as his mother. It was almost a year on in the Earl's second marriage, but a state of complete acceptance between stepmother and stepson had not been achieved.

> ..he is certainly happy at Eton... indeed enjoys it all – and gets on well with other boys. I think he is also desirous of working up to a higher place in school and as far as I can see the influence of Eton up to this time has been a good one and wholesome. I think I perceive an improvement in several respects. He is very fond of Elsie and she is quite charming to him and it would be strange if she did not win his confidence and affection...[521]

In many ways Lordy was happy at Eton, for he was away from Elsie and feminine company in general. But he felt insecure. Some of the Eton boys were rough and could be barbaric bullies. After a report was heard that Lordy was subject to an attack from another boy, a Duke's son who accused him of dumb insolence,[522] his older Wallop cousin, John (Jock) Fellows Wallop,[523] was obliged to nursemaid Lordy for several weeks.[524]

With several episodes of bullying and home-sickness behind him, Lordy scrambled through by building some good friendships, several of which endured for decades thereafter. The most important of these alliances being with Prince Victor Duleep Singh, the son of a Maharaja.[525]

The handsome, long-haired Victor (nicknamed Tulip[526]), only a few weeks Lordy's junior,[527] became the sickly Lordy's most prized companion. The boys became deeply attached to one another. During the vacations Victor was a staunch ally and Lordy's guest at his grandmother's London mansion. In their developmental years they were seamless friends, doing everything they could to oblige the other. There was a physical attraction from the start which almost certainly spilled over into innocent horseplay with a sexual element; at least exploring mutual masturbation as pubescent teenagers.[528] (See the epilogue for further context for Lordy's principal male–male relationships.)

The boys need for each other stemmed from experiencing a lack of attention and love during childhood. They had many other things in common. Both were outsiders. Lordy stood out as being no good at games, and he was constantly ill. Victor's father's Sikh heritage (albeit the Maharaja had reverted to being a Christian) dictated that his son wore his hair very long, and Victor's olive-skinned saw him dubbed a savage by his classmates. Neither boy was clever; both had harsh, domineering fathers; and they were fascinated by the idle pursuits of hunting, shooting and horse racing. But though they had much common ground, Victor was the stronger, the more confident. A rivalry formed between them that gave Victor the edge in entrapment and in enticing his friend to misbehave or just follow his instructions.

Victor's younger brother, Prince Frederick Duleep Singh,[529] was another friend at Eton. Although he remained outside the intimate coupling of Lordy and Victor, nevertheless he was a regular bystander who orchestrated his own carnal conquests in secret throughout his life.[530]

The overwhelming passion of all three boys was gambling, and they played for high money stakes, often against their fellows at Eton where only modest bets were the currency in the school yard. Whilst betting had always been a sport in which Eton boys indulged, no one had seen the enormity of wagers offered before the Singh brothers arrived there.

Ralph Nevill was a contemporary of Lordy at Eton College. His first year was, like Lordy, from 1879. Nevill has left behind a comprehensive narrative on Eton life, which includes some anecdotes and memories of the school's history, its masters and pupils.[531] In Nevill's book he describes how several boys from the school commonly broke the school rules by crossing from the banks of the river running through the school fields to attend the local horse race meetings at Windsor. Some of the boys even ventured as far afield as Ascot. "This was contrived by getting lifts on the way, and though some were caught and punished, quite a number indulged in what was to them an exciting adventure."[532] Two of these offenders intent on visiting Ascot and staking large bets there were Lordy and Victor. Ralph Nevill reveals the background to the tale:

> ..a new boy (the son of the Maharajah Duleep Singh, whose arrival at Eton created some sensation)... offered to bet... a fiver against a certain horse, which wager had been accepted. This was the largest wager we ever heard of as being made at Eton, and it was looked upon as extraordinary.[533]

The Carnarvons, meanwhile, were back at Pixton Park during November to see the youngest children, Ladies Margaret and Victoria, who had travelled from Eggesford with Eveline, Lady Portsmouth, who had been caring for them. The Earl was in contemplative mood. He records in his diary: "I have been looking over and burning a great many old letters. They are sad reading for they relate to times and persons and feelings now past away for ever."[534] Carnarvon was also suffering from recurring gout, which stopped him writing his diary between 11 November and 25 December. At that date he records "have been a prisoner of the sofa".[535]

Thirteen-year-old Lordy joined his family at Highclere on home leave, but soon wished for a return to Eton when he eavesdropped on a conversation between his father and stepmother. Elsie, it emerged, was expecting a child. As Lordy listened, thunder-struck, his father spoke delightedly of his hope for a boy, a Carnarvon heir in waiting, should Lordy not survive.

Chapter Sixteen

The Earl's Second Family

As the New Year of 1880 began Elsie was at Pixton Park, making arrangements to provide a grand treat for the children of the union workhouse. On 2 January, under a brilliantly lit Christmas tree, there were three presents for each of the inmates. Lordy took part in these proceedings with his stepmother and Winifred, distributing additional gifts of sweets, nuts, cake and oranges.

The Honourable Aubrey Herbert, Lordy's half-brother, was born at Highclere on 3 April 1880. How threatened Lordy must have felt as his father doted on the new child, showering him with love and attention. [536] Said one commentator: "The birth of Lady Carnarvon's son is an event of some interest, as by his first marriage with Lady Evelyn Stanhope, Lord Carnarvon had only one son, who is a delicate little boy..."[537]

As it turned out, Aubrey was as fragile a specimen health wise as Lordy and was afflicted by poor sight, in part as a result of the inbreeding of his father and mother.[538]

Whilst Lordy returned for the new term at Eton, nurses tended the newborn Herbert baby and the Earl, Elsie and Lady Winifred went up to London on 19 May for the season.

The year to date had taken its toll on the Earl and Countess. Elsie's confinement had not been without incident, and she was told by doctors to seek rest and quiet. (As we shall see later, she required surgery arising from complications of this birth.) The Earl was exhausted too, and had been laid up with gout. The year was also a troublesome one for the Earl in the public arena. He had been at the centre of damning claims of vote rigging in a by-election in Nottinghamshire, for requiring his tenants there to vote conservative.[539] A major political initiative on his part for developing the idea of national insurance for workers, sickness benefit and old age pensions was little reported, which disappointed both him and his allies.[540] The year was also a busy one for attending Conservative party rallies and Masonic meetings.

Once the new Herbert child's baptism was over, a much needed respite was sought.[541] A trip was planned to Wildbad, Germany, to take the waters. The idea was to give Elsie some time to gather her strength again post-childbirth, and to improve the Earl's still failing state of health. Lady Winifred accompanied her father and stepmother; it was Winifred's first time out of Britain.[542] On 2 July she celebrated her sixteenth birthday.

Elsie was very poorly. The party was forced to remain at Wildbad until 18 July, but by the time they set out on the homeward stages and reached the Rhine on 21 July, the Countess's condition was much worse. At Cologne, Carnarvon and Winifred searched frantically for an English physician, Dr Hall of Rohrergasse, mentioned in *Bradshaw's Guide*. Hall thought that the party could reach Rotterdam without Elsie's condition deteriorating. However, Carnarvon was at his wits' end. He importuned Hall to accompany them all the way to England, which he agreed to do.

They arrived at the port of Harwich on 23 July and headed straight for London, where Carnarvon immediately summoned Sir William Gull to examine his wife. Another medical man, Sir James Paget[543], was brought in for a further opinion. Elsie needed an urgent operation for a gynaecological problem that had been overlooked at the time of Aubrey's birth. The procedure was successfully carried out.[544] The pressure proved too great for Carnarvon. Sir William Gull ordered him to rest.

Finally, on 3 August the Earl and Countess were thought well enough to travel to Highclere to see their newborn son and the other children.[545] They found Lordy unwell with "a nasty sore throat".[546] Dr Douglas of Newbury had attended him and "applied Caustic and glycerine".[547] Now that his father and Elsie were back, Lordy was keen to escape. He left to go to his grandmother's safe haven of Bretby, accompanied by his holiday tutor, Robert Harrison.[548]

Despite the ill health of the Earl, a stream of visitors passed through Highclere, including the Heathcotes (who were, as close friends, naturally concerned about the Carnarvons). Another notable social visitor was the American historian Francis Parkman.[549]

On 6 September Lordy returned from Bretby Park. While at Bretby his grandmother had been kindness itself, but his aunt, Lady Bradford, had spoken frankly to the boy (and to his tutor, Harrison) about him seeking early improvement in his studies and attitude and spending much less time at the races.[550] Such a harsh comment was unlikely to backed up by Lordy's grandmother, Lady Anne. She was one of the "racing ladies well known [and] popular at Newmarket" [551], and Lordy, in confidence, relied upon her to give him and Victor valuable (though not always successful) horse tips.

Meanwhile, Elsie became ill again with complications arising from the earlier surgery. The Earl's feared history was repeating itself and that he was about to lose another wife. Lordy returned to Eton (from London) on 15 September. Meanwhile Elise needed a second operation, which was carried out in London by a Dr J. Smith, assistant to Sir James Paget, after which she returned to recuperate at Highclere.

Through his sister Eveline, the Earl had been introduced to Dr Michael Grabham of Madeira[552] who was visiting England. Grabham persuaded Carnarvon that under his personal medical supervision, on the island of Madeira, the Earl and his wife would soon recover their faculties and strength.

The return of his gout meant the Earl was having dire mobility problems. The spread of the disease also affected his hand. He records in his diary: "my right hand is half crippled with a sort of fit of gout".[553] Sir William Gull had once remarked to Carnarvon that "Life was a heavenly problem to be worked out by earthly materials".[554] This saying – which became a favourite fall-back quotation for the Earl at times of adversity and physical incapacity – somehow spurred in him a will to continue. The Earl took stock of himself at this point in his life; he was feeling depressed but hoped the forthcoming trip overseas would help him recover his stamina.

In early October Dr Smith approved the concept of the trip to Madeira and the Earl waved Elsie off at the station as she and six-month-old Aubrey travelled to Greystoke Castle, Cumberland. Elsie wanted to head north to show off her child, but also to say a fond farewell to her own family, as the planned trip to Madeira was to run through until the spring of 1881.

Meanwhile the Earl said his own quiet goodbyes to family and friends.[555] Dr Alan Herbert came from Paris to give his support to his brother and sister-in-law on their move to Madeira.[556]

To Madeira, and Then Back

Lordy returned from Eton to hear the news of the final plans for the health flit abroad. It was proposed that he would travel out to Madeira for the New Year school holidays with his cousin, Lady Lillian (Lilias) Wallop. Presumably, the announcement that his parents were leaving the country had little impact on Lordy, who saw little of them as it was.

On 24 October, the night prior to the Earl and Elsie going up to London to join their ship, the houseguests at Highclere were numerous, including several family members and friends.

The Carnarvons left Highclere on Monday 25 October to go to London to connect with the twin screw mail steamer *Kinfauns Castle* at East India Dock which would take them to the island of Madeira.[557] After a rough, stormy crossing Elsie's maid, Mrs Osmond, proved a good sailor, but during the tossing about on the high seas the children (and in particular Winifred, Margaret and the baby, Aubrey) suffered in the conditions.

The family arrived at Madeira on 4 November. The presence on the island of a former colonial secretary was marked by attendance on board the ship by British Consul Mr Haywood, together with a welcome greeting from Dr Grabham and Carnarvon's old tutor, John Kent, who had settled on Madeira some years before.[558]

The children were excited by their new surroundings. However, the baby was unwell with a high temperature, and Grabham was called out to examine him.[559] Bronchitis was diagnosed.[560] The rest of the household were greatly suffering too with heavy colds, with Elsie in particular poorly for several days.[561] An emergency arose when Elsie then sprained her foot and ankle slipping on the patio. The Earl records it thus: "A great alarm this morning with Elsie who slipped on some stones. It gave me a horrible turn... but thank god no real harm done... foot and ankle sprain."[562] Then the baby's condition further deteriorated. Dr Grabham was called immediately and treated little Aubrey "with iodine and cod liver oil".[563]

Everyone had recovered by 23 November, when the first exploration of the island became possible, but Grabham was constantly on call. John Kent also spent long stretches giving help and advice to the Earl and his family.[564]

By mid-December, the Earl was still not feeling well. One of the mail ships brought news that Lilias Wallop, who was to accompany Lordy out to Madeira for the Christmas and New Year holidays from Eton, was grounded in England, suffering from measles. On 16 December Lordy travelled from Southampton with only a manservant on the *SS Arab* to join his family, arriving on 21 December.[565] His father noted in his diary: "he was looking very well and enjoyed the voyage. The Captain and officers had been very kind to him and everything had gone well."[566]

His family's illnesses and bad storms marred Lordy's short time on the island. Still, he enjoyed sharing the sixth birthday of his baby sister Victoria (now recorded as Vera) on 30 December, although it brought back the grief over his mother's death.

At the start of 1881, a constant deluge of rain made the Carnarvon family prisoners of the weather on Madeira for many days. Lordy bade farewell to everyone on 16 January, on board the mail ship *The Trojan* and arrived safely back in the UK, which was experiencing tremendous snow and frost, the worst on record since 1838.[567] Lord Carnarvon's close friend, Sir Robert Phillimore stepped in to offer Lordy sanctuary overnight on his return from Madeira prior to heading back to Eton.[568] Lordy accepted the invitation. Phillimore wrote to Lord Carnarvon on 5 February 1881: "You will have heard how charmed we were with 'Porchey', a pleasant better bred boy I have seldom seen..."[569]

The rest of Lordy's family were on a sailing trip around Madeira on *The Fez*, under Captain J. Forwood. The trip was largely miserable, as conditions were choppy with lots of rolling of the boat. Frequent port calls did little to improve morale.

Still struggling with his health, the Earl allowed Grabham to subject him to a course of shock treatment using galvanism.[570] This (and other treatments) culminated in a long diary entry by Carnarvon about the state of his health and the prognosis, according to Grabham.[571] The good doctor convinced Carnarvon he was getting better. Moreover, he was told he had made sufficient improvement that he may resume a reasonable amount of work, in politics, back in England.

Whilst in Madeira Carnarvon kept in touch by letter with England. Several colonial friends, including James Froude,[572] with whom he shared a watching concern over the troubled events in the South African Wars, also visited him.[573] The Earl now relished the prospect of finally getting back to England and engaging in debate again in the public arena. However, before leaving Madeira he recorded in his diary: "The scene of English and indeed all politics is so perplexed, so blotted, so blurred, so full of what I dislike that I hardly desire to take much part again in it as an actor..."[574]

Two weeks before the return, Carnarvon was in happy mood. He recorded in his diary: "Elsie is almost herself again and the children are all wonderfully well... and I am very grateful..."[575]

News was eventually spread of the expected return of the Carnarvons to England on about 15 April 1881, with a report that "they have much benefited in health by their stay in Madeira".[576] The trip back on the *Dunrobin Castle* was uneventful.

Chapter Seventeen

Back into the Swing of Society Life

The news of the hour was that Carnarvon's old foe, Benjamin Disraeli, was dying. The Earl was told on enquiring that the former prime minister's condition was grave but stable. Catching up with his cousin, Robert Herbert (who was an official in the Colonial Office), and his old mentor, Sir Robert Phillimore, brought the Earl the latest intelligence on the diplomatic and political scenes. But illness struck him once more, and he was unable to attend Disraeli's funeral.[577]

Since the removals from the Earl's diary are numerous for the period that followed, this must have been a harrowing time.[578] Both Carnarvon and Elise were feeling unwell and knocked back by their recurring bouts of bad health. Elsie was in seclusion with her mother at one of the Howard family homes: Hampton Lodge, Farnham, Surrey.[579]

Elsie had not fully recovered from the trauma of undergoing several operations following Aubrey's birth. The time on Madeira had been long, and mostly pleasant and enjoyable – although this different way of living caused pressures, with everyone closely huddled together, unlike at Highclere and London where the Earl and Countess were able to spend time together alone. The relationship with her husband was at the centre of Elsie's life, and she also wanted more children. Elsie's latest health scare (which is not specified in the diaries) meant she was separated from the Earl, albeit in the loving arms of her own family. The Earl wanted Elsie to return to Highclere to recuperate and extract some time together at Milford. He records: "I came down [to Hampton Lodge] in the morning and found dear Elsie on the whole certainly better and I think looking stronger."[580]

To great relief Elsie's ill health receded, and the Earl was able to fulfil a number of London commitments to free up a reunion with Elsie. They were reunited as a family at Highclere's Milford Lake just as the children left to stay with the Portsmouths for the Whitsun holidays.

> Elsie and I came down here [to Milford]... The place always brings back to me whenever or something happens... so many recollections of past days that I hardly know whether the sadness or the pleasure

predominates.[581]

On 3 June the Earl and Elsie visited Eton to see Lordy. A good report was given as to the boy's progress by his housemaster, Mr Marindin.[582] The Earl joined his son for the 4th of June celebrations at Eton, traditionally held on the river Thames. Later that day, Carnarvon saw Elsie off to spend some restful time at Greystoke, Cumberland, whilst he visited Lady Chesterfield at Bretby Park. He found his late wife's mother in a quiet, sombre mood.[583] The Countess's melancholy seems to have had an effect on the Earl's own emotional state, as Elsie cut the next pages out of the diary. One can only muse that whilst at Bretby again he was reminded of the times spent there with Evelyn.

The Earl left Bretby to meet Elsie at Penrith. After a short stay at Lyulph's Tower, they returned to London on 13 June.[584] On Thursday 29 June the Carnarvons held a dinner which gave them an opportunity to see family members and old friends and also announce their intention to again take their place on the London social scene.[585] They were back at Highclere from 8 July, and then travelled back to London for a garden party at Holland House, which was one of the most brilliant of the season. There, the junior members of the Carnarvon family joined their royal counterparts to enjoy a Punch and Judy show.[586] A series of society dinners and events filled much of the rest of July. One highlight was when Carnarvon's sister, Eveline, gave a party at Prince's Gate.[587] Finally, on 20 July, the Carnarvons made their contribution to the season with a large reception.[588]

The Bruton Street residence was sold in favour of obtaining a larger, more spacious family home, and a period of house hunting followed. The Carnarvons vowed to friends and family that they would resume entertaining activities once a new home was found.

As well as seeing to matters at Highclere, the Earl attended the House of Lords to speak. Elsie was on hand in the Ladies' Gallery during one fierce debate on the Irish Land Bill.[589]

Elsie had a grand plan afoot to give a large garden party on the lawns at Highclere. She roped in Lady Winifred (much to her father's pleasure) and they jointly planned the event. The hugely successful party duly took place on Saturday 20 August. The weather was pleasant and there was a good attendance by the gentry, civic authorities and clergy of the neighbourhood. A military band from the 32nd Regiment performed a selection of music, and there were entertainments inside the castle. Numerous house guests (including family, with Lordy home from Eton and Alan Herbert, from Paris) tested the full might of staff at Highclere to manage the resumption of full-scale operations for receiving visitors after a long time lapse. Highclere's glory days under the last Countess, Lady Evelyn, were still a memory cherished from the previous decades.[590]

On 7 September, Lordy was ushered off by his father, Elsie and Winifred to return to Eton.[591] There was panic for the boy when he could not find his pet snake (a gift from Victor) which accompanied him everywhere and lived in a desk at Eton during term time.[592] A footman came to the rescue when the animal was found clinging to the drapes of the library. Meanwhile, the Earl, Elsie and Winifred went to Bretby Park to see Lady Chesterfield.[593]

Even the short burst of activity during the summer months had taken its toll on the health of both Carnarvon and Elsie. A spa treatment was sought with a planned stay over at Buxton in Derbyshire.[594] Later, feeling better, the Carnarvons spent time with Elsie's mother at Greystoke Castle.[595] A family wedding, of Elsie's brother, brought some good cheer.[596]

And End to Eton

Carnarvon was distressed by a report from Eton about Lordy's latest antics. He tried to resolve matters by visiting the school, staying over to consult with his friend Sir Robert Phillimore at The Coppice near Reading.[597] The authorities at Eton were gravely concerned about the shortcomings of Lordy in his day-to-day affairs and the excesses of a fifteen-year-old who was observed in the company of London bookmakers' agents and money lenders. Lordy had no defence to offer. He wisely kept silent about his partner in crime, Victor Duleep Singh, whose counsel he had already sought in order to prepare for the full weight of his father's wrath .

Lordy was temporarily removed from the school, and accompanied his father and stepmother, in disgrace, back to Highclere. It was a low point in the relationship between the Earl and his son and heir. Being estranged from Victor was the real, harder, punishment to bear. Lordy was grounded at Highclere in a miserable, friendless state.

In January 1882, Lordy accompanied his parents and Lady Winifred on a tour through France and Italy accompanied.[598] They left Biarritz in early January for Pau, on the northern edge of the Pyrenees, where the plan was to stay for about two months.[599] A few days later they visited Lourdes.

On 9 January, at the town of Monpellier, Lordy's father chose his moment to tell his son he would not be returning to Eton after the Easter holidays. The diary entry is sombre: "I had a serious talk with Porchey as to Eton and announced to him that he would not stay after Easter. It was on the whole a more satisfactory talk than I had anticipated."[600]

The Earl had mastered the art of recording in his diaries only what he wanted the likely reader to know. Words chosen by him in reference to his children were always slanted in his favour, showing him usually, if not always in the very best light, as a caring, conscientious and loving father. He was, but he was also a strict patriarch and disciplinarian. He often ranted and raved at Lordy, pointing out his fundamental character weaknesses.[601] The effect of this hostility from his father was that the boy would get upset and then sick.

Lordy fell ill on 13 January. A doctor was called, but it was only a shivering fit with a slight chill was diagnosed.[602] Reading between the lines, the Earl had almost certainly reduced his son to tears and hysterics. But it was not unusual for Lordy to play up, something that his wife Almina recounted in later years.[603] On this occasion in France, Lordy's illness resulted in a delay of a day in the family's planned tour, but they reached Avignon on 16 January.

By the end of the month they were all on the move again, spending time at Cannes and moving on to Mentone.[604] They ended the trip at Porto Fino, a location the Earl was exploring for a holiday villa to buy.

Lordy was anxious to break away from the family pack. He enjoyed Porto Fino for the access it gave him to boats, allowing him to indulge his passion for sailing. Although he experienced a few mishaps putting sails up and down and navigating squalls when sudden gusts swept down from the overhanging mountains[605], nevertheless he gained a proficiency here, something immensely lacking in his make-up in other ways. Besides which his father's man-servants were favoured for their ability to assist him in bringing his boat safely back into harbour.

The holiday over, the Carnarvons all returned home to England, via Paris. One of the Earl's staff, Weiner, accompanied Lordy and Lady Winifred back home separately, in order to accelerate a quicker return.

The Earl and Countess finally returned to London on 1 March.[606] The Earl had purchased a new London town ouse at 43 Portman Square.[607] However, some building work was needed there, so the couple's few London engagements were fulfilled by staying in hotels such as Claridge's and Hallam's.

Meanwhile, Lordy returned, demoralised, to spend his last weeks at Eton College.

During early March the Carnarvons spent some time together at their Somersetshire seat of Pixton Park, Dulverton, remaining there for Easter.[608] Elsie wanted her husband to consider spending more time at Pixton, with its "beautiful views of Exmoor... [and] richly wooded park sloping steeply to the rivers Exe and Barle".[609] Since the death, six years previously, of Lord Canarvon's mother, who spent much of the years of widowhood at Pixton, improvements had been carried out on the property. The estate was always rich with herds of wild red deer roaming its surrounds. Carnarvon's brother-in-law, the Earl of Portsmouth, was a figure of repute in the Devon and Somerset staghounds and he always relished staying at Pixton to hunt stag and foxes.[610] Lordy also adored hunting. However, his father's health, coupled with his marriage to Elsie, had stopped him indulging as much as he once did in sport.[611]

Lordy's dearest grandmother, Lady Chesterfield, often provided a safe refuge in London and Bretby Park for him. He was to be found languishing with her in the weeks culminating in his final severance with Eton, after being at the school for almost two and half years. But whether he liked it or not, Lordy had to face the music with his father. He eventually summoned the courage and returned to Highclere on 8 April.[612] The next day at he kick-started a great alarm because he was displaying signs of suffering from scarletina (a form of scarlet fever). Newbury's Dr Collins was called in, but doubted such an extreme illness; however, as a precaution Lordy was quarantined to the upstairs rooms in the top part of the castle. Meanwhile the whole house was fumigated with carbolic acid. By 11 April Lordy was "emancipated".[613]

A tragic family death on 13 April in London diverted attention to the plight of little Rolf Herbert. The nine-and-a-half-year-old son of Carnarvon's brother, Auberon, died of consumption.[614] There had always been talk of the boy being like Lordy; neither child was expected to live to adulthood.

But there was some good news to temper the bad: Elsie told the Earl that she was expecting another child. Lordy was aghast again.

Private Tuition

As summer approached the Carnarvons went up to their revamped London townhouse at 43 Portman Square for the remainder of the season, which included Elsie attending one of the Queens' drawing rooms.[615] The occasion, at Buckingham Palace on Tuesday 9 May, was to present her step-daughter, Lady Winifred Herbert.[616]

Meanwhile Lordy was packed off to Milford Lake House with his tutor, Robert Harrison.[617] The boy was not allowed to fritter away the summertime; he would have to study, learn and generally improve.

On 14 June the Earl dined with an old Eton chum, William Fremantle, a rising figure in the Church of England.[618] Fremantle gave advice on how to handle the situation with Lordy, including sharing with the Earl his opinion on the moral standing of the public schools besides Eton.

But before any action could be advanced to place Lordy in another school (Uppingham and Winchester were both being considered), come the end of summer the Earl was distracted. He fell unwell again, he was worried about the failing health of his sister Lady Gwendolen[619], and he put himself under pressure to finalise plans for renovations on a villa in Porto Fino, Italy.[620] Everyone was excited at the prospect of having a home in Italy. Elsie and Winifred were both taking Italian lessons.[621] It was also during this period that Carnarvon made a number of purchases of property and land in Australia, intending these as long-term financial investments for himself and his family.[622]

In August Lord and Lady Carnarvon, together with Lordy and Lady Winifred waited on tables, serving treats to guests from schools within the Kingsclere Union Workhouse.[623]

Carnarvon's health was better and his morale was lifted by a visit from his old physician, Dr Michael Grabham (of Madeira). The good doctor suggested a change of climate, although with Elsie expecting, going overseas was unthinkable.[624] Instead, the Earl and Elsie went up to Greystoke, with Winifred going ahead of them, whilst Lordy was allowed to go to Bretby Park for a short holiday. With the prospect of the freedom afforded by staying with his grandmother, Lordy was jubilant, albeit his sisters Margaret and Vera were also in tow[625] as was his tutor, Harrison.

Mr Harrison was unable to control his charge, and when his back was turned Lordy resumed contact with Victor Duleep Singh. The sixteen-years-olds formulated a plan to meet, and they soon fell into their old ways, attending the local races at Derby and enjoying pursuits around Bretby and Gedling – fishing, walking, shooting and riding together on land owned by Lordy. Harrison was left wondering where Lordy had disappeared to for large parts of the day.

The Earl was informed of Lordy's covert activities, and that he was avoiding his studies. On return to Highclere in October, the issue was addressed. The Earl's diary reflects how this went:

> A conversation with Porchey this morning. I tried very hard to set before him the duty of at least a little more work and of caring for others as well as himself... and his own amusements. He took it all well and I think what I said touched him... the difficulty is that the good intention palls too often with the words...[626]

Supported by Lady Chesterfield, Lordy request to continue living at Bretby Park was granted.[627] When he eventually returned to Highclere on 8 December, it was to a snow-covered scene, which allowed for some fun skating with his sisters. On 15 December Lordy organised a shoot, and because his father was unwell, Lordy had a great chance to shine as one of the guns.[628]

There was the usual movement between London, Pixton Park and Highclere during the period October to December.[629] Some of this was socialising, but an effort was made to give Elsie a period of calm, away from society, before her second child was born.

After a happy family Christmas and celebration of their wedding anniversary, Elsie gave birth to a second son on 27 December at Highclere.[630] It had been "an anxious and wearing night"[631] for everyone. The child was given the name Mervyn Robert Howard Molyneux Herbert.[632] There was great relief when Dr Douglas reported he was "perfectly satisfied"[633] with Elsie's progress. The Earl wrote simply: "Everything – thank God – going on well."[634]

During Elsie's confinement and its aftermath it must have occurred to Lordy that almost exactly eight years before his own mother's life had hung on a thread after her last child, Lady Victoria, was born. To take his mind off this painful memory, he was whisked away to carry on his studies at Milford with Robert Harrison.[635]

**Greystoke Castle, Cumberland
Seat of the Howard Family**

Eton College

Prince Victor Duleep Singh, 1877

EMBLETON VICARAGE

Embleton

Chapter Eighteen

Lordy Proves a Handful

On 16 January Lordy met with a unpleasant accident. He had been out riding with his father and on return went back to Milford on his tricycle. On the way it broke down and he was thrown off, cutting his kneecap severely. On learning of the accident from a servant, the Earl rushed down from Highclere and found Lordy trying to walk about. The injured boy was taken up to the castle and examined by Dr Douglas. There was no cause for huge concern, but Lordy's leg was put in splints.[636] For the next weeks he was grounded, with only his stamp album to help him pass the hours away.

The Earl was angry that Lordy's tutor, Harrison, had allowed his charge to spend time away from studies playing on his tricycle. He used the opportunity to confront Harrison further about the state of Lordy's progress. He was not impressed by Harrison's responses. He records:

> An explanation with Harrison which shows that with many good qualities, he is wanting in judgement and on some subjects very silly. He also cannot exercise the authority delegated to him. I fear that his connection with P is virtually at an end. It may endure for a few weeks or even months, but cannot last.[637]

On Sunday 28 January, Mervyn, the latest addition to the Carnarvon family, was christened at Highclere Church in the presence of his elder half-brother Lordy, all his half-sisters and his little brother, Aubrey.[638] Winifred was in good spirits, having returned home after spending time at Charlton attending two balls. Lordy's knee was healing well.

The Earl and Elsie were planning a European tour through France and Italy. Before leaving a showdown with Lordy's idle tutor, Harrison, was inevitable. The Earl records:

> P and Harrison are in the house. I had a talk with Harrison on the subject of our previous conversation. Strange to say he seemed to have forgotten a great deal of it... The matter was left on the footing

that all should go on for the present as it is but at Easter we should consider the whole position."⁶³⁹

The truth was that Lordy was running hoops around Harrison and was seeing Victor whenever he could, even at times when Harrison was asleep.

On 6 February, the Earl and Countess of Carnarvon left Highclere to spend time abroad.⁶⁴⁰ They enjoyed a grand tour visiting Paris, Lyons, Avignon, Cannes, Mentone, Genoa, Milan, Venice, Verona and Lake Lucerne. Letters from England kept them informed about the family. They returned to London on 16 March, although Elsie came back very ill, with the symptoms she had displayed after having her first child. By April, the pace of the season meant the family were travelling regularly between Highclere and their new London headquarters at 43 Portman Square.⁶⁴¹ Lordy returned from Eggesford after a brief stay. ⁶⁴²

Lordy continued to do what he wanted to do, and Harrison said nothing. But the boy's health soon collapsed as the activities with Victor descended into drinking episodes. Lordy was seen around race courses and sightings were reported to those close to the Herbert family. The Earl was informed and intervened. Lordy was sent to the Continent, for a trip through Germany, including a walking tour with Robert Harrison by way of improving his health at the spas and enlarging his command of the French and German languages.

On their return, the Earl made it clear to Harrison that his services were no longer required. The Earl's diary for 4 April, written in London, records: "An important conversation with Harrison – settled and understood that I am quite free to enquire as to a private tutor for P and if necessary arrange with him to take P after the summer holidays."⁶⁴³ Two days later, on a visit to Hatfield House, the Earl discussed with one of his Cecil friends securing a more competent private tutor for the purpose of getting Lordy into Oxford University.⁶⁴⁴

One of Robert Harrison's last assignments was bringing Lordy home from Germany. This was accomplished, Lordy arrived at Highclere on 7 August "very well and much grown".⁶⁴⁵

Lordy had proved a handful, and needed a different, stricter regime. His whole existence was about to go through an unpleasant period of upheaval, instigated by his papa, and supported, with relish, by his stepmother. Although Elsie had shown kindness to Lordy and wanted to get on with him (at least this attitude was displayed to her husband), when Lordy erred or was lazy, Elsie invariably sided with the Earl or said nothing.

The arch-censor of the Earl's diaries makes no effort to shield the story set out in the diaries of Lordy bringing the family name into disrepute. The boy did at times make her life and that of his father sheer misery. Many of the passages that Elsie cut from the diaries (about her husband) were spliced *after* the 5th Earl's death, showing she wished to demonstrate Lordy's failures. Occasionally, the Earl weeded the diaries, adding at the height of one period of chaos over Lordy's conduct: "I have destroyed – having read over – some parts of my journal – a painful task…"[646]

Embleton Days

Carnarvon was keen to place Lordy under a much stricter tutorial regime than that provided by Harrison, one that limited his social contacts and virtually ended any liaison with Victor. Thus Lordy spent "some months at Embleton under the tuition of the future Bishop of London, Dr Creighton to whose memory he [Lordy] remained much attached…"[647]

Embledon Vicarage stood halfway between Edinburgh and Newcastle. It was occupied by Mandell Creighton,[648] a straight-laced clergyman who took in sons of the nobility to help them prepare the path for taking Oxford University entrance examinations.[649]

Despite its grand exterior, with castled turret, Embleton was a near seminary, and although spacious, spartan conditions prevailed compared with Lordy's country-house lifestyle at Highclere and Bretby. Embleton was not like Eton College, but more akin to Dotheboys Hall. There was always a long list of applicants to go to Creighton, so Lordy was favoured because of his father's position and funding. The boys (in many cases these were more young men) included a mixed bunch of politicians' sons and aristocratic juniors.

Creighton provided residential care and an environment for reading and quiet self-study, with his very able wife, Louise,[650] a mother of seven, providing the essential welfare support to the inmates. Embleton was a hot bed of activity and a centre for the development of bright and budding young men in their early to mid-twenties.[651] At only seventeen, Lordy had virtually nothing in common with these other fellows. This learning hub at Embleton was described later by the wife of one of the inmates as being a teaching regime "carefully adjusted" by Creighton for "the embryo statesmen in his care".[652]

Since Louise wrote letters to her mother (which have been published) a record survives of some her husband's charges.[653] Among the other residents was Lordy's older cousin, Newton Wallop[654], Lord Lymington (later 6th Earl of Portsmouth) and Stopford Brooke, the son of an Irish clergyman. Brooke was later a member of Parliament.[655] Louise thought Lord Lymington "very greedy" and was irritated by the "untidy, slovenly ways" of Porchester and Brooke.[656]

There is no doubt that the young, shy, less academically minded Lordy was unhappy here, and the other, much older males, with their sharper wits, confident airs and bullying taunts, left him wanting, physically, sexually and intellectually. In this circus ring all members were a product of the invidious public school hierarchy of the youngest being put upon and mistreated – they were no more than fetchers and carriers.

Lordy accepted his fate. He was placed with Creighton just before the Earl, Elsie and Winifred left Britain for a tour of Canada.

Carnarvon's Canadian Tour

After his two terms as British colonial secretary, Carnarvon could delight in achieving one great triumph: he was the main architect of the plan which brought about the Confederation of Canada. This plan had proved successful (albeit a later plan for South Africa to be configured along similar lines was a most dreadful failure, and contributed to war), and in later years was deemed "a permanent memorial to his statesmanship".[657]

Carnarvon shrewdly attempted to cash in on this popularity by making a business trip to Canada to explore some personal land and property investments. On Thursday 23 August 1883, Carnarvon, Elsie and Winifred left Liverpool on the Allan Mail steamer *Sardinian* for Quebec. They were to be the guests of the governor general at Ottawa, with a tour, if time allowed, through Western Ontario and Manitoba. Aubrey and Mervyn were being cared for at Greystoke, while the older girls Margaret and Vera were farmed out elsewhere.

By 8 September intelligence was received at Highclere that the Carnarvons had arrived safely in Canada.[658] Their host there was the Marquis of Lorne and his royal wife, Princess Louise, a daughter of Queen Victoria.[659] Lorne was the outgoing governor general (who had been replaced by the Marquis of Lansdowne). To seize the chance of purchasing land alongside the railways in north-west Canada, the Marquis arranged banquets, as did the directors of the Canadian Pacific Railway and prominent citizens of Montreal.[660] Away from the receptions and dinners, where the real business of investing was conducted, Elsie was well looked after by the Marchioness of Lorne.[661]

Carnarvon's work as colonial secretary, which had centred on Canada's confederation, was frequently toasted on the trip.[662] Carnarvon later eulogised that Canada was "a place containing more chances for success than England for men of sobriety, energy, pluck and perseverance".[663]

The visit to Canada swept in pleasure trips to Quebec, Montreal, Ottawa, Toronto, Niagara and the Military College, Kingston. It was followed by a short stay in the USA, where the Carnarvons spent time in Boston, Newport and New York.[664]

On 10 October, on return from Canada, Carnarvon and Elsie went up to Greystoke, where the report was: "Good news of all the children – everything to be thankful for...".[665]

Getting into Oxford

On 13 October, the Earl went to Embleton to see Lordy and discuss his progress with Creighton. This provoked a long diary entry:

[Creighton] repeated to me what he had written – that he did not think that he could guarantee P getting through the Oxford examination and that it would be better with a view to his degree that I should place him in the hands of a regular crammer but in saying that, in the course of the conversation, that provided P worked really well for his degree I should be satisfied and that if asked when the time came he was unequal to it I should withdraw him from the exam and from Oxford...

He said... that he was willing to keep P if I wished it, and if I held him perfectly blameless if, when the time came P could not pass. This of course smoothed the way entirely and so it was finally settled that P should stay with him and read on for the exam but with the intention on my part of withdrawing him... later.[666]

There was some discussion about the exact Oxford College that would best suit Lordy, with Balliol being favoured,[667] where representations could be made in due course to its master, Benjamin Jowett.[668]

Lordy spent a few days happily shooting with his father at Bingham, staying over at the Chesterfield Arms.[669] Shooting was a sport in which Lordy fiercely competed; he was a great shot. Lordy and his father then visited together with Elsie's family at Greystoke Castle, before returning to their London home at Portman Square.[670] Lordy was able to visit Highclere, where his "health was drunk"[671] at the harvest festival.

On 3 November, Mandell Creighton went to Highclere. It was settled that the Earl and Lordy should write to Jowett and ask him to take Lordy's name for Balliol College, Oxford. Lordy then went back to Embleton, from London, on 9 November.

But something happened which scuttled the application to Oxford. A letter survives amongst the Carnarvon papers in the British Library from Jowett to Lordy's father dated 12 November 1883. The answer might be that the admission to Oxford was delayed by Jowett imposing his own timetable, with an offer to Lordy to try for admission in October 1884: "My dear Lord, I shall be very happy to admit your son as a in College Resident at Balliol in October 1884."[672] Jowett refers to preparations and the entrance exams and encloses "a memorandum relating to admin fees at Ballioll", which he said he would also copy to Creighton.[673]

Lordy came back to London on 21 December, saw his father there, and made excuses as he had plans to see Victor, who always succeeded in lifting Lordy's mood. He later went down to Highclere,[674] where the ceaseless talk was now of Lordy trying for entry into the Army instead of going to university.[675]

Lordy had also returned from Embleton addicted to smoking cigarettes. Creighton had a habit of sharing rolled-up cigarettes with his charges. Lordy partook of these and soon became hooked.[676] He was a heavy smoker for the rest of his life.

At Elsie's command, on Friday 28 December, Lordy was obliged in take part in a Christmas concert at Highclere, with his sister Winifred and a mass of their Howard cousins, by the Highclere and Woolton Hill Workmen's Club Room.[677]

As the year finally closed the Carnarvons were planning to escape to the South of France and then go on to Italy for two months, to avoid the worst of the English winter.[678] The villa, built for Carnarvon on the hills above Porto Fino near Genoa, was nearing completion. It was named Altachiara and described as "an Italian Highclere upon the cliffs, overlooking the little land-locked harbour of Portofino".[679]

**Elizabeth Howard, Fourth Countess of Carnarvon
Known as Elsie
[Leadbetter Collection]**

Chapter Nineteen

Lordy Trains for the Army

In January 1884 Sir Stafford Northcote, who led the Tories in the House of Commons, hit out at Lord Carnarvon in a speech at Exeter. It was a sad indictment of the soured relationship of these one time close friends.[680] Northcote was clearly furious with his old chum:

> How Lord Carnarvon ever came to be a Cabinet Minister is a mystery. He has not got a single quality of Statesmanship. He has neither foresight nor experience, and his speeches are dreary twaddle...
>
> ... Lord Carnarvon has not yet mastered the elementary principle that in the progressive party of this country there must necessarily be an advanced as well as a moderate section.[681]

To add to Carnarvon's depression, his relationship with Lordy was at a low point. The Earl had sounded out several of his closest coterie to find a long-term solution to Lordy's continuing idleness, obsessions and character weakness. One of these mentors was his brother Auberon. In a letter in January he offered advice on Lordy's addiction for playing cards for money:

> May I end my letter by putting in a plea which I had intended to make in person. I think there is an old prohibition about Porchey's playing at cards for money. I think it would be so much safer to let him get over the first little excitement of it at home. If he once gets in the way at home of playing for moderate stakes, it is possible he may not wish to exceed elsewhere but the change will be great from playing for nothing to playing for what he likes...[682]

The proposal put forward before Christmas that Lordy should try for entry into the British Army was now under active consideration. On 14 January Lordy went up to London with his father. The Earl had consulted with Joseph Garnet, Viscount Wolseley,[683] a long-standing military commander and friend from the Earl's days in the colonial office.[684] The decision was to taken to see Captain Walter James[685] of

"Jimmies", a crammer in London's Cromwell Road. Jimmies specialised in getting boys to pass the entrance tests for officer training at Sandhurst Military College.[686]

> I went up to London with Porchey to settle as to his entrance into the army – I had a talk with Wolseley first, afterwards with Captain James and as good as settled with him to take P...[687]

Lordy did not want his freedom curtailed by living in at Jimmies. He requested lodgings in London. This freed him up to continue to enjoy his own choice of non-Army friends and general socialising; but would his father buy it? Surprisingly, Carnarvon agreed to the boy's request, but wrote to Lady Antrim, a family collateral of Elsie,[688] with a view to Lordy staying with her for the following "six weeks, or so".[689] A further arm of inter-family support was provided by Schomberg McDonnell, one of Lady Antrim's sons, acting as Lordy's tutor and minder in London.[690] The Earl recorded in his diary for 20 January 1884:

> Highclere: Schomberg McDonnell is here and going up to London tonight with Porchey. He has undertaken the charge of him and I trust that all will now go well. I like him much. He is clear, quick, intelligent and most anxious to do all that he can. I discussed everything with him and proposed payment at the rate of £300 per annum...[691]

At the end of January, the Carnarvons travelled to Santa Margarita on the Eastern Riviera for a much needed period of rest and seclusion. On 27 February, the Earl, Elsie and Lady Winifred returned to their London townhouse from Paris.[692]

During May, Elsie hosted several dinner parties at Portman Square for family members and a number of her husband's political friends.[693] It was the third debutante year for Lady Winifred and she was now earnestly looking for a husband. Elsie's dinners continued through June. Many young men were invited along, but there was no sign of Winifred being involved yet with a suitor.[694] Winifred was a cultured girl, though, and had impressed one middle-aged journalist who was visiting Highcere for a Saturday to Monday stay-over:

At dinner I had the honour to take in Lady Winifred, whom I found to be a very clever girl, highly cultivated, and well read in modern literature. Our conversation turned chiefly upon books, and I found that her knowledge of French and German literature far exceeded my own.[695]

In this period Lord Carnavon secured various property investments in Australia and large areas of land in Western Australia, which he saw as being a safe refuge if his family ever needed to emigrate. The Earl formulated a detailed contingency plan for this eventuality.[696] Carnarvon purchased property in Melbourne, and also a large estate in Sydney. The plan was to set aside these as investments, and the greater part of any return was for the use of Aubrey when he came of age. Lordy was deemed to be (as heir) already taken care of, as the successor to his father's settled estates as well as (at the death of his grandmother, Lady Chesterfield) the heir to Bretby and Gedling properties, with estimated rentals of over £30,000 a year.[697]

In early April Lordy was on a break from Jimmies, staying at Eggesford to ride with his uncle, Lord Portsmouth, master of fox hounds, for a meeting of hunters at Sampford Courtenay.[698]

A further watershed was reached over the prospect of Lordy entering the army. It centred on the lacklustre feedback the Earl had received from McDonnell. En route to London, Lordy stayed over at Highclere. It was an opportunity for his father to tackle him head-on: "A long talk with P in which though I spoke as kindly as I could, I did not spare him. He seems disposed to do well..."[699] Later in the month Lordy's tutor McDonnell discussed the latest progress at Jimmies. There were issues concerning Lordy's behaviour requiring medical and health matters. A Dr Wilkins[700] was working with Captain James and his assistants on these issues, which are not specified.

On 25 June Elsie acted as hostess at a soiree at 43 Portman Square for her husband's colleagues from the Society of Antiquaries, who were drawn from right across the country.[701] In her five-year reign as Countess of Carnarvon, Elsie had become a popular figure. One observer remarked: "I could have echoed the words of Burke in which he describes his first vision of Marie Antoinette. But her personal beauty was perhaps the least of her charms."[702]

On the same day that Elsie captivated the Earl's close coterie, Captain James discussed with the Earl the latest position over Lordy's future:

> A conversation with Captain James as to Porchey. He confirmed strongly all that he had previously said as to Dr Wilkins,[703] both as a man and as a teacher... and said that... he was most happy to do anything he could to work in with Dr W as regarding P.[704]

On 5 July, the Carnarvons went down to Faircroft, Putney, where Lady Gwendolen was far from well. In the evening they hosted a dinner party in London as a thank you gesture to the Marquis of Lorne and Princess Louise, Marchioness of Lorne, their Canadian hosts of the year before.[705] The other guests included Lady Winifred, Lady Portsmouth, Mrs Howard of Greystoke Castle (Elsie's mother) and the poet Robert Browning.[706] Elsie (like her predecessor, Lady Evelyn) was fast building up a reputation for attracting major literary and political contemporaries to her receptions. Her sister-in-law, Lady Portsmouth, acted as an introduction bureau to such luminaries as Browning and the novelist Thomas Hardy; both men were regular guests at Eggesford.[707]

Lordy's progress at Jimmies was continuing. But in July, the Earl met with his son's mentor, Schomberg McDonnell, to satisfy himself on progress. The diary suggests there was some secrecy surrounding Lordy's actual whereabouts: "Meetings with McDonnell, avoiding letters etc.".[708] Ten days later it became clear that Lordy was to leave England for a further stay with the mysterious "Dr Wilkins" (who was finally revealed as a clergyman based in Hanover, Germany, who took in young gentlemen training for Army entrance exams). The Earl saw Wilkins face to face. The diary entry adds "[I] had a conversation with Dr Wilkins as to P... settled that [he] should go to him again in September and I paid him £60 for expenses of one term."[709] Lordy set off for Germany on 30 August 1884, to study with Wilkins.[710]

During August, the Earl and Elsie escaped London for rural rides through Yorkshire and Nottinghamshire, then spent two weeks at Pixton, where the Earl was poorly with a sharp attack of gout requiring visits from a local doctor from Taunton. The Carnarvons stayed at Greystoke, Cumberland in October, during which Schomberg McDonnell paid a visit, with more words being recorded surrounding Lordy's training abroad:

> I had a long conversation with [McDonnell] and he explained his difficulties and doubts to me... they were really very simple and easy to answer and the principal advice that I gave was "patience"... I think is doing well.[711]

The Earl and Elsie returned to Highclere.[712] It was Elsie who fell sick next, requiring attendance by Sir William Gull.[713] On Thursday 11 December, Lord and Lady Carnarvon, together with Lord and Lady Cairns, dined with Queen Victoria at Windsor Castle.[714] This marked an important forgiveness by the Queen which had been a long time coming since the Earl's resignation from office six years before.

> It is the evidence of a reconciliation on her [the Queen] on her part after six years of absolute silence... the Queen was most gracious... had a long chat with Elsie... and asked about the children... [with] a book and photograph given for Vera...[god daughter].[715]

Lordy was back home at Highclere for Christmas. His father had met him in London and reported that his son was "in a very good mood and talked very sensibly about Wilkins and his reading".[716] There was a hopeful prospect of enjoying a family Christmas.

On 23 December Elsie gave a tea to some local women, during which Lordy showed a change in his attitude as he "played his banjo, sang a song or two and helped much..."[717]. The Earl added:

> Nothing indeed can be more amiable or pleasant than his whole conduct since he has been at home. It is a marvellous transformation and gives me more delight than I can express. Whatever the cause – Germany – growth of good sense and good feeling... it is a breath of sunshine that is indescribable...[718]

On the strength of his successful appearance at one show, Elsie asked Lordy to participate in a musical concert at the Workman's Club on New Year's Eve. A report on the latter event was recorded by the Earl, together with a reflection on the performance of his two eldest children: "it was a great show... Winifred sang very well on this her first appearance in public... Porchey also... he seemed to be cool and at his ease."[719]

Since Lordy's majority was looming, he was kept aware by his father of financial and estate issues relating to the Bretby and adjoining properties. The Earl's diary states: "I had a talk with him about Notts property matters."[720] Porchey, the boy, was growing into the next Lord Carnarvon.

Lordy!

Chapter Twenty

Lordy's Rebellion

In early January 1885, Lordy went to Bretby to visit his grandmother, Lady Chesterfield, in what were to be the last few months of her life. The Earl records in his diary that his son was "in very good mood and we were all sorry... to say goodbye to him".[721] After receiving and entertaining a succession of visitors at Highclere, and attending to some Masonic duties, the Earl and Countess left London, for Paris, to travel to their remote hillside retreat at Porto Fino.[722]

Lordy was due to return to Germany to continue his studies in Hanover with Dr Wilkins. But he was planning to upset the applecart by throwing away all he had been working for over many months. He abandoned all the costly training that his father had arranged in Hanover, and claiming ill health, returned to England, to Highclere, to rest and recover. The truth was that, although unwell, he did not feel cut out for the military. As time went on the pressure had intensified, and he felt suffocated, bored and anxious, with a craving to see Victor again. He could not resist giving in to other cravings too; he especially missed sailing and travelling.

Later, on hearing of his son living frivolously again in London and additional rumours that he was conducting himself badly, the Earl's support for this carefree, selfish attitude and that of the equally delinquent, pleasure-seeking Victor (who was also training as a cadet at Jimmies[723]) ended. As neither boy seemed to want to grasp any level of responsibility, the two friends were kept apart. The Earl read the riot act to Lordy, not least pointing out the money that was involved in the process and making clear that his obligations were first to his family and that his income from his estates could not be frittered away.

The Earl's nerves were shattered, not helped by the loss of his beloved friend, the great admiralty judge Sir Robert Phillimore, who died on 4 February 1885. Another personal problem was brewing: at nearby Milford Lake the Earl's old tutor, the behaviour of John Kent was a cause of concern.[724] To the Earl's great relief, Kent returned to live on the island of Madeira.

Lordy, meanwhile, conceded to spend Easter at Pixton Park with his father and Elsie.[725] House guests included the Earl and Countess of Harrowby and Lady Camilla Wallop, who had been one of Elsie's bridesmaids and a house guest at Highclere in the New Year holidays. Elsie took the lead at steering the nineteen-year-old Lordy into taking some interest in Lady Camilla, the second daughter of the Portsmouths. Like Lordy, Camilla had about her a hint of being withdrawn from others, but she was a kind and clever woman and would have made a Countess comparable to Lordy's own mother.[726]

Lady Camilla Wallop continued to be a frequent invitee at London dinner parties in Portman Square[727] at Highclere and in 1885, when Lordy's father became lord lieutenant (and viceroy) of Ireland,[728] she remained an invited guest. An illustration of this is a visit to an afternoon performance at Hengler's Grand Cirque in Dublin one Saturday in late June. This witnessed the attendance of Lordy, Lady Winifred, Aubrey Herbert and cousin Lady Camilla. They all arrived in a open carriage ahead of Lord Carnarvon and Elsie to enjoy the show, comprising horses, acrobats, jugglers and highly trained dogs.[729]

Exile and Loss for Lordy

Given Carnarvon's chequered history of a resignation and health-related hysteria, his Irish appointment was a controversial and surprising one. His acceptance of the role of viceroy followed a personal request by the prime minister, Lord Salisbury. [730] Ireland was a troubled land accepting the title was an especially brave decision by Carnarvon, coming as it did in the shadow of the Phoenix Park Murders three years previously.[731]

When Carnarvon headed for Dublin, he could naturally be certain that Elsie would act out being the perfect hostess and valued partner. The family, including Lordy, were also mobilised to live in Dublin. Lordy appealed to go to stay at Bretby with his grandmother, but his track record had shown he was only going to waste time and money out of his father's sight, so he was given no choice but to suffer exile in Ireland.

The Earl drew comfort in calculating that having Lordy with him in Ireland might give his heir an impetus to think about mapping out his own career by perhaps serving his country in some administrative capacity. It was a naïve thought. Lordy had no interest then, or ever, in public service. He had no desire to have his wings clipped and turning out day after day, night after night, at the many presentations, openings and official functions as fitted in with the busy duties of his bullying father, the Irish viceroy.

Soon after the Earl and family were in place at Dublin, grave news was received from Derbyshire: Lady Chesterfield was gravely ill. The Dowager Countess of Chesterfield had first been struck down with a sore throat. The next day she went for a drive, feeling better. However, she was worse the following day, with an acute attack of bronchitis,[732] and attended by a surgeon, Mr A. Hooper, from Burton on Trent. Later her London physician, Dr Sims of Mayfair, was telegraphed and arrived to see her. Lady Bradford, her sister, came to her bedside.

On receiving the telegraph imparting news of his grandmother's decline, Lordy hastened to Bretby. But he was too late; the last significant link with his mother was severed with the death of Lady Anne on Monday 27 July 1885. She was aged eighty-two.[733]

One of those who knew her well, for thirty years, was Lady Dorothy Nevill, who records in her memoirs:

> Lady Chesterfield was... a high-born lady of the old school – so aristocratic and always so kind... Her last years were very sorrowful, losing her husband, then her son – a most interesting young man – and then, lastly her only daughter, to whom she was so fondly devoted...[734]

Publically, it was stated that with Lady Chesterfield's death her Derbyshire and Nottinghamshire estates, including a large expanse of coal mines in the district, had become the property of Lordy, albeit he was still an infant in law, aged only nineteen. In her will the Countess had left a personal estate of £118,000. She left legacies to Lordy's three sisters, and she left Lordy her leasehold house in Hill Street, Berkeley Square, London, as well as "her plate, pictures, jewels, books, furniture, horses, carriages, farming stock and the residue of her personal estate".[735] The downside was that it was all to be held in trust until Lordy was twenty-one. In effect, the 4th Earl would manage Bretby and the Countess's legacies on Lordy's behalf until he came of age in 1887.

Anne had left Lordy very wealthy, on top of which he had the house and estates to come from his late mother. When his majority was reached, Lordy would be (on paper at least) worth more than his own father.[736]

Though he would benefit from her death, Lordy was deeply saddened by his grandmother's passing. She was the only one who had understood his grief over the loss of Lady Evelyn. Often during Lordy's excursions to Bretby the two of them would go to the nearby church where the Countess would play the organ to relieve her woes – and that process would lift the morale of her grandson.

Lord Carnarvon and Lordy attended the funeral together at Bretby. Lordy bitterly resented how things had turned out. He had never wanted to go to Ireland with his father; and had he been allowed to go to Bretby instead, he would have spent the last his grandmother's last weeks at her side. But he had been forced to stay in Ireland and been denied a last chance of seeing his grandmother alive. Now Lady Anne was gone, Lordy was increasingly lost in a sea of loneliness and hatred.

In September 1885 it was announced that Lord Carnarvon had "let Bretby Hall... to Mr Hamar Bass, MP for a term of three years".[737] Whilst Bretby was Lordy's property, he was underage and not legally capable of conducting any such transactions. This let to Bass was later denied.[738] There is evidence of discussion with Lordy on this issue.[739]

Back in Dublin, Carnarvon's job subsumed his whole life and that of his wife and family. There was constant travelling for everyone between London and Ireland.[740] Elsie begged Carnarvon to engage her brother, Esme Howard[741] (who had newly passed the diplomatic service exam), in some role. He was therefore taken onto the staff at Dublin as the Earl's assistant private secretary. There was something more sinister to Elsie's move than mere nepotism: her chief motive in putting her brother forward was that he might observe and report for her upon the activities of her stepson, Lordy. The two cousins found themselves virtually manacled to each other. Howard reflects in his memoirs: "I used to ride frequently in the Phoenix Park with Carnarvon's eldest son Porchester... [We] were invited to shoot woodcock, and on one occasion we went to Galway to fish for salmon..."[742]

Lordy was numb during the round after round of dinners and ceremonies his father and stepmother dragged him to day in, day out. On 29 November one such event was an investiture for two Irish luminaries to receive the accolade of knights of St Patrick. One of the recipients was Viscount Wolseley, a famous soldier who had been involved behind the scenes, with Lord Carnarvon, in Lordy's brief spell pursuing a potential military career via Jimmies crammer.[743]

1886

At the beginning of January 1886, Elsie represented her husband at various vice-regal events. The Earl had been suffering for some while from the strain of work and the constant travel to and from Ireland, and a complete physical and mental breakdown resulted. Elsie had to leave her husband in order to fulfil his engagements.[744] This left him feeling bereft. He records: "I hope Elsie will be back tomorrow. I miss her terrible."[745] Reports carefully recorded that Carnarvon was suffering from a form of "general anxiety" which had overtaken him.[746] He was also gravely worried about Robert Herbert's affairs. [747]

Running concurrently with this headline of the Earl's ill health was an alternative picture, with rumours of the overwhelming horror that had gripped some of Carnarvon's Cabinet colleagues (including the prime minister, Salisbury). The lord lieutenant had blatantly expressed a sympathy towards making concessions to the political aspirations of the Irish Nationalist leader, Charles Stewart Parnell.[748] He had also engaged in direct talks with Parnell. But Ireland was not Canada, where Carnarvon's brand of federalism had worked, and the majority of the Cabinet were against Parnell's plans and ambitions on any scale.

As the remainder of the month passed it was clear that Carnarvon would almost certainly have to resign as lord lieutenant of Ireland on health grounds, but this only told half the story: the real reason for the resignation was political, since Carnarvon was seen as a supporter of

Irish home rule. As Salisbury's government fell on 28 January 1886, Carnarvon's last post was sounded: he was finished as a Cabinet Minister and never served in government again.[749]

A few months after Lady Chesterfield's death, Lordy was separated from his family. He secured a university place at Trinity College, Cambridge, and his enrolment there began in the October term of 1885.

The Earl and Elsie left Ireland on Thursday 28 January 1886. "The streets were lined with troops, and bands played the National Anthem as they passed, while the crowds along the route cheered most enthusiastically."[750] One commentary on the Earl's tenure says:

> Lord Carnarvon will be remembered as one who, coming to this country at a critical time, discharged his functions in the most inoffensive manner possible, used his judgement in general prudently, and at the end refused to be forced for party purposes into countenancing a policy which his political and administrative experience and his common sense alike condemned.[751]

The Earl and Elsie made a surprise visit to Cambridge University, from London, on 4 February to check up on Lordy's new life at Trinity College and to say goodbye as they were due to retreat for several weeks to Porto Fino. The diary entry records:

> Elsie and I went down to Cambridge to see Porchey... and on the whole it was all satisfactory... His rooms are nice ones and he seems to be settling down fairly and doing some work... the tutor Rev A Stanton seems a good quiet man.[752]

Lordy was expected to join his family at Porto Fino for Easter.

On Wednesday 10 February the Carnarvons, with several of their children, including Lady Winifred, left London for Paris and then onward travel to Italy.[753] At the end of February Elsie's health deteriorated, giving cause for concern. "We have had two or three very uncomfortable not to say anxious days," wrote the Earl. "Elsie has had a great deal of fever and a very bad cough..."[754]

Lordy arrived at Porto Fino on 11 April after an exhausting journey.

Porchey arrived last night about midnight having walked all the way from Rapallo... He had mistaken the station and missed the boat... he arrived exhausted and famished and with a troublesome cold... but he slept on to 12 o' clock today and revived...[755]

No sooner had Lordy arrived than grave news was received from England about the Earl's sister-in-law, Lady Florence "Dolly" Herbert, wife of Auberon. She was dying.[756] They all returned to England on 1 May to attend the funeral,[757] which took place at Highclere Cemetery, "the grave being dug beneath a cluster of beech-trees, close to the place where her eldest son [Rolf] was buried". After Dolly's funeral the Carnarvons returned to London, whilst Auberon and his children took up residence at Milford House, the cottage on the banks of Highclere Lake which was often occupied by Auberon and his family.[758]

As well as keeping up appearances in London at state balls, dinners and receptions, Carnarvon was keen to keep himself involved in colonial affairs. He had made many friends across the whole of the British Empire. In June, Carnarvon and Elsie entertained a hundred prominent colonial visitors from the executive commissioners of the colonial and Indian exhibition[759] at a garden party at Highclere.[760] Lordy was not at home, but his siblings Winifred, Margaret, Victoria and Aubrey and several Wallop and Howard cousins took part, helping to serve the refreshments in a spacious marquee.

Highclere Park was also the setting for gatherings of the Primrose League, an organisation supported by Elsie which spread Conservative principles in Britain.[761] Carnarvon used such occasions as a platform for addressing some of the political issues of the day.[762] He was a politician who used newspapers and editors to good effect; he was always assured of his speeches being reported in the press, and where he wished to add to what others were saying (especially about his own speeches), he wrote letters to the newspapers that were published.

The next large-scale event at Highclere was on Tuesday 13 July. This time it was following a Masonic meeting at Newbury. As pro grand master of the Freemasons, Carnarvon carried considerable weight and influence. He offered the hospitality of Highclere to the brethren, and they were graciously received at the castle by Elsie, Lady Margaret Herbert and other members of the family.[763]

Cambridge and Living the High Life

Lordy was reading Modern Languages and Mathematics at Trinity College Cambridge.[764] His tutor was Reverend V.H. Stanton, MA, DD.[765] Lordy had a good knowledge of French and German,[766] and was receiving support for the Mathematics element of the course.[767] At first he had rooms at the College, but he later moved into lodgings in Cambridge town.[768]

But after a period of less than a year (including breaks away from Cambridge), Lordy tired of student life and his attendance at lectures virtually ceased. He preferred loafing about with Victor, who was also enrolled at Cambridge. Their re-acquaintance could not be hindered, despite the whiff of scandal and rumour attached to closeness and destructiveness of the relationship.

Whilst on leave from Cambridge, they decided to leave Britain: they would share a pleasure trip of travel, sailing and sport in America.

Lordy was confident in his decision to travel with Victor. Amid his grief over losing his beloved grandmother, his anger against his father for keeping him in Ireland, his growing resentment of Elsie's interference and surveillance (demonstrated in Ireland), he had good reason to escape abroad. And as the wealthy owner of land and property with his forthcoming majority looming in 1887, he had clout enough to challenge his father and be taken seriously about spending the summer in the USA.

The *Reading Mercury* of 31 July 1886 records: "Lord Porchester has gone to America for several months, in company with a friend. Intelligence of his lordship's arrival on the other side of the Atlantic reached Lord Carnarvon this week." The "friend" in question was, of course, Prince Victor Duleep Singh. At the time the news about Lordy's arrival in America was received the Carnarvons were entertaining the French ambassador and Madame Waddington at Highclere for a Saturday to Monday stay. On the Tuesday Lord Carnarvon went up to London to attend a meeting of the Conservative Party and he returned to Highclere the same evening.[769]

The Earl had misgivings about Lordy's general lifestyle. The writing was on the wall: reports from Cambridge painted a less-than-worthy picture of the Carnarvon heir dodging unpaid bills.

My Lord I enclose Lord Porchester's College bill, which by some inadvertence was not sent, as it should have been 10 days ago. If it had been it would have reminded him of the proper day of return, though he should have known this otherwise.[770]

Lordy's tutor also marked him out for "his ease loving disposition and disinclination to study".[771] The Earl hoped his son might return from America with a greater sense of purpose and responsibility.

Whilst Lordy was enjoying himself with Victor sight seeing,[772] yachting horse racing and hunting in America, his father and stepmother went to visit to his place at Gedling. Lordy had inherited Gedling Lodge, in Nottinghamshire, which was a more private location than Bretby, from the Chesterfield estate.[773]

In October Lordy is still described as "travelling in America".[774] During that time the Carnarvon heir visited the parlours and marinas of the east coast. Victor acted as leader, his royal standing making him attractive bait (better than a mere viscount). Any wife of Victor's would, of course, become a princess. Lordy was in any case a reluctant companion when Victor's goal was to explore the matrimonial stakes by meeting Yankee heiresses who were under the protection of their mothers. Lordy always accepted Victor's more dominating character in such matters, but preferred to stay in the background or conceal himself in the darkness of a New York theatre.

Lordy was back in Britain in November, and was observed with others at Brighton on a seafront thronging with fashionable assemblage. One of the draws was a desire to see Mrs Bernard Beere as Peg Woffington in *Masks and Faces* at the Brighton theatre.[775] Of course there was also the horse racing at Brighton. [776]

The Carnarvons left Highclere to spend a few days in London: they later spent Christmas also at their London townhouse.[777]

Lordy's private life, meanwhile, was spiralling out of control, with numerous bouts of spending on art and ceramics and into debauchery as both he and Victor slipped into a twilight world of frequenting London's gaming clubs and brothels. Lordy was seen by observers as trying to imitate the lifestyle of his playboy sidekick, Victor. He was still a student at Cambridge, but he had neglected, indeed abandoned his studies. The university published a list of examination results in which a "fourth class" was recorded against "Lord Porchester, Trin".[778] Lady Winifred describes this descent by her brother into self-indulgence:

> His studies were interrupted (indeed replaced) by pleasure seeking and speculative purchases and a series of ambitious gambling sprees... sport... was the main interest of the young man's life, and it is feared that he was more often seen at Newmarket than at lectures.[779]

This latter comment represents the *only* departure by Winifred into making any critical aspersion about her brother in her posthumous tribute of 1923.

As 1886 closed, alongside Victor, Lordy had become branded as a lover of the high life. Life centred around society parties and, almost always together, fraternising in private gambling dens. In public they could be seen rashly entertaining amongst the era's horse-racing cliques. Lordy was running up large debts on the anticipation of his fortune to come from his dead mother and grandmother. However, he was not good at keeping a tally of what was owed. Constant squabbles between Lordy and his father became more heated, always over Lordy's extravagance, life style and lack of prudence.

Some concerns also arose in the mind of Rev Stanton, Lordy's tutor at Cambridge when the Carnarvon heir announced plans to move out of his rooms at the University, to take up lodgings in the town. This prompted a letter from Stanton to the Earl.[780] In the same letter is evidence of Lordy suffering bleeding from the mouth. [781]

Porto Fino, Near Genoa, Italy

Auberon Herbert and Lady Dorothy Nevill

Countess of Chesterfield, Lordy's grandmother

Lady Gwendolen Herbert [Leadbetter Collection]

Chapter Twenty-one

Self-indulgence

The Carnarvons spent the New Year of 1887 celebrating at 43 Portman Square. However, Lordy had been burning the candle at both ends. He succumbed to total exhaustion, lying helpless in his bed with a high temperature and fever. In his diary for 2 January, the Earl is waspish in attributing blame:

> Lordy is very far from well. We sent for [Sir William] Jenner[782] who says he has a very bad throat... he has brought it on himself... It appears the doctor told him on no account to go out and he went out to dinner and never returned till midnight. It is a troublesome case anyhow.[783]

Lordy's serious condition (suspected to be a form of diphtheria) prevailed for several anxious days, with Elsie putting off a dinner party scheduled for 4 January. But still Lordy still went out drinking, whoring, entertaining and gambling.

By Sunday 9 January Lordy was back on his feet and the family's attention turned to Lordy's sister, Lady Winifred, who was about to get married. She accompanied her father and Elsie to St Paul's Cathedral for her very last family outing with them as a Herbert. In a progress report on Lordy recorded in the Earl's diary that day he makes no bones of stating that he thought Lordy was unlikely to mend his ways: "[Lordy] came into the next room for the first time – much better but very weak. I hope the illness has been a lesson to him, but I hardly believe it..."[784]

The year 1887 marked Lordy's coming of age, at age twenty-one. The legal milestone was signalled by the *Court Journal*, as was the majority of several other "eldest sons of peers".[785] It should have been a defining moment, of great family pride. But relationships were strained.

After the scare over Lordy's illness, the key event of January was the wedding of Lady Winifred[786] to Captain the Honourable Alfred John

George Byng, 7th Hussars, fifth son of the Earl of Strafford. Byng was fifteen years older than his bride to be and a soldier who had fought in the South African wars. He had also been an ADC to Lord Carnarvon during his time as viceroy of Ireland. The families announced beforehand that it would be a quiet affair and room would be restricted at the church.[787]

The ceremony took place on the tenth of the month in the Chapel Royal, Savoy in London's Strand, where Winifred's mother, Evelyn Stanhope, was once a frequent worshipper. Winifred was given away by her father, and her sisters Margaret, now aged sixteen, and Victoria (Vera), eleven, were bridesmaids along with two of the bridegroom's sisters. As the bride arrived there were gasps at her beauty; she was attired in duchesse satin and wore diamond ornaments. But Lady Winifred was cautious and feeling nervous. She dropped her handkerchief no less than three times on the way from the coach to the altar. It was said this was a indicator that either the union would be a lucky or, more likely, an unlucky one.[788]

Naturally, the Earl (and Elsie) hoped that Winifred's marriage would be a very happy one. Lordy did not attend the church service, for he was still confined (by his illness) at Portman Square. The official bulletin read that he was "suffering for some weeks from bronchitis".[789]

The Carnarvon heir was at his wits' end with boredom and craved his own time to partake of more lively gentlemanly pleasures, but he was pleased that his sister seemed happy enough. Elsie hosted a function at 43 Portman Square for the newly married couple, and Lordy appeared at "the tea-reception in invalid garb".[790]

Later the newlyweds spent the start of their honeymoon at Highclere Castle. As Winifred's husband had spent his entire life in the army, he actually had no home of his own. His father[791] had died the year before and the Byng family were adjusting to this fact. It was envisaged that Winifred and Alfred would live at Bretby Park, Lordy's estate, in Derbyshire, at least until Lordy, on coming of age, decided on Bretby's future. The couple were assured of privacy for a while, because as soon as Winifred was married the Carnarvons announced they were leaving London for several months to stay at their hillside villa in Porto Fino, Italy.[792] They reached Paris on 14 January, and Italy the next day.

With the family gone, Lordy was free to suit himself, but after some days and late nights on the London scene, during which his severe throat infection worsened, he was grounded again at Portman Square, although he eventually left England on Thursday 20 January to join the rest of the family in Italy.[793] Lordy arrived with what was proving to be customary chaos, which irritated his father, who wrote:

> [Lordy] arrived – having caught a fresh cold on his way here. He stayed in Paris three days and then went to Monte Carlo and to the theatre and with this and various other foolish acts got a bad cold. It is very sad.[794]

Lordy relaxed at Porto Fino and around the port of Genoa, sailing and trying to avoid a head-on collision with his father and stepmother. However, the Earl could not help but notice his son's antics when he had a close shave with modern-day pirates who attempted to join his yacht, which he'd left lying off the coast far out at sea. Lordy had hired a boat to take him to the yacht and on the quayside he picked up two Italian youths to row, but they later turned nasty. Lady Winifred picks up the story from here:

> the two ruffians gave him the choice between payment of a large sum or being pitched into the water... [Lordy] listened quietly, and motioned to them to pass his dressing bag. They obeyed, already in imagination fingering the English "Lord's" ransom. The situation was, however, reversed when he extracted, not a well-stuffed pocket book, but a revolver, and pointing it at the pair sternly bade them row on, or he would shoot.[795]

Further drama followed in February when the family experienced the discomfort of the aftershocks of a mild earthquake which passed through an area near Pegli, close to Genoa. But they all returned safely to England in late March.

Further Disgrace

The Earl records in his diary the birthday of his son: "Dear Aubrey's 7th birth. God bless him."[796] In the same week he tackled Lordy over his obligations on coming of age in June.[797]

Bouts of illness struck Lord and Lady Carnarvon, and before the 1887 London season broke they went down to Bournemouth for a change of air.[798] At about the same time Lordy returned to study at Cambridge, in what was to be a final dismal display on his part of his association with Trinity College.[799] Ill health (gout) prevented Lord Carnarvon (second only in seniority to Bertie, Prince of Wales) attending the annual grand festival of Freemasons, but his reappointment by the Prince of Wales as pro-grand master (a senior rank in freemasonry) was confirmed.[800] Meanwhile Sir William Jenner,[801] a physician of outstanding brilliance who attended Queen Victoria, was often called in by Carnarvon to judge the state of each illness, new and old, that hit the Earl himself, as well as attending Elsie, Lordy and all the children and staff.

Then, as if his father weren't already pushed to the limits, Lordy brought disgrace upon the family name once again. He was obliged to leave Trinity College, Cambridge, in 1887. His tutor, Reverend V.H. Stanton, MA, DD, made it clear to his father that there was *no* future for the Carnarvon heir within its hallowed walls.[802] The underlying issues, as with Lordy's removal from Eton, were financial skulduggery combined with a general laxity in his coursework. Stanton spelt out in a letter to the Earl that Lordy would not have the capacity to complete his study.[803]

The Carnarvon heir was deemed reckless in his spending and forgetful about repaying his borrowing. A bill for the paintings that adorned his walls and the furniture for his rooms at Cambridge was among several unpaid demands reported to the Earl. Living beyond his means, Lordy sought out money lenders, who now hung around him like vultures swooping over a dead carcase. Although Victor was in the same begging boat, having overspent on his allowance, he had a cunning plan to find a comfortable refuge in the Army.

Lying low from the money lenders, at loggerheads with his father over the Cambridge debacle and with a threat made by his father to embargo his right (not least because of the added expense and certain hypocrisy) of celebrating his majority, Lordy was brooding over these rebuffs. To escape, he left London at the end of May to go to Paris with Victor,[804] who had initiated his attempt to get into the Army by being presented at one of the Court levees.[805]

A Disappointed Father

In June the nation celebrated Queen Victoria's golden jubilee: fifty years on the throne. On 23 June there was a jubilee thanksgiving service at St Paul's Cathedral, on the 25th a state banquet at Windsor Castle, and on the 28th a jubilee ball at the Mansion House, at which four kings were present, together with members of the Royal Family. The celebrations continued the next day with a garden party at Buckingham Palace. Lord Carnarvon attended the mass turnout of over 6,000 freemasons for the celebrations in London at the Albert Hall on the 13 June. Alongside the Prince of Wales, the Duke of Connaught, Prince Albert Victor and other distinguished freemasons, he moved the adoption of a loyal address to the Queen, a ritual in which the organisation pledged its loyalty to the monarch. At the close of he presented the Prince of Wales with a Masonic jewel.[806]

Carnarvon was proud of his Masonic rank. It was also almost certainly in his mind how proud it must feel when a son became a freemason, following his father's links with that historic organisation. When he spoke on moving the address of the succession of members of the Royal family who had been Freemasons, generation after generation, sons following their father, his inner, most bitter disappointment (and he viewed it with a certain shame) was that his eldest son, Lordy, displayed no interest whatsoever in following in the same Masonic footsteps.[807]

Lordy had provoked his father on several counts. Carnarvon responded brutally, lashing out with words and deeds. This caustic behaviour from the Earl ran contrary to the public face of the man, albeit there was an element of the disturbed soul about both faces.

Carnarvon is described in one newspaper centrepiece as "a nobleman of mild speech and beaming manner".[808] Among his erstwhile Cabinet colleagues, he was seen as something of a lame duck, often called "Twitters", a name assigned him by Benjamin Disraeli. Carnarvon's reputation for indecision and constantly threatening to resign were the chief gripes about him from others in Parliament. Queen Victoria was often appalled by his squeamish behaviour, especially for not standing up strongly enough to several of Britain's cunning adversaries abroad.[809]

Twitters Carnarvon was, by 1887, effectively finished as a public figure. One commentator reflecting on the decade before this concluded that "good but nervous and somewhat weak and sentimental"[810] summed him up neatly. It is also recorded that he had a nervous, irritating little cough.[811]

The ailing Twitters had several confrontations with his son over money, his lifestyle and the future shape of the Carnarvon name and legacy. Carnarvon loathed confrontation. But it's clear he was intent on being vile, since Lordy would not easily compromise and the promise of reform came too late. The heir to the Earldom of Carnarvon would therefore be denied any celebrations to mark his 21st birthday. Such a ban as this by an Earl upon his eldest son was rare. Officially it was stated "the festivities with which such an auspicious event would be celebrated are postponed on account of the Jubilee celebration and Lord Porchester's contemplated tour abroad".[812]

To stop the inevitable gossip pointing to the real reasons for the brutal slaying of Lordy's right to have his majority recognised, a further statement was leaked to the press that "the celebration will take place at Highclere later in the year, and most probably at the conclusion of the London Season".[813] But another report deferred any celebrations until the following spring, in part on account of the Earl's poor health.[814]

On Sunday 26 June 1887, the 4th Earl made no attempt in his diary to mark his eldest son's coming of age that day. The actual entry is terse and curiously incidental: "Elsie and I went to S Pauls..."[815] Further illumination of what was behind the Earl's remarkable snub is revealed several weeks later. Complaining of the pressures upon him, the Earl writes:

> a very heavy and constant [burden]... property... local and family... This last has been most painful – P of course the cause – and I know

not what to hope on the [future] I have everything to fear – nothing humanly speaking to encourage..."

He subsequently adds:

> I have had a terrible time with P's money matters. Today I have settled it, and have engaged to pay everything on certain conditions which are to be embodied in a deed... It is a dreadfully painful affair...[816]

Lordy was slow to offer any full, convincing apology or justification to his father or comment upon his follies. In short, he was addicted to gambling and high living. He knew there would have to be a further showdown with his father.

It was another week before any element of closure is identifiable from the Earl's diaries. From the passage that follows it's clear that Lordy not only faced an ultimatum over his financial and other excesses, but his father's further scorn.

> I had at last explanation from P and told him disdainfully that my help now had been given for the last time and that if he got again into trouble he must not look to me to extricate him again...[817]

The additional punishment meted out on Lordy extended to requiring him to decline invitations to the twenty-first birthday celebrations of two of his closest, former Eton chums, the respective heirs to the Lords Beulieu and Ashburton.[818] Lordy was comforted by Victor, whose own coming of age fell on 10 July 1887 but whose father and mother were estranged and had, like Lordy, to accept only private festivities. The two wounded heirs escaped to Paris to celebrate together.

Lord Carnarvon closed other bolt holes to suppress Lordy's big day. He intervened to stop a dinner being held at Newbury to mark Lordy's birthday, citing the "Queen's Jubilee and other circumstances" as the reason.[819] But he could not prevent a later congratulatory address being presented by the town clerk to his lordship to register the happening, and congratulating Carnarvon upon the coming of age of his son and heir, Lord Porchester. However, only the Earl (not Lordy) gave any reaction, although he said he spoke for his son too.

43 Portman Square, 11 July 1887

My Dear Sir – I have to acknowledge your communication on the part of the Mayor and Corporation of Newbury, and I must ask you to convey to them my very sincere thanks, and those of my son, for their congratulations and good wishes for him on his recent coming of age. He begs me to express for him his high value of their good opinion and regard, and his earnest desire that he may always retain their esteem.[820]

Another Rebellion

Lordy was back from France, staying over at Highclere. At the end of July it was officially announced by Queen Victoria, at Windsor Castle, that Lord Carnarvon was to be the new lord lieutenant of Hampshire. The leader in the local newspaper declared: "Everyone in Hampshire will recognise the wisdom of the appointment just made by Her Majesty."[821]

Victor's gambling debts subsumed him, under " a howling society scandal" [822]. Lordy was to be disciplined further: he was coerced into joining his father and stepmother on their forthcoming and long overseas travel to South Africa and Australia.[823] Consequently, in August Carnarvon, Elsie and Lordy left Britain for a long sea voyage.[824]

Eventually, Lordy rebelled against being treated harshly (as he saw it) and being virtually held captive. He escaped, impulsively promising to comply with his father's new guidelines. He was back in England in September 1887 on the Isle of Wight, making ready for a long yachting cruise.[825] On Thursday 29 September he left Cowes on board his yacht *Aphrodite*[826] bound for Lisbon and Madeira. The intention was to then make for the West Indies and subsequently South America and Australia. In reality the plan was to seek a long exile with Victor (who was recovering after the death of his mother[827]) so that both rebels might avoid family ties for some considerable time. The voyage around several continents, with the *Aphrodite* under Captain Caws, a sailor from a family of notable sea captains, was estimated to take eighteen months.[828]

The initial plan was to make for Lisbon, then Madeira and the West Indies, but bad weather and navigation problems set them back, with alarm bells going off as to the ship's whereabouts in the Atlantic.[829] Lady Winifred's record of 1923 is helpful in describing this adventure-packed "cruise around the world". She writes:

> From Vigo he sailed to the Cape Verde Islands, the West Indies, paused at Pernambuco and then let drive for 42 days on end through the great solitude of the tropical seas till be brought up at Rio.[830]

Eventually, *Aphrodite* made for Buenos Aires, Argentina, where news of Lordy's trip and the crew's endeavours had made such a splash that Lordy gave a grand reception on board the 110-foot yacht for the Argentinean president. [831]

Probably the most accurate version of the South American adventure is that recorded in *Baily's Magazine*.[832] This reflects Lordy's own account – not Winifred's diversion, for she would make us believe that her brother languished throughout the trip with his heads in books. The emphasis of the piece in *Baily's* was that the trip was about Lordy letting off steam, whilst officially the chief purpose of the voyage was to improve his delicate health. Anyway, the narrative records that the time away did him "a world of good".[833]

Death of Alfred Byng

On 8 November 1887, Captain, the Honourable Alfred Byng, Lady Winifred's husband of only ten months, fell ill at their adopted home of Bretby Park. After being treated by the local family doctor, Mr A. Hooper, he was seen by Sir Andrew Clark[834] and Sir James Sawyer.[835] However, Byng gradually became worse and died "from stoppage of the bowels".[836] He was aged thirty-six. Byng's remains were brought to Highclere by train to be buried on a bleak Saturday, 12 November.[837]

Winifred was accompanied by her aunts, Eveline and Gwendolen, who travelled by an earlier train direct to Highclere station and drove to Milford Cottage on the Highclere estate, where beds had been arranged as the Castle was having repair and drainage works carried out.[838] The comfort and support from her two aunts saw Winifred through the terrible ordeal. The Earl's agent Mr McCraw also helped. [839]

The rest of the family were away abroad. Her father and stepmother were touring in Australia; Lordy was on a yachting cruise with Victor in the West Indies, and her sister, Lady Margaret, was in France.[840]

News of Byng's death reached the Earl and Elsie in Melbourne. The Earl records: "my heart bled for poor Winifred and I dread to think of the crushing blow that it will be to her – poor child – nine months of… unexpounded sunshine and then to be all over…[841]

**Grave of Lady Evelyn Stanhope
Fourth Countess of Carnarvon
Highclere Cemetery
[Julia&Keld Collection]**

Chapter Twenty-two

More Partying, More Debt

The Carnarvons enjoyed an extensive tour of Australia. They left Brisbane in January 1888 on the penultimate leg of their long trip. At Melbourne, they were booked on the P and O steamer *Shannon*, to finally return to England.[842]

On the evening of 5 April, they reached Florence, where Queen Victoria was also visiting.[843] They were back in London, at Portman Square, by 2 May.[844] It was reported that they were both in excellent health as a result of their trip.[845]

Whilst his father and stepmother were absent abroad, Lordy had spent time away with Victor, including a short holiday together at Torquay in April.[846] Following the long Christmas holiday Victor had left Sandhurst Military College and was gazetted to the Royal Dragoons "quartered at Aldershot",[847] but he continued to lead an extravagant life in London.[848] Victor always fancied himself as one of the smart set. The two friends slipped away whenever they could to Paris, or in England joined up with the few close chums with shared interests (usually contemporaries from Eton or Cambridge) for a day's riding, hunting and shooting.

Lordy enjoyed this freedom and Victor's company in the same measure. Sometimes this meant the Carnarvon heir was forced to endure Victor's choice circle in London. The boys went out regularly together, dining well (Victor ate far too much) and gambling (both of them wagered far too much). As well as frequenting several gentlemen's clubs, they were leading lights in the *International Club* whose club house stood on the corner of Northumberland Avenue and Trafalgar Square.[849] It was foremost the lure of the gambling houses.
[850]

For more fun, and when seeking company, they occasionally went out dancing at one of the capital's hotels, but of an evening they would usually end up in the male-only card school circuit. Afterwards, having invariably lost more than they'd won, they would stagger (tanked up on champagne other delicacies[851]) back by hansom cab to

Victor's home at 120 Mount Street in the wee small hours, sleeping well into the next day. [852]

The two of them were always borrowing money, when broke or owing money. When their schemes failed, there were debts to pay to betting rings and money dealers. Debts were met by further loans from financers, all on the strength of their future allowances. In Lordy's case he had constantly offered as security his land and property portfolio. Now he was of age, he was confronted by large claims which he realised had to be met.

The two friends also frequented the theatre as first-nighters, and Victor had a hobby of writing love lyrics – which he hummed, recited or sang to the accompaniment the piano. The Prince had gained a reputation as one of the fashionable London figures; he was seen at many functions, including many at Court (he was Queen Victoria's godson) and was deemed the latest Mayfair host of particular note. Cynics remarked, on seeing him in the full exuberance of youth, that he ought to tone down his lavish hospitality for his own good.[853] Besides which, the Mount Street flat had an expensive upkeep, and it was soon disposed of when the Prince (as an officer in the Royal Dragoons) was posted to Canada in the following year.[854]

Lordy's appetite for London society's trite rituals, receptions, balls, dinners and the season's events was not as absorbent as Victor. Lordy was lacking in social graces. Unlike Victor, who was a dandy in dress, Lordy hated displaying himself. It was not his ideal scene, and he often snubbed invitations. When he did attend (as his wife Almina later discovered when he was forced to be something he detested), he could be rude and boorish.

Pulling Away from Family

Like Victor, Elsie was also playing the celebrated London host. She was plunged into a series of prize-giving sessions for good causes, including awards to the girls of the Royal Masonic Institution at the Albert Hall in the presence of the Prince and Princess of Wales.[855] Concurrently, the Earl attended a meeting of the United Grand Lodge of England to give his verdict on the state of Masonry in Australia.[856] In addition, the Carnarvons called on the King and Queen of Sweden on a visit to London,[857] and the Swedes took part in a ceremony of prize-giving with Lady Carnarvon.

On 22 June it was announced that the Countess was unwell and had pulled out of a commitment to open at bazaar at Lillie-bridge Hall in aid of St Oswald's Church, Fulham.[858]

During July, Lordy accompanied Victor on a trip to Paris and Cannes.[859] These places were among their regular haunts; the attraction of the nightlife and the casinos was a lifelong passion, but they also enjoyed tennis, sailing, shooting and the fine dining.

In August it was announced that the Carnarvons were to hold a garden party at Highclere "to which all the leading county people" were invited.[860] Then, in early September, the Carnarvons left Highclere to go and stay at Bretby Park.[861]

Lordy was again abroad with Victor. He received telegrams outlining the Earl's worst days in the autumn of 1888, with long stretches of immobility and pain which saw Carnarvon confined to his rooms on returning to Highclere. This period marks the point of the Earl's general decline in health; thereafter he was on borrowed time.[862]

Lordy travelled around the world, ignoring requests to come home. One bulletin from 1 September 1888 reported this update: "Lord Porchester, the eldest son of Lord Carnarvon who left England about a year ago for the West Indies, has recently arrived at the Cape, and intends to go up country on a hunting expedition."[863]

Lady Winifred reveals more about one of these hunting trips for elephant, where her brother got more than he bargained for:

> the parts of hunter and hunted were reversed. Accompanied by a single black, he lay in wait in the jungle for an elephant, and in due course the beast made his appearance. Porchester, generally an admirable shot, fired and missed him, and after a time, seeing no more of his quarry, slid down the tree where he was perched, intending to amble quietly homewards. To do this, he had to cross a piece of bare veldt which cut the forest in two. He was well in the middle of this shelterless tract, when he perceived that he was being stalked by the elephant, saw he had no time to re-load, and took to

his heels with a speed he had never imaged he could compass. His rifle, his cartridge pouch, his glasses, his coat were all flung away as he ran for dear life. With the vindictive beast pounding on behind him [latterly] he reached the friendly jungle again climbed a tree and was saved...[864]

Well enough to attend a local function, on Tuesday 30 October Lord Carnarvon gave an extended address in the town hall, Newbury, on "the Australian Colonies".[865]

Lordy was back in London in November and leading his own life. His health was still causing him problems. His father saw him in London on 12 November, "going on well but having had an evidently sharp attack – a severe chill".[866] A visit at Highclere on 17 November prompted a record by the Earl of his son: "looking better but not strong".[867]

It was announced in December that the Carnarvons were intending to leave England for Porto Fino, Italy, for several months, largely for the benefit of the Earl's health. Accordingly, they left London for Paris on 6 December and travelled to Genoa.[868] They arrived at their hillside retreat on 10 December in good time for Christmas and to celebrate their tenth wedding anniversary.

After the way he had been treated by his father and stepmother, it is not surprising that Lordy was unconcerned about the deterioration in his father's health. He stayed as far away as he could from centre of the drama. If he held on, he would be the next Earl and could then completely please himself, totally. He secretly hoped (albeit not callously) that his father would die whilst he was abroad. He thought the Earl a sorrowful sight.

Before his father left for Italy, Lordy saw for himself that his papa remained seriously ill but hanging on to every inch of life. Lordy's own health had been affected by his over-indulgences at home and abroad with Victor, and when Victor abandoned him to return to his Army career, the resulting loneliness was difficult to bear. However, there had been some return to health. The *Reading Mercury* of 8 December 1888 records: "We are glad to learn that Lord Porchester's health has undergone considerable improvement during the past week or two. His lordship left Highclere Castle in the early part of the week for town."

Captain (later Admiral Sir William) Kennedy

Chapter Twenty-three

The 4th Earl Deteriorates

Lordy's plan was to join his family at Porto Fino, after Christmas. However, he wanted some time on his own. He preferred to defer the proposed family gathering as long as he possibly could. Christmas and New Year always brought a reminder to Lordy of his mother's loss. He could not find it in himself to rush to Porto Fino to add his insincere fervour on the wedding anniversary followed by his sister Vera's fourteenth birthday. So he left London, looking for a diversion, and on the Belgium frontier he found it when he was "robbed of 600 francs"[869] en route to Milan.

On 28 December he reported from Milan news of the robbery to his father by telegram, saying he was delayed, and on 30 December, saying he could not come on yet to Porto Fino owing to illness. The Earl's diary entry for 30 December reads:

> A letter and telegram from P at Milan... he is laid up with a return of his London illness... but he reports himself better and the doctor satisfied though he cannot come on at once. I have offered to go to him and have written and telegraphed...[870]

On 1 January 1889 the Earl received a telegram from Lordy (or rather, his valet, Mr West) saying he was better and expected to be at Genoa in a few days. He duly arrived on 3 January.

> He had come to Genoa yesterday evening slept there and came on today. I had intended to go into Genoa to meet him and induce him to see [Dr Breiting][871] but I was poorly yesterday and the day before with an incipient sore throat and did not dare to go this morning. He arrived however – but the account which he gives of himself does not satisfy me. He has seen Breiting and I wish I could get at his opinion.[872]

The Earl later records: "P in good spirits but not I think strong."[873]

Lordy felt under pressure from the depth of his father's constant enquiries about his health, friends and social activities. So he left Porto Fino for Genoa on 7 January, on board the family yacht, for a sailing trip to Nice. But the wind failed and he had to cancel the trip.

Ignoring medical advice, Lordy went on by rail to Genoa, and despite missing the train and experiencing a wait of two hours at the station, he went on to Nice for a rendezvous with pleasure, eventually returning to Port Fino on 21 January when, according to his father, he was "looking better".[874]

The Carnarvons returned to England separately. Lordy went back first, after spending some time in Paris and Cannes. The Earl was required to sort out some political and legal matters in London and left Elsie behind at Porto Fino with the younger children. On 4 February, whilst dining with Winifred and friends, the Earl suddenly became ill. He records: "I had a fainting fit as we left the dining room which was very disagreeable. Dr Hart was called and insisted on going home with me."[875]

Lordy could not stand the prospect of more interrogation from his father, and now the wait and depression at home for his father to resume better health. A bulletin from Highclere dated 17 February 1889 records: "Lord Porchester is about to start on a tour through Egypt and Africa. He will be absent from England several months."[876]

Elsie returned to England to witness for herself the precarious state of the Earl's health, which was fast declining. The Earl reported to his wife and daughter that he was getting better, but on 19 February he had a long talk with Dr Robson Roose[877], who diagnosed a complaint which was said to be "everywhere" in his body.[878] As was common place, doctors lied in order to spare the patient more unnecessary worry and distress. Lies were especially common when the press reported on the health of a public figure. The true extent of Carnarvon's poor prognosis was not revealed to him at this stage. Since ultimately the Earl's final medical condition and resulting death was from liver cancer, it seems likely that the label of "gout", from which he suffered intermittently, was a convenient euphemism for the appearance at this time of carcinoma mitosis.[879]

Certain rituals, meanwhile, could not be postponed. Elsie presented her stepdaughter, Lady Margaret Herbert, at the Queen's drawing room on Tuesday 26 February 1889.[880] The Earl records: "Margaret presented. She and Elsie looked very nice in their dresses when they went to Court."

Whilst Lordy was abroad his name had been linked (it seems fraudulently) with the purchase of a yacht in England. The Earl was furious and records: "A disagreeable affair... some scamp has obtained £80 from a yacht builder in London under Porchester's name. It is very doubtful whether we can catch him but I must try to do what is possible..."[881]

Then the Earl was given another reminder of his mortality with the death of his chaplain and Highclere friend, Reverend George Portal:

> Poor George Portal's death. It must have been very sudden. Another strong link in my life's chain snapped... I have no one now living of my old Ch Ch [Christ Church, Oxford] friends except two with whom I was really very intimate – Sandon [Earl of Harrowby] of whom I see little and Salisbury, who as a friend has no longer any existence... for me. With G Portal on the other hand as life went on the friendship had grown stronger and to me the blow is very great...[882]

The Earl was recommended a new treatment for his nerves, involving the stimulation of his muscles using an electric current. It was similar to Grabham's use of galvanism in Madeira. The new physician was Dr Mortimer Granville[883] whose engagement was continued for some months.[884] A recuperation period followed at Eastbourne, during which Granville diagnosed a probable earlier occurrence of "blood poisoning".[885] Despite recording "my imprisonment continues" [886], the Earl forced himself to resume attendance in the House of Lords.[887]

Granville was the Earl's choice since he had written a book on gout.[888] He was one medical man of the day who maintained a constant message of hope for incurable patients in his charge. He believed it was better to tell a patient who was beyond treatment or dying that all was well, rather than giving him a death sentence. As a result, the lives of some patients was prolonged.[889]

A brush with death

In May 1889 Lordy returned to England from Egypt.[890] In transit he had at last caught up with Victor, who had returned from his Army post in Canada, leaving, somewhat true to form, a less than worthy trail of chaos and unpaid bills. As soon as the boys were back in London they received a warm welcome from old friends, and were "visible in one or two of... [their] favourite theatrical haunts".[891] Each was full of lively tales about their respective life experiences abroad.

Victor returned to Halifax, where he was in post as aide-de-camp to General Ross, the man commanding the British forces based there.[892]

Each of the boys had enjoyed their share of wild ways.[893] They'd sown their oats jointly and severally over several continents. But in their frantic search for carnal pleasures the two friends had laid themselves vulnerable to being afflicted by the scourge of sexually transmitted disease.[894]

Lordy had kept quiet about the exact state of his health. But a life-threatening condition gripped the Carnarvon heir. He lay poleaxed at the family's London townhouse in a terrible state, with a high fever and, much worse, suffering from hallucinations. He had entered a region of horrid hell and was in and out of consciousness.[895] On 16 July Elsie, along with Lady Margaret, went up to London to attend a ball at Devonshire House and found her stepson far from well.

Lordy's flirtation with pleasure had caught up with him. But the tame diagnosis of Lordy's malady was recorded as "a bad quinsy".[896] This almost certainly masked the real nature of the condition. In reality, the disease was one that was an ever-present danger thereafter to Lordy, and to anyone with whom he was intimate.[897] He had contracted syphilis of the mouth and face. He had almost certainly caught a venereal disease in one of the whorehouses of Germany or Cairo or London. The debilitating symptoms of Lordy's condition had affected him for some time, but he had confided this to no one, and the unpleasant affects of the disease had been left untreated.

Under pressure from the family, Lordy ultimately presented himself to Dr Robson Roose.[898] Roose did not identify the venereal disease. At this time, blood tests were primitive, with no diagnostic blood test yet devised for syphilis.[899]

The Earl recorded in his diary:

> Porchester has called in Robson Roose. He is better now but Roose considers he must go ahead to San Moritz and spend the winter in some warmer climate. It is very sad for it might have been so easily avoided as far as one can tell. Roose says he has really poisoned himself with over smoking.[900]

The malady contracted in Egypt caused Lordy progressive health problems, physical and mental, and there were at least two later occasions when as a result his life lay dangerously close to extinction.[901]

The Earl was sorry to see his son in such a serious condition. But their relationship was past the point where the father felt he could help the son.

Even on property matters relating to Lordy's hideaway home at Bretby, the Earl was loathe now to interfere in his son's legitimate control over his own affairs. The Earl records in the diary: "An offer for Bretby from Grogan but P. [Lordy] is evidently disinclined unless the price is phenomenally high and I have said that I will not in any way press or advise a sale unless he desires it."[902]

Lord Carnarvon and Elsie returned to Highclere in October, after a great absence, and were joined there by Mervyn and Lady Victoria (Vera).

Meanwhile Lordy had gone to Bretby to recuperate and examine the offer for sale on that property.[903] He was later joined there by his father and Elsie (almost certainly at Lordy's request). Looking for a way of taking his mind off his debility, the Earl was busy editing for publication the original 4th Earl of Chesterfield's letters to his godson. For the last time Lordy and his father found a brief together. The Earl's diary records his excitement at Lordy's researches (in the Bretby Archives) that had turned up important information that had a bearing on his father's pending reprint of the Chesterfield Letters.[904]

Lordy left Bretby for a short trip to Paris. He was expected to return from his travels to spend further time at Bretby,[905] and he was reported there at the beginning of October, hosting a shooting party over his father's managed estates at Stockefield, Shelford and Bingham, Nottinghamshire.[906] He then accepted invitations to shoot and hunt on other estates, including Beaulieu, with his old Eton contemporary, John Douglas-Scott Montagu.[907] This shooting party later led to court proceedings being taken against Lordy by the authorities for failure to apply for a gun licence.

But the return to fraternising with old school chums was a brief one for Lordy, who had further travel plans, this time to spend several months in South Africa and Australia.[908] In a touching entry in the Earl's diary he records:

> Porchester left for London, whence he starts tomorrow for Dartmouth to sail on the *Rosslyn Castle* for the Cape. I am very sorry to say goodbye, but I hope that he may gain in health and in many other ways from the journey. He was himself sorry to go.[909]

This emotion did not preclude Carnarvon from asking for a watchful eye to be kept on his precious son, Lordy by any friends of the Earl visiting in the Cape. [910]

The Earl perhaps sensed his own death was near, and that he might not see his eldest son again. In a diary entry after Christmas he recorded more sentiment:

> It is 6 years since we kept [Christmas] here at Highclere and we have been, with the exception of Porchester, the whole of the family collected here together. I too have been feeling stronger than I have been for a long time and I am very thankful for all the blessings and happinesses which are around me...[911]

Chapter Twenty-four

A Farce at Hyde Petty Sessions

Just before his return home from his travels abroad, which included glimpses of Hong Kong, China,[912] Japan, Australia[913] and America, Lordy's name was blackened in a minor court case.

In late January 1890, the Excise department brought a speculative action against him at Hythe Petty Sessions. Naming him as "George Edward Stanhope Molyneux Herbert (Lord Porchester)", he was charged with using a gun for the purposes of taking partridges at Beaulieu on 5th November 1889 without having the necessary gun licence.

Lordy was abroad when the action was set in motion. He was represented at the hearing by Messrs Godwin and Louch, who had agreed to accept service of the summons on his behalf.

Edward Brennan, an excise officer stationed at Lymington, claimed that he was in the neighbourhood of Bergeries farm, Beaulieu, when he said Lordy carrying a gun and in pursuit of game in the company of a party of other gentlemen. There were keepers, beaters and dogs, and the witness saw several partridges shot. The bench asked Brennan to justify his claim, but the evidence produced of identification was flimsy. Neither had the excise man spoken with Lordy to establish whether he possessed a licence. No checks had been made of the registers to see what licences (if any) were issued to Lordy. One magistrate said he was irked that the excise laws were being brought into disrepute by an excise officer interfering with a shooting party taking place on private lands.

The discussion of the case revealed many omissions by the unlucky, over-zealous excise man in his handling of the affair. Although it was concluded that as the case was not proved it must be dismissed, the verdict and comment by the bench caused a furore, with letters to newspapers complaining of favouritism towards toffs at the expense of those who could not afford lawyers to argue the case for them. The same magistrates fined a man forty shillings, with fourteen shillings costs, a few weeks later where it was claimed in answer to not having a licence that the accused was only scaring the birds on land owned by his brother. The headlines of "Rich Man's Law" were bad publicity for the Carnarvon heir. His father was far from pleased, especially given Lordy's absence abroad.[914]

Living It Up Down Under

While all the fuss was being played out before Hythe Petty Sessions, Lordy's extended travels (with a new valet, George Fernside) had taken him from Cape Town on to various ports, towns and cities of Australia. In early February he travelled from Melbourne to Sydney. Before starting for Sydney he spent a few days with the Earl and Countess of Hopestoun at Government House. The Earl (John Adrian Louis Hope) was governor general of the state of Victoria.[915] The Hopestouns were well known for their lavish hospitality.

The news soon spread fast and wide that the Carnarvon heir was "making a tour of the Australian colonies".[916] On 6 February 1890 Lordy was entertained at a grand civic luncheon given by Sydney Burdekin, mayor of Sydney.[917] Because of Lord Carnarvon's past colonial status, the city fathers were keen to do the honours for the celebrated Earl's eldest son and heir.[918]

Deep down Lordy knew these well-meant but long, dreary rituals of hosting and attending dinners and receptions – which he had seen at close quarters in Ireland when his father was viceroy – would be the shape of his life as the future Lord Carnarvon. It was not a fact he relished.

An Unexpected Family Wedding

As the last months of the 4th Earl's life drew to a close, Lordy was still travelling through the Far East and on the homeward leg through USA.[919] As the year proceeded, a "perfectly unexpected"[920] family wedding was planned, that of the widowed Lady Winifred to an up-and-coming and wealthy Liberal MP, Herbert Gardner.[921] This event was assured to cheer up Elsie and Lord Carnarvon, whose illness was clearly terminal. His cancer was now beyond treatment, eased only by "Granville's pills and champagne".[922] He records suffering "sharp pain in my side, great malaise, difficulty to draw breath, altogether poorly and in pain".[923] In the weeks before his death the Earl was a patient of E.B. Turner, FRCS,[924] and it was he who broke the news to the patient that his condition was hopeless.[925]

Carnarvon's rapidly deteriorating health prompted the bringing forward of Winfred's wedding.[926] On Tuesday 4 March she was married in a very private affair at Brighton. Her father gave her away. Two entries in the diaries reveal the Earl's thoughts:

> "Dear Winifred, I trust it will be a happy marriage – everyone speaks well of him [Herbert Gardner] and I like what I see of him but can't pretend to really know him and I feel that there has been a very short time for W herself to know him. She has made the choice for herself...
> ...
> Very fine morning though the snow is still lying. Dear Winifred was this morning married at St Peter's, the old parish church. Everything went off well. I had the carriage and horses from Highclere but somehow the whole thing felt very strange.[927]

As soon as the wedding was over Lord Carnarvon and Elsie returned to London to travel on to Porto Fino via Paris with the three younger children. The stay was to help ease the Earl's condition and allow him to rest far away from the public's gaze.[928] The Earl was optimistic: "In our Mediterranean home – Now for the next 6 weeks I hope that we shall have a time of pleasant quiet, reading and writing and fresh air..." [929]

Despite some health setbacks – with the children and Elsie and servants all falling ill – the Earl passed some of the weeks there writing a memoir of the Herberts. He was greatly cheered by the arrival of Winifred and her new husband from their honeymoon tour of Europe.

The time at Porto Fino ended with the family's return to England on 28 April, via Milan and Weisbaden, where they were to meet up with Lordy. The plan did not, however, go well:

> 21 April: Milan: In the evening after dinner a tiresome telegram from Porchester at Weisbaden saying that he was leaving there on

26th April having given one the understanding that he would be there till the end of the month. All our plans are consequently changed and one must travel day and night to get there on time. Perhaps there is some real reason for this, he has not behaved well. Arrived Weisbaden 23rd...[930]

The Earl's last diary entry was on 15 May 1890. Since Lordy's return to Britain is also reported as being 15 May, it's not clear whether he met with his family at Weisbaden, but he had certainly angered his father again.[931] But although Lordy was bitter about many things, he finally agreed to one concession to please his dying papa: being presented at Court.

The Unconventional New Earl of Carnarvon

Lordy was never one for convention, nor for following the expected rituals of his class, or for putting effort into defending the family name or willingly fulfilling his duties. His many foibles caused grief and sadness to his father, who was nearing the end of his life. The Carnarvon heir had long delayed going through his presentation at Court. In the years since coming of age and the added responsibilities of being the inheritor of the Chesterfield lands (the succession to which had been in part curtailed by the need for his past debts to be settled), Lordy refused to comply or be regimented. He would not be told what to wear, and any command to attend functions dressed in accordance with Court etiquette, as he had been obliged to wear in Ireland, resulted in his non-appearance. He was not a copy of his father or grandfather; nor was he willing to model himself on any of the previous Lord Porchesters. He had also refused the family hope of Lord Porchester being presented at Court by his father.[932]

However, just two weeks before his father's death, on the afternoon of Monday 16 June 1890, at St James's Palace, Lordy was one of the young men presented to His Royal Highness the Prince of Wales, who was standing in for the Queen at the levee. Lordy was presented by Viscount Lascelles.[933]

The 4th Earl died in London on the evening of Saturday 28 June [934], two days after Lordy's twenty-fourth birthday. Lordy's closet ally, Victor, was with his regiment at Colchester at the time.[935] He was immediately granted extended special leave to rush to support the new Earl of Carnarvon in his hour of need.[936]

Lordy was numbed by his father's death. This was a combination of natural grief and the great burden of responsibility that now rested on his shoulders as the new Earl and Squire of Highclere, Bretby and Pixton Park. His first duty was to bury his father.

In La Sua Volontada e Nostra pace

On 2 July the 4th Earl's body was removed from Portman Square in London to Paddington Station and conveyed to Newbury by train. Elsie travelled by the same train with several members of the family. Lordy stayed behind in London, and made his way to Highclere later that evening. At Newbury there was a great gathering of people who had come to pay their respects. The coffin (of polished oak ornamented with brass coronets) was taken by carriage to Highclere Castle, where it lay in state in the North Library. The lid of the coffin was inscribed:

Henry Howard Molyneux Herbert, fourth Earl of Carnarvon, born 24 June 1831, died 29 June 1890.

Thou wilt keep him in perfect peace whose mind is stayed on Thee, because he trusteth in Thee.

A brass shield, also on the coffin, read *In La Sua Volontada e Nostra pace*. (*In His will is our peace*).

The funeral, the next day, was to the Carnarvon vault in Highclere Cemetery. The long procession was led by Lordy, whose grief was dignified and contained, but with every respect shown to his late father.[937] As well as family, friends, political and Masonic colleagues, the civic authorities of Newbury and surrounds and the Earl's estate workers, the Earl's great friend the 3rd Marquis of Salisbury (the prime minister) attended the internment.

Queen Victoria sent a wreath, attached to which was a card bearing the words – written, it was stated, by herself – "A mark of regard from Victoria". The Prince of Wales was represented by Lord Suffield, and also sent a wreath, "As a token of sincere friendship and regard."[938]

In London a commemorative service was held for the 4th Earl at the Chapel Royal Savoy, where he was associated his whole life. As soon as the funeral proceedings were over, Lordy asked Victor to join him at Highclere a few days later. With the Herbert family in mourning, Victor was the perfect companion and had all the skills to charm and sympathise with Lordy's grieving relatives.

Victor attempted to resign his Army commission, giving as a reason his own father's serious ill health.[939] The Maharaja had suffered a stroke and was living in exile in Paris.[940] However, Victor was not close to his father, and really this was a ploy, now that Lordy was the owner of extensive properties, for the two friends to be together. There was no privacy at Highclere, so they discussed the options, taking first a respite at Dulverton for some black game and partridge shooting.[941]

On 11 September the new Lord Carnarvon performed his first public act as an Earl. He opened a "commodious parish room"[942] which had been set aside by the 4th Earl as a memorial to Reverend Canon R.G. Portal, his old college friend and mentor, for many years rector of Burghclere and the Earl's personal chaplain, who had died in 1889.[943] Carnarvon made a short speech, highlighting the friendship between his father and George Portal. He then left England for the Continent.[944]

In October, the reading of the will of the 4th Earl was scheduled to take place. All wings of the family assembled with the widow, Elsie, at Greystoke Castle, Cumberland.[945] Winifred Gardner was already there with her stepmother and her new husband. Lordy arrived from Bretby. The late Earl's last provisions for his family were just to all. He acknowledged Lordy as the eldest son and heir with no adverse comment or provision. Elise was left well provided for as were all the late Earl's children from his first marriage and sons from the second. There were no grounds for dispute and everyone felt a sense of relief and gratitude.[946]

On leaving Greystoke, Lordy (to the great delight of his sister, Winifred) invited his brother-in-law, Herbert Gardner, to shoot pheasants with him and Victor at Highclere.[947] As in years gone by, Winifred remained on call to offer her brother support if he desired it.

Lordy escaped with Victor to Paris for the Chantilly autumn race horse meeting.[948] As Victor was being pursued by debtors (despite being on an allowance of £8,000 a year from the India Office), he was contemplating staying permanently in Paris.[949]

At the year drew to a close, Elsie (effectively banished[950] although comforted by an overwhelming number of letters of condolence for her husband's loss[951]) was still at Greystoke Castle, Cumberland, with the family of Carnarvon's two younger sisters and two half-brothers. They remained there until after Christmas, later moving to Paris for several months until Pixton was available in April of the following year, to provide the Countess with a roof over her head.[952] At the same time Lordy hosted his planned seasonal shooting party at Highclere, with Victor, Lord Chesterfield, Lord Manners, Lord Burton and Herbert Gardner.[953] This November shoot at Highclere became a regular annual event thereafter. [954]

Last Days of Freedom for Lordy and Victor: 1891-95

Lordy's health was erratic during his early years as Earl, sometimes grave. The origin was the malady he was infected with during his ill-spent youth.[955] The new Earl also travelled extensively in Europe. [956]

A regular flow of notable and inquisitive guests roamed through Highclere throughout these early years. [957] There were those who had advice for Lordy about many subjects concerning the future, for the better running of the Highclere estate, and there were those who dared to give him advice about where he might look for a wife. A second large wave at one November house party at Highclere comprised many with old links to the family and some active on the London scene. The subject of conversation was of Lordy finding himself a Countess, and thus creating an heir.[958]

At his worst hour, Lordy had to face the fact that (like Victor) he was greatly in debt. Despite the consequences that would follow in letting a woman into his world, he knew he must find himself an heiress.

Victor was recovering from the events leading to his father's death, which had occurred when Lordy and Victor were travelling together through Germany. (See Epilogue). In November 1893 Lordy gave the orphaned Victor refuge at Bretby. There was perfect privacy and tranquillity for two friends there to hide away behind all the world's expectations of them: Lordy the head of the Carnarvon dynasty, Victor the head of the Singh dynasty.[959] Theirs was a leisurely life of mutual pleasure and bliss with no one breathing down their necks. Yet all too soon they faced the responsibilities of birth.[960] The trouble was always the same: money woes. Both of them had become heavily indebted to the gentry's bookmaker, Richard (Dicky) Fry, and had to face the harsh consequences of their inept actions.[961] A possible further reason for the constant bleeding of Lordy and Victor's funds which cannot be entirely dismissed is that one or both of them were being blackmailed by opportunists who knew a great deal about the proclivities of the two men over their several years as dandies on the London, Paris and Riviera scenes and at sea.[962]

Victor presented his brother, Prince Frederick, at Court on 10 May 1894. By the summer months of 1894, the time was closing in on Lordy and Victor's frivolous, wayward bachelor days. [963] For Lordy, marriage to Almina Wombwell was his inevitable lot. For Victor, any further libertine days were numbered; he had an eye on further service in the Army.[964] He realised that, sooner or later, he would have to find himself, like Lordy, an artificial marriage, with a show wife.[965] He was nurturing a legal case against the India Office, for more appropriate allowances to be paid to him and his siblings. If successful that action would restore his fortunes.[966]

But first, one last fling for the friends. The prospect of a sailing trip together in the Mediterranean and Atlantic islands brightened their gloom. In their last free time together they got up to their usual antics playing the tables at Monte Carlo and Cannes. They were never to enjoy this same peace, although their close relationship continued until Victor's death in 1918. During those years Victor saved the Carnarvon marriage from falling apart.

In early 1895 the Carnarvon yacht *Katarina*, under Captain J. Berry of Southampton, moored off Orotava, north of Tenerife. This was for a rendezvous between Lordy and Victor and the millionaire banker Baron Alfred de Rothschild, the latter arriving from his brother's boat. In the year before, Lordy had become engaged to Almina Wombwell, [967]whose guardian and benefactor was Alfred, a close friend of

Almina's socially conniving mother, Marie Boyer. [968] It was Alfred who became Lordy's financial saviour. The banker snubbed Victor; he would do nothing to bail out the Prince from his losses, and counselled Lordy, with his new wealth, to resist doing so either.

The bizarre meeting at sea secured the terms of the final negotiations for Almina Wombwell's hand in marriage and established the structure of the Rothschild–Carnarvon marriage settlement.[969] This included a base fund of £500,000 and payment by Alfred of Lordy's debts of £150,000.[970] In return for Alfred's investment, Almina became an instant Countess, the 5th Countess of Carnarvon, when on 26 June 1895, on his twenty-ninth birthday, she married Lordy. Victor Duleep Singh stood as the best man.

Thereafter three people were locked together inside the marriage: Almina, Lordy and Victor Duleep Singh.[971]

Almina Wombwell and George Herbert

From 1895 The Fifth Earl and Countess of Carnarvon

Prince Victor Duleep Singh and Lordy!
[Leadbetter Collection]

Epilogue

Lordy's Quest to See His Mother Again

Lordy grew up affected by superstition, and consequenty he developed an obsession with the afterlife. His father told ghost stories[972], revelling in relating unexplained tales that he'd read or heard about whilst travelling in his youth in the Middle and Far East. The Earl of Malmesbury records in his memoirs:

> December 8, 1862: thence to Highclere, where we were very kindly received. Lord Carnarvon [Lordy's father] and I talked about necromancy and spiritualism. He told me that he had read a great number of books upon the Black Art, and in some found formulae of so horrible a nature that they quite haunted him.[973]

In 1864, Lord Iddesleigh, another guest at the house, refers to being "consoled with an evening of ghost stories" about the Highclere bogy. Iddesleigh "expected a visit from Grampus, the Highclere bogy,[974] who, it is true, had been laid in the Red Sea for a hundred years, but his time was now nearly expired".[975]

Tales also abounded in Lordy's family of close encounters with the dead. [976] One of the old Lady Carnarvons was said to have appeared in her family house at Petworth eleven years after her death in 1826.[977] And when Dr Alan Herbert was lying at death's door at Highclere, suffering from typhoid fever, his dead mother, Henrietta, was seen at his bedside by one of the nurses attending the patient. Winifred Burghclere and others verify this sighting.[978]

But it was in Berlin in 1893, when sojourning with Victor, that Lordy became fully convinced of the actuality of this other transitory world and was drawn into pursuing a quest of seeing his own dead mother. On 21 October, Lordy and Victor were playing the casinos and ogling around the sin dens of the German capital. They went back to their hotel just before midnight to go to bed. Victor always slept with a light on. Lying awake, his eyes were attracted to a picture on the bedroom wall. He then saw the face of his father filling the entire picture frame, his eyes gazing out intently. Victor got out of bed and approached the picture, only to find it a small portrait of a young girl leaning out of a balcony, holding a rose. [979]

Victor told Lordy of the strange vision at breakfast the next morning. Such was the bond between the two boys that if one of them experienced a strange phenomenon, the other would believe it without question. Later that day a telegram arrived to inform Victor that his father had suffered a stroke the previous evening; he had not regained consciousness and had died in the small hours. When Victor had seen his father's head in the picture, he had been either close to death or already gone.

Lordy envied his friend's remarkable experience, and it gave him hope of seeing his mother, Lady Evelyn, once more. Lordy mused that if Victor had seen his dead father, there must be some means whereby he could once again gaze on the face of his mother. He'd missed her every day of his life. Winifred Burghclere records that their mother's death "was a lifelong loss"[980] to her brother.

Over several years, Lordy held séances at Highclere. This was linked to a wider public interest and an enthusiastic following for spiritualism, which had caught on in Britain after widespread coverage in USA. The séances were described by a Highclere housekeeper in her book,[981] and also by the 6th Earl.[982] But when put under scrutiny the results of the latter's séances seems far-fetched, as phoney as the participants.[983]

There is no evidence that Lordy ever satisfied his wish to see his mother. It is poignant, however, that in his last will and testament he asked that in the event of not being able to be buried on Beacon Hill (where he was entombed in 1923), he desired to be laid to rest beside his mother in the ground at Highclere Churchyard.

Romantic Friendships with Victor Duleep Singh and Howard Carter?

Homosexual men in Victorian society are to be found in all walks of life and in sizable numbers amongst the ranks of the aristocracy, schoolmasters, the universities and both Houses of Parliament.

A.L. Rowse names many in *Homosexuals in History*[984], including several men who feature amongst the 4th Earl's social and political contacts. Highclere, Eggesford and Pixton Park played host to a succession of these closeted gay men. [985]

Among the Herbert family one of their own, Robert Herbert,[986] shared a house in the Australian outback with John Bramston.[987] The house's name, Herston, was a fusion of the two men's names. Their "romantic friendship" has been the subject of much curiosity.[988] Bramston's obituary declares "his life was greatly influenced by his close personal friendship with... Robert Herbert".[989]

The Wallop collaterals to whom Lordy was allied whilst growing up include a string of confirmed bachelors, colonial exiles[990] and childless couples. The Wallop line rattles with a number of men who as boys came under the spell of Oscar Browning[991] – a notorious Eton master (just before Lordy's time there) with a sexual proclivity towards young men. Browning once held tutorials in his bath with the boys standing around.

From the age of thirteen Lordy enjoyed a close friendship with Prince Victor Duleep Singh. The evidence points to it being a far from simple relationship. Theirs was a bond of emotional need and of rare devotion that endured for four decades. The two boys found a symmetry and means of survival in a union with each other, and as men they would regularly meet at Bretby Park to spend long periods of time together alone, but for a few retainers.

It is mischievous and impertinent to assert that there was any more than some pubescent horseplay in their private lives. Yet their life stories would be incomplete without a reference, at least, to this important aspect of their relationship.

After exploring "wild ways"[992] in his youth (largely at Victor's encouragement) at Eton, Cambridge and on the Continent, Lordy contracted a venereal disease.[993] The assumption is that this was from sexual contact with a woman, but that is not certain. The matter is left open in *The Life and Secrets of Almina Carnarvon.*

Lordy had a deeply held mistrust of women. He was never confident in their presence. His mother, though remote, had left him when he needed her most, and he shunned other women, even outlawing them on his yachts. [994] But certainly, both Victor and Lordy had sexual relations with women (though in Victor's case, his marriage to Lady Anne Coventry was based on mutual celibacy). [995] After Lordy married Almina Wombwell, she had two children. It is implied (in *Secrets*) that *if* their marriage was consummated, it was done so late. Documentary evidence on Highclere headed notepaper (seen by the author) cites the paternity of Almina's son as being his best friend, Prince Victor Duleep Singh, but declares that Lordy is without doubt the father of Almina's daughter, Lady Evelyn Herbert.[996]

In addition, there is evidence that Lordy's sexual proclivities settled on the female form. He liked gazing upon woman – clad and otherwise – in his photographic studio in London[997] and on stage in darkened theatres.[998] Lordy was attracted to women who painted their faces, stage actresses and the early film actresses. The portraits of his dead mother had come to represent a warped idea of beauty. This beauty was inanimate, one sided, unreal; the women he photographed fell into the same category.

Such fragments as exist point more to Lordy being heterosexual with only flimsy evidence lining up of any homosexual leanings.

But what of Howard Carter? The author was informed in an email on 21 October 2011 that Lord Carnarvon and Howard Carter were gay lovers. The text is clear:

> I suspect you know that the 5th Earl of Carnarvon and Howard Carter were "an item". I was reliably informed of this by a friend of mine whose Godfather was intimately involved with that couple. Do let me know if you would like me to forward a letter on to him.

Was there an affair with Carter? Almina certainly hinted as much to her godson.[999] The two men lived together in Egypt, and Carter stayed frequently in Britain at Highclere, Bretby and Seamore Place Mayfair. Carter's house (built from his design) in the Valley of the Kings was made in part from precious Bretby stone, which was Lordy's idea. [1000] Did Lordy have these bricks brought out from England for a love nest with Carter? Had the similar curious coupling between his father's cousin Robert Herbert and John Bramston been a model?

The author Paul William Roberts has encroached on Carter's apparent celibacy to some conclusion;[1001] now was this startling evidence of a closer relationship between the two a base to sustain an insolent claim? The controversial email was from a verifiable source, a respected literary figure.[1002] The author followed up the assertion up with a letter, emails and a telephone conversation with the informant. The contact cautioned that he was not the original source; the actual source was a man *from inside the Carnarvon family*.

The reluctant source is a well-placed figure within the family of Lordy's half-brother, Mervyn Herbert.[1003] The latter was a British diplomat in the residency at Cairo, Egypt, throughout the period 1915-23. Mervyn knew and undoubtedly witnessed at first hand the nature of the relationship between the sponsor, Lord Carnarvon, and the man he had sponsored, Howard Carter. On making representations the outcome was that the Carnarvon family member "didn't want anything to do with the enquiry". It was an understandable block.

Is such a relationship conceivable? Between an employer and employee, with such a class divide? The author raised the issue with the American Alfred Jones PhD, a (British-born) psychologist acquainted with men who knew Carter and someone who has closely studied what makes men like Carnarvon and Carter tick. His opinion is as follows:

> In my opinion Carnarvon and Carter could best be described as "a very odd couple indeed". Walter Emery[1004] and others thought Carter strange in the extreme. He was "asocial". A man who would fly off the handle at the slightest provocation. At that time, one's sexual behaviour was taboo. Viewing him (based on your premise) as a psychologist many say that he was a man of many conflicts. The question of a "relationship" between himself and Carnarvon never occurred to me, but if it did, I suspect that Carnarvon would have been the aggressor in so far that this type of behaviour was viewed in a far more accepting manner than within the ranks of the other classes.
>
> The English public school system was a very pathological entity in many ways as was the nurture and admonition of upper class young gentlemen. A boy from a public school background would have a much more accepting opinion.

I don't think that Carter could "love" anyone. Homosexual behaviour in and of itself does not always imply "love" but psychological needs. Lust, if you will, as was perhaps the case with Oscar Wilde who was a sexual opportunist.

Any type of sexual behaviour, homosexual, heterosexual or bisexual is very complicated with many variables.

Look to Taylor's book *Sex in History*[1005] in which he postulates that our sexual behaviour depends on whether any particular culture worships the Moon or Sun.

The Victorians were very anti-sex which made the subject more clandestine and titillating.

Based on your picture of these complicated circumstances, I would suspect that Carnarvon could best be described as "amorphous sexually" which is a term used for those individuals with no single sexual orientation, but (like Oscar Wilde) a sexual opportunist capable of directing their sexual drive in many directions but with a strong homosexual component.

I previously described Carter (based on the information given to me by those who knew him) as having a character disorder. Carnarvon had the same psychological profile (based on your findings), which are very typical of those with almost total self-serving needs. There were many other such men from within both the Royal family as well as within the aristocracy. The sons of King George V and Queen Mary were examples. Children were attended to during the formative years by servants and often abused in many ways. There have been lengthy studies regarding these circumstances in which there are studied cases of children who were separated from their mother at birth and given over to surrogates. They spend their entire life with the preoccupation of total self-indulgence. I would suspect that there were developmental features that set in motion Carnarvon's adult behaviour. The mores of his social class would have precluded the type of sexual promiscuity as seen with Carnarvon (and his peers).

Fortunately, psychologists are not permitted to sit in judgement, but apply social knowledge based on developmental factors alone. The fact remains that these people often go through life as their own worst enemy. The character neurotic cannot seem to learn from experience and go through life making the same mistakes over and over again. They have zero capacity for self-inspection and evaluation. The relationship between Carter and Carnarvon was apparently very neurotic and almost anything could have transpired between them.

Dr Alfred Jones's compelling introduction to this book supplements these comments. He rightly cautions that private lives should be kept just that, private.

In fact, Howard Carter's personality is an easy target to exploit. One reviewer puts Carter amongst a vulnerable group of men: "Any [public] figure who remained unmarried, had close same sex friendships or acted in a way perceived flamboyant by modern standards is automatically presumed homosexual."[1006] There is no clear evidence to support the theory of a homosexual relationship between Lordy and Carter. Yes, they were joyless men in their relations with women, and their relationship was sometimes fraught, but it seems a stretch to think rows were from a place of passion.[1007] Carter's devotion to his work was the most important thing of all;[1008] he was a "master of resource".[1009] As for Lordy, the record is unclear, but there is no satisfactory, written proof that he was a closet homosexual.

Some Corrections to the Historical Record

In the *Life and Secrets of Almina Carnarvon* I revisited several events in the Carnarvon–Carter–Tutankhamun timeline leading to the discovery of the tomb.

For instance, Lordy did *not* go to Egypt as a result of a car accident in Germany in 1901 or 1902. He spent time in Cairo in February/March of 1901 as part of a wider tour.[1010] He was a frequent traveller to the Nile delta from many years before this, starting at end of the 1880s when he visited with Victor Duleep Singh whose mother's family were based there. Lordy did fall ill in the summer of 1902, but the infamous car accident in Germany was in 1909, by which time he and Carter had some years of association and digging already behind them.

What was the spark to ignite the blue touch paper and have Lordy turn his attentions to Egypt? Chapter 4 of *Secrets* describes Lordy's visit to the USA in 1903, and aims to establish a case in favour of the influence of ex-Senator Jeremiah Lynch,[1011] globetrotter, Egyptophile, one of the leading members of San Francisco's Bohemian Club[1012] and an author of books on Egypt and mummies.[1013] Lynch, a veteran of dozens of visits to Egypt and well known in Cairo, undoubtedly fuelled Lordy's own knowledge of that country's history. They both adored the idea of finding a rich, undiscovered tomb in the Valley of the Kings.

Another area of confusion is what Howard Carter actually said as he peered into the tomb. According to Almina, Lord Carnarvon called in impatiently, "What have you found, Carter?" And from the depths of the unparalleled find Carter cried out, "Marvels! Marvels! Wonderful Things!"[1014]

A further detail in Lordy's history to revisit is his cause of death, which was reported as being severe blood poisoning and pneumonia as a result (and it was only ever presumed to be[1015]) of an insect bite.[1016] The cause has been exhaustively explored, with theories as varied as a curse of the pharaohs to poisoning from the dust of bat droppings.[1017] Inferences may be read into the reason(s) why the skills of the particular doctors attending the Earl's sick bed were needed. [1018]

In fact, at the time of the alleged bite Lordy was already dying from cancer of the throat. Lordy's widow, Almina, revealed this truth years later.[1019] A surviving octogenarian[1020] who knew Almina as a young man in the 1940s, and whose mother worked for the Countess, is adamant on this matter. He told the author in July 2012 :

> [As to] Lord Carnarvon's death. I remember clearly my mother telling us that Lady Carnarvon told everyone the rumours appearing in the press about the cause of his death, being insect bite/or a curse because he and Carter had opened the tomb, were nonsense. She said that he died of throat cancer. That's what I remember and this was repeated over many years when recalling those times.[1021]

Given the countless instances of Lordy's attacks of mouth and throat infections (evidenced by his father's diaries and correspondence[1022]) it is not a surprising outcome. Lordy was also addicted to cigarette tobacco, which Almina disliked but tolerated.[1023]

This startling revelation of a terminal illness must beg the question whether it was Lordy being *in extremis* that led to him giving Carter notice that he would fund only one more year's excavations, and not that the Earl's impatience (not one of his redeeming traits) at ever discovering a treasure trove. Also worth considering is that Almina, with her nursing experience, had the means of administering a quick and peaceful death, notwithstanding that her sister-in- law Winifred Burghclere, and her mother-in-law, Elsie, commented that Almina had done everything she could to save Lordy's life.[1024]

Did the bite, if it happened, merely accelerate an incurable condition? Or was the bite used as a decoy in order to suppress truth? Cancer held a stigma; it was the disease that dare not speak its name.

No challenge has ever been raised on the veracity of the bite from a mosquito. But there was one lone voice at the time that, upon hearing of Lordy's insect bite, was edged with disbelief. This testimony has been languishing in the long grass for ninety years. It came from a close friend of Lordy, who had frequently travelled abroad in his company.[1025] This comments are noteworthy and cast reasonable doubt on the official story:

> There is an additional note of tragedy in the sad death of Lord Carnarvon when I read that it was due, in the first instance to the bite of a mosquito, for he had endeavoured to avoid these pests all his life. There is an excellent hotel in Paris in which he would never set foot, as he had once been bitten there; while in every new place he ever found himself his first visit was to the local chemist to buy something or other in case there were any mosquitoes about.
> Some 30 odd years ago we were on a shooting trip to South America, together with the late Prince Victor Duleep Singh. One day a wealthy estanciero [a Latin American estate owner] invited us to his ranch, situate an hour outside Buenos Aires, where he informed us, there were thousands of ducks waiting to be shot. We turned up early in the morning, and while we found that there were literally thousands of duck on the lagoons and swamps there were also millions of mosquitoes. After an hour of glorious sport we were in such pain, and our faces and hands were so swollen, that it was

impossible to continue. We held a council of war and the majority of two decided that the only thing to do was to go back to the ranch and seek relief and respite under the mosquito curtains in our bedrooms until the hour fixed for the fiesta which our host had specially prepared for us. Carnarvon would not hear of this, and after further discussion, he borrowed the peon's horse and galloped across the pampas to the nearest railway station, where he chartered a special train and returned to Buenos Aires. Next day, when two pitiful figures of fun with heads and hands swollen to the size of pantomime masks reproached him about his defection, [he] smiled sweetly at me and informed us that as long as he lived he would *never* remain five unnecessary minutes in a place where he was liable to be bitten by mosquitoes.[1026]

An additional and intriguing point arises on the reason for the appearance at Luxor (albeit after the tomb was opened) of an American surgeon named Hugh Hampton Young.[1027] Tony Leadbetter (Almina's godson) understands that Almina *asked* Young to examine her husband and to suggest possible treatments that were available in USA (not Britain) for Lordy's ailments.[1028] The evidence is obscure in Young's autobiography, but suggests that Young was only probably on a pleasure trip to Europe and visited the Valley of the Kings. In London Young certainly had sought out Almina, who had given him a letter of introduction to her husband.[1029] Young's medical speciality was urology, and he was also a leading figure on the prevention and treatment of venereal disease. Lordy's life had been blighted by this, which caused recurring body sores. One informant (a credible source, since his family have long links as tenants on the Highclere Estate) asserts that the Earl "received regular injections of a mercury-based compound in a plight to ease a life long malady".[1030] The same informant is certain that Lordy suffered prolonged and serious side effects from the regime, including the loss of his teeth and difficulty taking nourishment.[1031]

What Happened to Lordy's Family and Associates?

Elsie (Elizabeth, Countess of Carnarvon; stepmother): She made a sterling contribution in the Great War, based in Alexandria, Egypt, and aiding the war wounded in the Dardanelle's Campaign. She became (with her son Aubrey) a notable figure in Albania, founding hospitals and schools and generally improving the health of that country, where she was affectionately known as "Mother". Her beloved son Aubrey died a few months after Lordy in 1923. In her last years Elsie welcomed her close family and friends to stay at Porto Fino, Italy, where she died in 1929. Her son Mervyn died in Rome a short time after his mother. There remain surviving issue descended from Elsie's two sons.[1032]

Lady Winifred Burghclere (sister): Her second marriage to Herbert Gardner produced four daughters. He predeceased her in 1921; she survived until 1934 and completed several literary works. Issue survive.

Lady Margaret Duckworth (sister): She married civil servant George (later Sir George) Duckworth. He predeceased her in 1934. She died in 1958.[1033] Issue survive.

Lady Victoria Herbert (Vera; sister): Never married. Shared a London home with Elsie. She retired to Purse Caundle, Dorset, and died there in 1957.

Prince Victor Duleep Singh (friend): The two friends saw each other in England and abroad and especially at times of personal and marital crisis. Victor and his wife Anne were exiled to Paris,[1034] where they lived during the Great War, but with pleasure trips to Monte Carlo, where Victor died in 1918.

Alfred de Rothschild (benefactor): After creating the half-million pound fund for the Lordy-Almina marriage settlement of 1895, he continued to support them. When he died in 1918, Almina's share in the £1.5m will included the house at 1 Seamore Place, Mayfair, and £50,000 cash. Lordy was left £25,000 by Alfred.

Almina, 5th Countess of Carnarvon (wife and widow): Remarried in December 1923, Lt. Colonel Ian Onslow Dennistoun. She ran a serious of nursing homes from 1927-1943. Afterwards she retreated to Somerset. The last part of her life was spent in Bristol, where she died in 1969.

Henry, 6th Earl of Carnarvon (son): Henry took an American wife, Catherine Wendell, in 1922. Catherine had two children, a son, Henry (later 7th Earl), and a daughter, Lady Anne Penelope Herbert. Issue survive. Catherine divorced the 6th Earl in 1936 and in 1939 he remarried the dancer Tilly Losch. He died in 1987.

Lady Evelyn Herbert, later Beachamp (daughter): Evelyn married Brograve Beauchamp in 1924; he was a politician and businessman. They had one daughter, who survives. Lady Evelyn was the last surviving of those who entered the Tomb of Tutankhamun in 1922, and she was centre stage at the 50th anniversary of the discovery in 1972. The latter event was celebrated with an exhibition at London's British Museum. She died in 1980.

Howard Carter (colleague and friend): By the early 1930s Carter had completed his life achievements in Egypt, working (for Almina) under a new work permit/concession issued by the Egyptians. He also assisted Almina in the sale of Lordy's private collection of Egyptian artefacts to the Metropolitan Museum, New York, and her claim (on behalf of the Carnarvon family) for the costs against the Egyptian government of Lordy's years of excavation work.[1035] Carter died in 1939.

Inheritance

"An understanding of one's childhood is the key to the understanding of one's adult life." So writes Dennis Friedman in his book *Inheritance*.[1036]

The Victorian gentry followed a blueprint for managing their estates and rearing their children. This was a cold, harsh, unemotional regime. Since land and property ownership was critical to the family's continuance, the gentry were obliged to give particular attention to the running of their estate(s), which brought their income from tenancies, agriculture and mineral rights. Farm mangers and gardeners organised the growing of fruit and crops, and the keeping of animals; many estates had a large residence (sometimes several) with a home farm, making them essentially self-sufficient.

Children whose parents were landed/titled were usually placed in other people's hands. Servants, wet nurses and housekeepers fed them, and tutors and governesses educated them. The lord of the manor and his wife saw their children infrequently; they made decisions about them at arm's length. Where (as with Lordy's father) the landowner was a public figure, society fixtures (usually in London) took precedence over local duties, although the latter might be delegated or delayed. Since the regime depended on goodwill and regular sightings of them by local folk, some invitations could not be refused. In parish/estate affairs the chatelaine could arrange participation with her model children playing a part, learning the ropes of the job they would eventually inherit. Family values were important, and the children learned their place in the hierarchy.

Most of the next generation's gentry passed through this style of upbringing unscathed. But the process swallowed up the 4th Earl of Carnarvon's children, especially his eldest son and heir, Lordy. The regime was supposed to be a representation of dignity and stiff-upper-lip showmanship, but for Lordy it was a hellish, unfeeling machine that rendered him dysfunctional. His constantly poor health was mishandled, and he was never allowed to adequately grieve after his mother's death.

With the loss of a mother's love, he looked to his father. But the 4th Earl would not accept the boy as an individual or deal with him being less able intellectually. Although he was able to show proficiency in languages, sailing and shooting, his father was silent in praise. Lordy became the target of a harrying father and buckled under the weight of suffering and study.

His general shortage of ability was a block to accomplishing anything worthy at prep school, Eton and Cambridge, where he was branded weak-willed and shy. So he joined forces with an opposite kind of personality, Victor Duleep Singh, a more confident boy from an exotic background. Together they turned to frivolity and pleasure, risking their reputation in wild ways. They were blindingly negligent in financial matters; in Lordy's case requiring a bail-out from his father who reaped retribution by snubbing his son's coming-of-age celebrations. Lordy rebelled: despite grave health he took off around the world in search of travel and adventure and gratification.

When eventually he became Lord Carnarvon, Lordy's past was a dark shadow that haunted him. Malignant debt and ill health stalked him, and marriage to a rich woman was his only recourse, thus ending his carefree days and the life he really wanted.

But history had a special place reserved for the indulgent, never-do-well Lordy!

THANKS AND ACKNOWLEDGEMENTS

The author graciously acknowledges the various sources and/ or authors of material quoted in the text etc and their respective custodians, publishers and copyright holders. Such quotes used have been kept modest and incidental. Care has been taken *not* to exceed the spirit of the copyright principles laid down in the respective *"Permissions and Fair Dealing"* guidelines in terms of the limits under the criteria for " *the purposes of criticism or review"*. In the majority of instances- and this is reflected in the End Notes- non-copyrighted material has been used. All extracts used are considered legitimate and/ or allowable under exemption or expiry provisions of UK/ EU copyright.

The position regarding the quotations from the diaries and from the correspondence of Henry Herbert, 4th Earl of Carnarvon requires further comment. Some effort has been made to identify and clarify any specific obligations remaining to the copyright holder of the material, if there is one via the British Library. [1037]The rules on this are muddled and ambiguous and untested. There is no deliberate intention to breach UK/ EU copyright and indeed to commit any infringement. It is for others to otherwise initiate proceedings should they disagree and / or wish to test the limits of continuous or enduring copyright and the current state of the exemption(s) under the law.

Henry Herbert died over a century ago, in 1890. He left the diaries and other papers in his estate to his second wife, Elizabeth (Elsie) 4th Countess of Carnarvon (1854-1929), who in turn left them to her two sons Aubrey (who predeceased her in 1923) and Mervyn (who died in 1929). Thereafter it may be argued that the copyright on the diaries etc became orphaned.

The diaries were used and refashioned to compile Lady Burghclere's biographical sketch of her brother, published from 1923. They were used for compiling *The Life of Henry Howard Molyneux Herbert*, published in 1925. No provision for the disposal of the diaries is known of in the Will of the last co- owner traced, viz, Mervyn Herbert. The volumes were in fact rediscovered by an academic languishing at Pixton Park in the 1970s, after the death of Aubrey Herbert's son, Auberon Herbert in 1974 (see Professor Gordon's *The Political Diaries of the Fourth Earl of Carnarvon, 1857-1890*, published in 2009). On 24 July 1978 the Executors of Auberon Herbert sold a large collection of the 4th Earl of Carnarvon's papers at Sotheby's. This material which included the diaries was purchased by the British Library and is now designated Add 60757-61100. The diaries were also used extensively by Professor Jalland in *Death in the Victorian Family* (OUP) (1996). Curiously the acknowledgements in both these aforementioned publications by Gordon and Jalland cite the respective Earls of Carnarvon at the time before publication as giving " permissions", whereas the late 6th, late 7th and present 8th Earl of Carnarvon were/are not a relative in blood or blood descendant or legatee of Elizabeth, the 4th Countess, the original donee of the diaries by virtue of the 4th Earl's Will. As far as the author can determine there are also no living Executors under the late Auberon Herbert's estate.

Notwithstanding that the diaries and letters culled from here are over 122 years old and the author, the 4th Earl (and/or a few of his siblings and the very few other quotations from other individuals included) have been dead for a comparably long period- *certainly in all cases over 70 years-* the work has been produced to view by the British Library for the purposes of research. The work done in drafting the manuscript has been with a view to publication but given the lack of clarity on the copyright postion an attempt has been made by the author, in good faith, and as a matter more of courtesy to obtain permission from Alan Herbert of Tetton House Somerset, a direct descendant of Elizabeth, 4th Countess of Carnarvon, the original donee in the 4th Earl's Will, and of the only surviving grandson of Mervyn Herbert but this has brought no response, comment or objection. That said there might be reasonable grounds for assuming that UK/ EU copyright has already expired. The rules laid down in respect of UK/EU law are that an author's works are protected for 70 years only after death. One interpretation of this is that Henry Herbert's copyright (and that of his succeeding Estate) ended in 1960, allowing use from 1 January 1961. Another view is that as the 1923-5 publications of/from the diaries are later, copyright ended in 1990s.
1038

Notwithstanding any further enduring copyright or other legal or moral obligation the inclusion of such material as that contained herein is in any case considered a very small and incidental part of the full extent of the vast, expansive Carnarvon Papers as a whole with at least 344 volumes held by the British Library Manuscripts Collection and a large companion set of volumes in the Carnarvon Papers within National Archives, Kew. The use of the selected diary and correspondence here may thus in any case be duly covered by fair dealing provisions and since this retrospective stands to review the life of George Carnarvon, it can be further argued that the inclusion of such extracts for review and/or criticism is an acceptable, alternative exemption under existing UK/ EU copyright law. No one remains alive that is mentioned in the extracts from the diaries/ correspondence. Moreover the use of that material here is an essential and legitimate disclosure in the public interest in this anniversary year of the discovery of Tutankhamun, NOT for return, commercial gain or profit by the author but to extend the public knowledge of the whole life of George. 5th Earl of Carnarvon, and to reflect and review, and lay down with truth and accuracy and for the essential sake of history, his early life from the single most important source of reliability held within the nation's heritage. The British Library (where the Carnarvon diaries and correspondence may also be seen and copied by ticket holders without restriction) purchased these papers on behalf of the nation from the Herbert family (after these were offered for sale at Sotheby's) in 1978. It seems remarkable in fact and inequitable in law that the diary contents should be withheld or restricted from a wider, curious public, especially as the centenary of the discovery of Tutankhamun draws ever closer. The author believes it is/would be "repugnant" to aim to suppress this publication on the grounds of its inclusion of extracts from the 4th Earl's diaries and correspondence, which are in any case in the public domain and owned by the nation.

The author wishes to thank Anthony (Tony) Leadbetter, for his incomparable contribution to this further compilation on the Carnarvon family and collaterals and for providing photographs and images reproduced herein including those given by Almina, 5th Countess of Carnarvon to Tony's mother, Anne, who worked for Almina from 1945-1969.

Others who stand out in giving help and support and inspiration to this book are Monty and Tom Dart, Dr Alfred Jones (for his forthright Introduction) and Charlie Wilson (for editing services and advice on text structure). A special thanks to Bernard Pearson for indexing the text. In relation to the Epilogue the author would wish to thank Peter Bance and Brian and Phil (Bicknoller, Somerset) and

Julia and Keld for the photograph of the grave of Lordy's mother, Lady Evelyn Herbert in Highclere Cemetery.

None of the individuals named here have had *any* part in the process to reproduce the manuscript in book form, that is entirely the author's responsibility.

Among the public records to acknowledge is the material in Crown Copyright extracted from National Archives, Kew. Thanks are due to the staff of the British Library, London. The author acknowledges the kind permission of other UK etc repositories and collections and Internet sources named in the End Notes or individuals or bodies otherwise (unintentionally) omitted.

The opinions in the text are the author's alone. Also any errors in action or implied in the text etc are the author's and his alone. He welcomes corrections, with sources and any additional data to include in any future version of the book. He thanks also Newspaper Archive.com, Abe Books, Amazon Books, Google Books, Cumbria Archives, Somerset Archives, The British Library, including the Newspaper Library. Finally, he records considerable thanks to his wife Perry and family and fellow writers at NYO.

INDEX OF NAMES AND RELEVANT PLACES

10 Downing Street	55, 81
120 Mount Street	161
13 Weymouth Street, Portland Place	66
17 Bruton Street	38, 39, 75, 79, 86, 115
43 Portman Square	118-9, 125, 129, 133-4, 139, 150-2, 160, 175
66 Grosvenor Street	49, 50, 51, 54, 58, 60, 65, 75
Aberdeen, Lord	29,
Albert Hall	154, 161
Aldershot	160
Altachiara	130
Anson, Mrs	22
Antrim, Lady	133
Aphrodite	157
Archibishop of Canterbury	49
Ascot	106
Ashburton, Lady	29
Ashburton, Lord	156
Ashley Arnwood	84
Austrian Embassy Belgrave Square	76
Averst, Dr James	63
Avignon	117, 125
Babylon	27
Baden Baden	66
Bagehot, Walter	40, 82
Balliol College, Oxford	129, 130
Barle (river)	118
Barry, Sir Charles	14
Bass, Hamer M.P Mr	141
Bath Marquis of	50
Beachamp, Brograve	192
Beacon Hill	36, 78
Beaconsfield, Lady Mary	89
Beauchamp, Lady	60
Beauchamp, Lord	60
Beaulieu,	171
Beaulieu, Lord	156
Belgrave Square	60
Bernard Beere, Mrs	146
Berry, Captain J	178

Beust, Count	77
Biarritz	117
Bing, Captain the Hon. Alfred John	150-1, 158
Bingham	170
Bishop Poynet	36
Blanchford, Frederick	55
Boston	128
Bournemouth	153
Boyer, Marie	179
Bradford Lady	22, 67, 110, 140
Bradford, Earl of	67
Bramston John	183, 184
Breitling, Dr	165
Brennan, Edward	171
Bretby church	22, 52, 134
Bretby Park	14, 21, 36-7, 40, 43, 46, 50, 52, 60-2, 66-7, 70, 72-4, 77, 79, 81, 83, 87, 95-6, 99, 109, 115-6, 118, 120, 126, 137-8, 141, 146, 151, 158, 163, 169, 170, 175, 178, 183
Brighton Theatre	146
British Museum	192
Brooke, Stopford	127
Browning Robert	78, 135
Browning, Oscar	183
Brown's Hotel	86
Brussells	65
Buckingham Palace	28, 45, 56, 62, 80, 119, 154
Buenos Aries	158, 189, 190
Bunny, Dr Joseph	70, 71
Burdekin, Sydney	172,
Burghclere Church	61, 93, 94
Burghclere Lady Winifred (nee Herbert) later Gardner	9, 11-2, 15, 20, 28, 31, 43, 52, 56-7, 62, 76, 78, 84, 86-8, 90, 93-6,

	98-9, 101, 108-9, 111, 114, 116-9, 120, 127-8, 130, 133-4, 135-6, 139, 143, 147, 150, 158-9, 162, 166 172-3, 176, 181-2, 189, 191
Burghclere, Lord	88
Burke	134
Burrowes, Dr George	70, 71
Burton on Trent	140
Burton, Lord	177
Buxton	52, 116
Cairns, Lady	136
Cairns, Lord	136
Cairo	187
Cambridge House	38
Cambridge University	143, 145, 160, 183, 193
Cambridge, George Duke of	87
Cannes	117, 125, 162, 165, 178
Cape Verde Islands	158
Carlton	73
Carnarvon, Henrietta 3rd Countess of	25-7, 31, 34-6, 39, 46, 51-2, 58, 67, 76, 80, 87
Carnarvon, Henry 4th Earl of (The Earl)	10, 13, 15-6, 25, 26-7, 29, 30-2, 43-5, 50-2, 54, 56-9, 60-3 65-6, 68, 70 71-5, 77-9, 80-1, 83-4, 86-8, 90 93-9, 101-4, 107, 110 112-19, 120, 124, 126,

Carnarvon, 1st Earl Henry 1st Baron of Porchester	127-9, 130-6, 138-9 140-3, 145-6, 150-1, 153-4,156 157,159-63, 165-6 168-9, 170-1, 172-6, 181, 193
Carnarvon, Henry 6th Earl of	9, 15, 191
Carnarvon, Lady Elizabeth (nee Howard)(Elsie)	78,84, 89-90,98, 102-3, 107-9,110, 112-19, 120-1,124 126-28, 130, 133-7, 139, 141-2, 143-6, 150-1,153, 155, 157, 159, 165-6, 168, 171-73, 175-76, 188, 190-91
Carnarvon, Evelyn 4th Countess of (nee Stanhope)	12,14-7, 19, 20-2, 28-9, 30-2,34-5 36-9, 40-5, 49,51-3, 55, 56-9, 60-2, 64-6, 68, 70, 72-5 81-5, 93-6, 108,115-16, 141,151 158,182
Carnarvon, Henry 7th Earl of	191
Carnarvon, Henry George Herbert 3rd Earl of	14, 25-6,28, 36, 39, 49 52
Carter, Howard	5-7,9-10, 182, 184-88, 192
Caws, Captain	157

201

Chantilly	177
Charlemagne	25
Charles I	98
Charles Russells (the)	77
Chesterfiel, Philip, lst Earl of	19, 60
Chesterfield, 7th Earl of (see also Stanhope, Lord George)	67
Chesterfield, House (Mayfair)	19, 31,43
Chesterfield, 6th Countess of (nee Ann Forester)	14,16, 20-2, 30-1, 34, 37,39,51, 62,72-3, 81-2 87,95, 110.115-6 118,120, 134,138,140, 143
Chesterfield, 6th Earl of	14, 9, 20-1, 34,37 49, 50-2
Chesterfield, Philip 4th Earl of	19, 20, 169
Chevening	59
Chiswick	62, 72,75
Christ College, Oxford	26, 50
Claridge's (hotel)	118
Clark, Sir Andrew	158
Cole, Henry	76, 77
Coleridge, Rev. Edward	26
Collins, Dr	119
Cologne	65, 109
Connaught, Duke of	154
Cotton, Dr	67
Couper (Cowper) Lady Florence (Dolly)	65
Coventry, Lady Anne	184, 191
Cowes	73, 75, 84
Cowper, Lord	77
Cranbourne, Lord	55, 56
Creighton, Louise	127
Creighton, Dr Mandell (Bishop of London)	126, 127, 129,130
Cromwell Rd	133
Crystal Palace	29
Damascus	27
Dardanelles	95, 97, 190
Darwin, Charles	64
Delane, John T	40
Dennistoun, Lt. Col. lan Onslow	191
Derby, Countess of	30, 38,45, 86
Derby, Lady Mary	82-4
Derby, Lord	22, 29, 30,

	45, 52-3, 55-6, 72, 86,96
Devonshire House	168
Didcot	102
Disraeli, Benjamin (later Lord Beaconsfield)	22, 39,53, 56,57, 79, 80, 81,114, 154
Douglas,Dr	109, 121,124
Dublin	139, 140, 141
Duckworth, Sir George	191
Dufferin ,Lord	37, 60, 96
Dufferin, Lady	60
Duleep Singh, Prince Frederick	105, 106, 178
Duleep Singh, Prince Victor	105-6, 116-7, 120,125-6, 130, 138, 145-6, 147,153,156, 160-3,168, 174, 176-7 178-9 , 182-4, 187, 189, 191,193
Dulverton	175
Dunrobin Castle	113
East India Dock	111
Edward VI	36
Egerton Ryson, Rev	75
Eggesford House	11-12, 61, 73 ,83-4, 94-5 ,99,100, 106, 134-5
Embleton Vicarage	126, 127, 128,129
Emery, Walter	185
Eton College	12, 26-7 50, 85,101-8 112, 114, 116-9, 126, 153,158, 160,170 183, 193
Evans, Mary Ann Disraeli's wife	53
Exe (river)	118
Exmoor	118
Faircroft, 375 Upper Richmond Road, Putney	87, 135

Falkland, Viscount	98
Farre, Dr Arthur	81
Fellowes Wallop, John (Jock)	105
Fenton's Hotel, St James's Street	38
Florence	160
Forwood, Captain J	112
Frederick Richard West	50
Freemantle William	119
Freiborg	66
Freidman, Denis	192
Friedrich, Professor N,	65, 66
Frogmore	40
Froude, James	113
Fry, Richard (Dicky) Fry	178
Galway	142
Gardner, Herbert	172, 173, 176, 191
Gaskell, Milnes	94
Gedling	39, 120, 134, 146
Genoa	130, 152, 163, 165-6
George V	186
Gladstone, William	54, 57, 60, 79
Goodwood (races)	45
Gordon House School	101
Grabham, Dr	110-3, 119
Graham, Cyril	57
Grampus' The Highclere, Bogey	181
Granville Hotel, St Lawrence on Sea	76
Graves, Frederick Percy	85
Green Street	86
Greystoke Castle	13, 78, 103, 110, 115-6, 120, 128-9, 135, 176, 177
Grogan	169,
Gull (Dr) (later Sir William)	71, 81, 93, 109, 110, 136
Halifax	168
Hall, Dr	109
Hallam's (hotel)	118
Hampshire Quarter Sessions	40, 45
Hampton Lodge, Farnham	114
Hanover	135, 138
Hardy, Thomas	135
Hare, Augustus	77, 60
Harrison, Robert	109, 119, 120, 121, 124,

Harrowby, Countess of	125
Hart, Dr	139
Hatfield House	166
	31-2, 56,60, 125
Hauffmann, Dr	65,66
Haywood, Mr	111, 112
Heathcote, Sir William	37, 40, 55
Heidelberg	65
Hengler's Grand Cirque, Dublin	139
Henley	105
Herbert, The Hon William	25
Herbert, Lady Gwendolin(e),	12, 25,35, 55,63,67, 73, 83, 86, 88-9, 98, 100,119
Herbert, The Hon.Dr Alan	25, 34, 44, 64, 71, 76, 88-9, 93, 99, 111,116, 181
Herbert, Auberon	25, 65, 84,88, 119, 132,144
Herbert, Edward	57, 61,62
Herbert, Lady Anne Penelope	191
Herbert, Lady Evelyn	184, 192
Herbert, Lady Florence (Dolly)	84, 144
Herbert, Lady Margaret (later Duckworth)	12, 15, 62,83, 87-9, 90,98, 100,106, 111,120, 128 144,145,151,159, 165, 168, 191
Herbert, Lady Victoria	12, 14-5, 83,87-9, 90, 94-5, 98-9,106,112,120 121, 128,136, 144, 151, 165, 169, 191
Herbert, Mervyn, Robert, Howard Molyneux	121,124, 128,169, 185, 191
Herbert, Robert	142, 183, 184
Herbert, Robert G.W	26
Herbert, Rolf	84, 119
Herbert, Sydney	28
Herbert, The Hon Aubrey	108, 110-12 ,124, 128, 134,139,

Highclere Castle	153,190-1 11, 13-6, 26, 30, 35-6, 38, 40, 42-3, 45,50 52-4, 56-8, 60-2,64, 67, 71-4 76-7, 80-1,83, 88, 94-6, 98-9, 100-02 107, 109, 110-11, 115-8, 120-21,124 129,130, 133, 138-9,144, 151-5,157-8,162 163-6, 169,173, 175-6, 181-8 190
Highclere Cemetery	175, 182,
Hill Street, Berkeley Square	79, 140
Holland House	115,
Hooper, Mr A	140, 158
Hopestoun, Earl of	172
Howard, Esme	141
Howard, Lord Henry Thomas	27, 35
Howard, Mrs (Elsie's mother)	135
Hurstbourne Park	43,96
Hythe Petty Sessions	171, 172
Iddlesleigh, Lord	181
Ischl (salt baths)	66
Isle of Wight	157
James, Captain Walter	132, 133,134,135
Jenner, Sir William	150, 153
Jersey, Countess of	89
Jimmies	133, 134,138, 142
Jones PhD. Alfred	185, 187
Jowett, Benjamin	129
Katerina	178
Kent, John	111, 112,138
King and Queen of Belgium	52
King and Queen of Sweden	161
Kingfauns Castle	111
Kingsclere Union	57
Kingsclere Union workhouse	63, 120
Knightley of Fawsley, Lady	78
Knowsley	74
Lady Chesterfield wife of eighth Earl	87
Lady Georgina (West)	50

Lake Como	66
Landsdowne	128
Laverick Mrs	81
Leadbetter, Tony	190
Lebanon	26
Lewis Wyndham	53
Lillie-Bridge Hall	162
Lisbon	157
Lodge of Hope no 574	99
Londesborough House	67
Londesborough, Lord	60, 67
Lordy see also Carnarvon, George 5th Earl of (Porchey)	5- 9,10-6, 20-2, 25-6,28-9 34-9, 41, 51-3, 55, 61-4 65, 67,71-2,75-8, 80-1, 83-5, 89,94-5 96, 98-9, 100-08 109-12, 114,116-19, 121,124 126-9,130,132-7 138,140-44,146-7, 150-1, 152-8,160-3 165-9,170-5 176-9, 181-7 188-9 190-1,193
Lorne, Marquis of later the 9th Duke of Argyll	58.128,135
Losch, Tilly	192
Lothrop Motley, the Hon John	62
Lourdes	117
Lower Grosvenor Street	43
Lucerne	66, 125
Luxor	190
Lynch, Jeremiah	188
Lyons	125
Lyons, Admiral	30
Lyulth Tower	115
McCraw James	158
Mackenzie, Dr	66
Macleod, Reginald	95
Mademoiselle Rachel	21
Madeira	110,111, 113, 119, 138, 157
Malmesbury, Earl of	50, 181
Manitoba	128
Manners, Lord John	79

Manners, Lord John	177
Mansell, Dr	62
Mansion House	154
Marathon	61
Marie Antoinette	134, 135
Marlndin. G.E	102, 114
Marlborough House	49
Mayfair	161
Mayo, Lord	58
McDonnell, Schomburg	133, 134, 135, 136
Melbourne	134, 159
Mentone	117, 125
Messrs Godwin and Louch	171
Metropolotan Museum, New York	192
Milan	165, 173
Milford Park(Highclere)	35, 65, 78, 114, 119, 121,138,144
Military College Kingston	128
Miss Anson	21, 34
Molesworth, Lady	39, 40
Montague, John Douglas Scott	170
Monte Carlo	152, 178
Montpellier	117
Montreal	128
Murray John	40
Napiers, of Glasgow	95
Neuhaven	66
Nevill, Lady Dorothy	40, 42, 54
Nevill, Ralph	106
Neville, Lady Dorothy	140
Newbury	14, 16, 44, 52,70, 79,93, 102, 109, 144, 156 157, 163, 175
Newmarket	147
Newport (USA)	128
Niagara	128
Norfolk, 12th Duke of	27
Northam	84
Northcote, Agnes	95
Northcote, Sir Stafford	132
Northcotes (the)	77
Northumberland Avenue	160
Northumberland House	38
Northumberland, Duchess of	38
Orotova	178
Osborne Isle of Wight	58, 70

Osmond, Mrs	111
Ostend	65, 66
Osterley Park	89
Ottowa	128
Oxford University	125, 126, 129
Paddington station	175
Paget, Sir James	95, 109,110
Palmeston Lady Emily,	38
Panshanger	77
Pantaleoni	45
Paris	33, 43-6, 64, 71, 88-9, 93, 110, 115, 117 124, 133, 137, 143, 152, 154, 156, 160 162. 170, 176-8, 189, 191
Paris, Count of	45
Paris, Countess of	45
Parkman, Francis	109
Parnell, Charles Stewart	142
Pau	117
Peel, Sir Robert	20
Pegli	152, 191
Pembroke 8th Earl of	25
Penrith	115
Pernambuco	158
Petworth	181
Philimore, Sir Robert	103, 112, 114, 116,138
Phillimore, Lady Phillimore	103
Phoenix Park	139, 142
Pixton Park	13, 25, 30, 39, 46, 55, 60-1,63-5, 73,75-6, 80 83,87, 93-4 ,96, 99,106, 108, 118,121,135 139
Portal, Rev G.R	94, 176
Porto Fino	117, 119,130, 138, 143, 153, 163, 165-6, 173,191
Portsmouth, 5th Countess of, Lady Eveline Wallop	12, 25, 38,39, 43,55, 73, 82, 83-4,

209

Portsmouth, Lord	87, 94, 98,100,101 102, 103,106, 135 101, 118, 134
Prince Albert (The Prince Consort)	29, 40
Prince Albert Victor	145
Prince of Wales future Edward VII (Bertie)	41-2, 52, 58,62 , 67, 73,153-4 161, 174-5
Prince's Gate	115
Princess Louise, Marchioness of Lorne	128, 135
Princess Mary Adelaide	75,76
Princess Mary of Teck (later Queen Mary)	75, 186
Princess of Wales(Alexandra)	42, 52,62, 75 161
Pulteney Hotel, Albemarle Street	75
Purse Caundle, Dorset	191
Pyrenees	117
Quebec	128
Queen Victoria	13, 21, 28, 45, 49, 58, 70, 79, 80-3, 85, 86,136 153-7,160-1, 175
Rapallo	144
Rawson, Mr (or Rawston)	98
Rhine	109
Richmond, Duke of	60
Rio (de Janeiro)	158
Roberts, Paul William	184
Robson Roose, Dr	166, 168, 169
Rohregasse	109
Ross General	168
Rosslyn Castle	170,
Rothschild, Baron Alfred de	34, 178, 179, 191
Rowse, A.L	182
Ruthin Castle	50
Ryde	72
Salisbury, Lady	31, 42, 56
Salisbury. Lord, Marquis of (The Salisbury's)	42, 49,55-6, 58, 60, 83, 139, 142-4,175
Sampford Courtney	134
San Francisco's Bohemian Club	188
San Moritz	169
Sandhurst Military College	133, 160
Sandon Lord(Dudley Ryder)	26
Sandringham	67, 73,74

Santa Marghita (Eatern Riviera)	133
Sardinian	128
Savoy Chapel	83
Sawyer, Sir James	158
Sawyer, Sir Robert	36
Scarborough	67
Seamore Place, Mayfair	184, 191
Shah of Persia	75
Shannon	160
Shelford	19, 170
Sibthorpe, Mrs	101
Sims, Dr	140
Smith, Dr J. Smith	110, 111
South Kensington Museum	72
Sping Vale Oak Hil Ryde	73
SS Arab	112
St Andrews church, Greystoke	99
St George's Chapel Windsor	40
St James Palace	174
St James's Palace	28
St Michael and All Angels, Highclere	62, 124
St Oswald's Church, Fulham	162
St Paul's Cathedral	62
St Paul's Church, Knightsbridge	72
St Paul's Cathedral	150, 154, 155
Stanhope	19
Stanhope, Lord George (see also Chesterfield 7th Earl of)	20, 37, 45, 50,58-60, 73,80,85,177
Stanhope, Lady Mary	34, 42, 49, 58, 59
Stanley, Lord (later 15th Earl of Derby)	55, 60
Stanton D.D, Rev, V.H	145, 147, 153
Stokerfield,	170
Strafford, the Earl of	151
Strasbourg	66
Suffield, Lord	175
Sydney	134, 172
Syria	26
Tattersalls	50
Taunton	135
Tenerife	178
Tetton	25
The Ball House, Piccadilly	29
The Chapel Royal, Savoy, The Strand	151, 176
The Chesterfield Arms	129
The Coppice	116
The Fez	112
The Mansion House	52
The Mercia	73, 76
The Trojan	112

Thomas Jackson of Pimlico	36,
Thompson Gream, Dr George,	39
Toronto	128
Torquay	55, 63
Townsend, Meredith	77
Trafalgar Square	160
Trinity College, Cambridge	143, 153
Troutbeck, Cannon John	84, 96
Turner E.B	173
Tutankhamun's Tomb	5,9, 10, 192
United Grand Lodge of England	161
University of Bristol	6
Uppingham	119
Valley of the Kings	184, 188,190
Veale's Royal Hotel, Teignmouth	55
Venice	125
Verona	125
Victoria (Australian state of)	172
Vigo	158
Viscount Lascelles	174
Waddington Madame	145
Wallop, Lady Camilla	139
Wallop, Lady Catherine	34, 94,95
Wallop, Lady Lillian (Lilias)	111, 112
Wallop, The Hon Edward (Teddy)	101
Wallop, The Hon Frederick (Freddie)	101
Wallop,Newton Lord Lymington, (later 6th Earl of Portsmouth	127
Weiner	117
Weisbaden	173
Wellington Duke of (Arthur Wellesley)	20
Wembworthy	94
Wendell, Catherine	191
West, Mr	165
Western Ontario	128
Westminster Abbey	34, 62
White, Rev Henry	83
Wildbad	58, 65,109
Wilde, Oscar	186
Wilkins, Dr	134, 135, 136
Wilton House	25
Winchester	119
Winchester Abbey	35
Windsor	106
Windsor Castle	62, 79, 157
Woffington, Peg	146
Wolseley, Viscount (Joseph Garnet)	132, 133
Wolsley, Viscount	142
Wombwell , Almina (later) Carnarvon 5th Countess of	6-7, 9-10, 34, 117, 161, 178-9, 183-4

	187,188
	190,191
Woolton Hill Workmen's Club Room	130, 136
Yorke House, Twickenham	45
Young, Hugh Hampton	190
Zurich	66

Prince Victor Duleep Singh

Almina's son, Henry, 6th Earl

Sir Robert Herbert

Carnarvon and Carter
[Leadbetter Collection]

END NOTES

[1] Almina Victoria Marie Alexandra Wombwell (1876–1969). Her mother was French, her father English. From 1895 Almina was the 5th Countess of Carnarvon. Her guardian Baron Alfred de Rothschild pledged a marriage settlement of £12,000 a year on her and the 5th Earl.

[2] The nickname of "Lordy" or "The Lord" was applied to George Herbert by the native diggers in the Valley of the King where he spent a decade and more of his life in search of the ancient treasures of Egypt. Thus "Lordy" is the adopted use in this retrospective.

[3] See James, T.G.H.: *Howard Carter the Path to Tutankhamun*, Kegan Paul International (1992) and Winstone, H.V.F., *Howard Carter and the Discovery of the Tomb of Tutankhamun*, Constable and Company (1991).

[4] Reeves, C.N. and Taylor J.H., *Howard Carter: Before Tutankhamun*, Harry N. Abrams (1993).

[5] Burghclere, Lady Winifred, *Biographical Sketch of Lord Carnarvon* (1923).

[6] See Cross, William P., *The Life and Secrets of Almina Carnarvon* (2011), ISBN 978–1–905914–08–1 (3rd edition).

[7] The Carnarvon Papers in the British Library, London, hold the 4th Earl's "diaries, travel journals and memoranda" recording his years of youth (1852) through to the year of his death (1890). Ref: Add 60887–60935. The diaries total over 60 volumes.

[8] Hardinge, Sir Arthur [edited by Elizabeth, Countess of Carnarvon], *The Life of Henry Howard Molyneux Herbert 1831–1890* (1925). Oxford University Press. Three volumes. These volumes (together with the 1923 sketch by Lady Winifred) mark the first post posthumous publication of the Fourth Earl's diaries and general correspondence.

[9] See Fiona Carnarvon's *Lady Almina and the Real Downton Abbey, The Lost Legacy of Highclere Castle*. Hodder & Stoughton (2011).

[10] Eggesford House, Devonshire, one time seat of the Earls of Portsmouth. An Elizabethan house which stands on high ground commanding extensive views over the Valley of the Taw, with well wooded park of 300 acres, pretty gardens with the finest yew hedges. From *Washington Herald*, 9 July 1913.

[11] The mansion house of Highclere (or sometimes High Clere) owes much to the 3rd Earl of Carnarvon's vision. The design owes its spark to Sir Charles Barry, who went on to design the Houses of Parliament (despite the claims by another architect's family that it was a Mr E. Welby Pugin who gave Barry the concept). Highclere was described as "plainly an anticipation of the Houses of Parliament [by Barry] on a much smaller scale". See *The Lancaster Gazette, and General Advertiser for Lancashire etc.*, 14 September 1867. NB: Much of the interior of Highclere is credited to the architect, Thomas Allom.

[12] Based on an entry in the 4th Earl's diaries for 9 January 1879 in the British Library, Reference Add 60913.

[13] Based on a comment made by Almina, 5th Countess, to her godson, Tony Leadbetter.

[14] Lady Winifred Anne Henrietta Christiana Herbert (1864–1933). Lordy's elder sister. Lady Dorothy Nevill described her as "a woman of great literary gifts and quite exceptional cleverness…" (See *The Reminiscences of Lady Dorothy Nevill*, edited by her son, Ralph Nevill. Edward Arnold (1906))

[15] Referred to in Morris, Rev. Francis Orphen, *A Series of Picturesque Views of Seats of Noblemen and Gentlemen of Great Britain and Ireland*, W Mackenzie (1880). Volume VI. See note below.

[16] Of Eggesford House, Rev F.O. Morris writes: "It might well have been in the 'Happy Valley' above which this Country House stands, among surrounding hills covered with wood, that Rasselas may be supposed to have meditated, 'the world forgetting'..."

[17] Lady Eveline Alicia Juliana Herbert (1834–1906), a mother of 12 children of her own, was the first daughter of Henry John George Herbert, 3rd Earl of Carnarvon, by his wife Henrietta Anna Howard-Molyneux-Howard. Eveline married Isaac Newton Fellowes, later Wallop (1825–1891), 5th Earl of Portsmouth (from 1854). Eggesford Burghclere, Lady Winifred, *Biographical Sketch of Lord Carnarvon* (1923). House was in the parish of Wembworthy, Devon. It is recorded as a "House by Thomas Lee for Newton Fellows in the nineteenth century and dismantled 1917".

[18] Burghclere, Lady Winifred, *Biographical Sketch of Lord Carnarvon* (1923).

[19] Lady Winifred Herbert (1864–1933) who was later Lady Burghclere; Lady Margaret Herbert (1870–1958) who was later Mrs George Duckworth; Lady Victoria Herbert (1874–1957).

[20] Burghclere, Lady Winifred, *Biographical Sketch of Lord Carnarvon* (1923). Her obituary in *The Guardian* of 4 October 1906 records " Lady Portsmouth would be up at six o'clock in the morning in the country to go round her farm. In her youth she rode very hard and was a great whip."

[21] Ibid.

[22] Based on an entry in the Carnarvon diaries for 9 January 1879. British Library reference Add 60913.

[23] *Derbyshire Times and Chesterfield Herald*, 17 April 1880.

[24] Burghclere, Lady Winifred, *Biographical Sketch of Lord Carnarvon* (1923).

[25] Harris, S. Hutchinson, *Auberon Herbert: Crusader for Liberty*. London (1943) p. 26.

[26] A remove is a division in an English public school.

[27] Elizabeth Kitty Acland inherited the Pixton Park (famous for its splendid woods and its rookery and heronry) and also the Tetton estates in Somerset on the death of her brother, Sir John Dyke Acland, 8th Baronet, in 1785. In 1796 she married Henry Herbert, Lord Porchester, who in 1811 succeeded his father as the 2nd Earl of Carnarvon. Tetton is still occupied today by a member of the Herbert family.

[28] Henry, 4th Earl of Lord Carnarvon (1831–1890), was colonial secretary twice, in 1866 (when Lord Derby was prime minister) and in 1874 (when Benjamin Disraeli was prime minister).

[29] Elizabeth Catherine Howard's father, Henry Howard of Greystoke Castle (1802–1875), was a brother of Henrietta Anna Howard, 3rd Countess of Carnarvon (1804–1876), the mother of the 4th Earl of Carnarvon.

[30] Lady Evelyn Stanhope was the only daughter of the George, 6th Earl of Chesterfield, of Bretby Park, Derbyshire. Lady Evelyn Stanhope's married name, from 1861 onwards, was Herbert. She was the 4th Countess of Carnarvon, born on 3rd November 1834, and she died on 25 January 1875.

[31] Lady Evelyn died at 16 Bruton Street, London, the Carnarvon's townhouse. Society doctors attending her were consulting physician Sir William Gull (1816–1890), MD FRS [cited as a suspect in the Jack the Ripper murders in Whitechapel in 1888] and consulting obstetric physician Dr Arthur Farre (1811–1887), MD FRS, who was sometime professor of obstetric medicine at King's College, London. See also Cross, William, *The Life and Secrets of Almina Carnarvon* (2011), Chapter 2.

[32] *Bucks Herald*, 6 February 1875.

[33] Lady Evelyn's last wishes were fulfilled. She made these requirements known in her final days after she had learned of the death of her loyal housekeeper, Mrs Laverick, who had died in a railway accident at Shipton. The grave of Mrs Laverick lies nearby.
[34] *Reading Mercury*, 6 February 1875.
[35] Lady Evelyn's only brother, George, had died in 1871.
[36] *Reading Mercury*, 6 February 1875.
[37] A marriage of convenience with a homosexual (a dilettante was one euphemism to describe such men).
[38] According to the antiquary Camden: "the famous family of Stanhope originally drew their name from the town of Stanhope, near a forest, so called in Darlington Wapentake, and in the Bishopric of Durham." Though in later times their home and seat was at Shelford, in Nottinghamshire, and it subsequently being Bretby Park in Derbyshire.
[39] The letters *(Letters to His Son on the Art of Becoming a Man of the World and a Gentleman)* of Philip Dormer Stanhope (1694–1773) were written from 1737 until 1768. The 4th Earl of Carnarvon found some further versions at Bretby Park including letters by Stanhope to his godson. These were edited and published by Henry Herbert in 1889, co-incidentally when his own son, Porchey, had fallen off the edge (in his obsession with gambling and other vices) and whose lifestyle was then in grave need of a firm grip.
[40] Chesterfield House was built by the 4th Earl of Chesterfield, between 1747 and 1752 (with the architect, Isaac Ware). It stood in Mayfair on the north side of Curzon Street, between South Audley Street and (now) Chesterfield Street. The house was sold by the 7th Earl in 1869 to Charles Magniac. After this sale some of the contents of the house were transferred to Bretby Park. The house was demolished in the 1930s. See also Chancellor, Beresford E, *The Private Palaces of London Past and Present*, Kegan Paul, Trench, Trubner & Co (1908) and the same author's *The Lives of the British Architect*. Duckworth and Co (1909).
[41] *The Morning Post* of 6 November 1834: "BIRTHS: On Monday last, at Chesterfield House, the Countess of Chesterfield, of a daughter."
[42] The Chesterfield heir, George Philip Cecil Arthur Stanhope, born 1831, was entitled to call himself Viscount Stanhope, or as he more inclined to do, Lord Stanhope (not to be confused with the Earls of Stanhope, who also styled themselves as Lord Stanhopes). He became the 7th Earl of Chesterfield following his father's death in 1866, but died (unmarried) from the effects of a freak outbreak of typhoid fever, in 1871, contracted at the same time and place as his friend, Bertie, Prince of Wales.
[43] See *The Morning Post*, 22 January 1836.
[44] *Freeman's Journal and Daily Commercial Advertiser*, 2 April 1838.
[45] Hardinge, Sir Arthur [edited by Elizabeth, Countess of Carnarvon], *The Life of Henry Howard Molyneux Herbert 1831–1890* (1925), three volumes. Lady Winifred Burghclere contributed the memoir of her mother and wrote the greater part of the sketches of "Family Circle." Pages 181–4 are also written by Winifred.
[46] Jeffery, Reginald W., *Dyott's Diary 1781–1845*. Archibald Constable and Co. Ltd. (1907).
[47] See *The Morning Post*, 5 January 1850.
[48] See *My Recollections* by Adeline Louis Maria de Horsey (1824–1915), Countess of Cardigan and Lancastre, published by John Lane Company, New York, 1909. "Miss Anson" was probably Miss Isabel Anson or one of her sisters, all daughters of Hon. General George Anson (1797-1857).

[49] See *The Morning Post*, 6 July 1847. Rachel (1821–1858) was the first dramatic actress to achieve international fame in Britain, USA and elsewhere, with appearances in Boston and Paris, London and Moscow in the tragedies by Racine and Corneille.
[50] See *Derby Mercury*, 8 January 1851 and *Atlas*, 11 January 1851.
[51] *The Morning Post*, 30 April 1852.
[52] Ibid.
[53] Reference in an obituary tribute to Anne, Lady Chesterfield by "Sketcher" in the *Daily Telegraph*, 1885.
[54] Fanny Kemble, the famous actress (1809–1893), records in her memoirs *Records of a Girlhood* (2nd edition published 1883, by Henry Holt) says this about Anne and Isabella:

> They were celebrated beauties: (Anne) the elder, afterward Countess of Chesterfield, was a brunette; (Isabella) the younger, who married Colonel Anson, the most renowned lady killer of his day, was a blonde; and they were both of them exquisitely pretty. They had beautiful figures as well as faces, and dressed peculiarly and so as to display them to the greatest advantage.

See also Redesdale, Algernon Bertram Freeman-Mitford, *Memories*, Hutchinson (1915).
[55] There were five Forester sisters. Anne Elizabeth, Lady Chesterfield (1802-1885); Elizabeth Katherine (1803-1832) [who married Robert Smith (eldest son of Lord Carington) and who died of cholera. See entry for 22 July, 1832 in *A Portion of the Journal kept by Thomas Raikes Esq from 1831 to 1847* by Thomas Raikes.] Henrietta Marie (died 1841) Lady Conyngham; Isabella Elizabeth (died 1858) Mrs George Anson; and Selina Louisa (died 1894) Lady Bradford.
[56] *The Lancet*, 1860, page 271 records: "Hon. Mrs Anson took a vial full of laudanum by mistake for a gout draught. The vial was labelled 'poison' but she did not read it." The event date is given elsewhere as January 1859. It is fully described by Alfred Swaine Taylor in *On Poisons in Relation to Medical Jurisprudence and Medicine* (1875).
[57] Raikes' journal. See above.
[58] Lord Derby's marriage proposal was made in 1830, but rejected in favour of the Earl of Cherstefield. Disraeli's marriage invitation was made in later life after each party had lost their spouse.
[59] See *Sheffield Independent*, 1 March 1883. A local history says: "A memorial plaque in St Wystan's Church, rebuilt by Anne [Chesterfield] in 1878, records: 'In memory of Benjamin Disraeli, Earl of Beaconsfield. The foremost man of his age. Eminent in letters, in council, in debate. A statesman far-seeing and sagacious, a patriot zealous for his country's honour. A devoted servant of the Queen, by whom he was trusted, honoured and mourned. This tablet is erected by Anne Elizabeth, Countess of Chesterfield, a record of a much prized friendship and a lasting regret.'"
[60] See *The Life & Letters of Lady Dorothy Nevill* (edited by her son, Ralph Nevill). On the subject of Lady Chesterfield's proposal of marriage from Disraeli, Ralph Nevill asserts: "Lady Chesterfield, my mother declared, was only prevented from accepting Mr Disraeli by the strong objections of her daughter, Lady Carnarvon."
[61] *Lodge's Peerage*, 6th Edition (1838).
[62] Balch, Elizabeth, *Glimpses of Old English Houses*. Macmillan and Co. (1890).
[63] Henrietta Anna Molyneux Howard (1804–1876), 3rd Countess of Carnarvon, member of the Howard (Dukes of Norfolk) family.
[64] The 4th Earl's siblings were Hon. Alan Percy Harty Molyneux Herbert MD (1836–1907), a doctor who lived most of his life in Paris; Hon. Auberon Edward William

Molyneux Herbert (1838–1906), member of Parliament for Nottingham 1870–74, a leading (and eccentric) figure in politics and philosophy; Lady Eveline Alicia Juliana Herbert, later Wallop, 5th Countess of Portsmouth of Eggesford House, Devon (1834–1906); and Lady Gwendoline (sometimes Gwendolen) Ondine Herbert (1842–1915), another eccentric, who campaigned for vegetarianism.

[65] *The Manchester Guardian*, 13 December 1925.

[66] In 1843, when Henry was twelve years old (and so Lord Porchester), he made a speech to great approval at the Exeter Hall in front of 3,000 people: "That the subject of humanity to animals should be made a matter of special instruction in our National Schools." See *The Cornwall Royal Gazette, Falmouth Packet and Plymouth Journal* for 10 March 1843.

[67] Ibid.

[68] Harris, S. Hutchinson, *Auberon Herbert: Crusader for Liberty* (1943) London. p. 20.

[69] This cause of death "spinal affliction" was reported in newspapers of the time of the 3rd Earl's death. From the evidence in the diaries of the 4th Earl's regular immobility, and of receiving treatment for nerves, the disease was almost certainly of a neurological kind and was an inherited gene over several generations.

[70] Preface (written by the 4th Earl) to *Reminiscences of Athens and the Morea* which includes his father's *Travel Journal in Greece, in 1839* (1869).

[71] *The Gentleman's Magazine and Historical Review*, Volume 187.

[72] Coleridge is cited as being an inspiration to both these Herbert boys in the paths they chose in their professional lives: colonial service. T.S.H. Escott says in *Personal Forces of the Period* when referring to colonial administrators in Australia:

> Chief among these has been Sir Robert G.W. Herbert, whose local experience of a high office in Queensland was of the utmost service at the Colonial Office, not only to himself in his duties as Permanent Under-Secretary, but to that cousin and chief Lord Carnarvon, whose sympathetic clearness of vision and administrative ability made the Colonial regime of the two relatives memorable abroad and profitable at home.

[73] Sir Robert George Wyndham Herbert, GCB (1831–1905). Colonial administrator in Australia and later a permanent under-secretary at the Colonial Office. A constant contact of the 4th Earl on personal, political and family affairs, he was involved with Elsie Howard in compiling the first draft of the biography of her husband.

[74] The 4th Earl's guardian was Sir William Heathcote (1801–1881), 5th Baronet, Hampshire MP and who later represented Oxford University in Parliament. Carnarvon's private tutor at Eton and Oxford and lifelong friend was John Kent (1810–1905). Reference to John Kent in the 4th Earl's diaries indicate he was a shy man, sometimes mentally unstable personality, given to eccentricity, but to whom Henry Herbert was devoted. His early life was spent in Canada, where he was a master at the Upper Canada College. See *A History of Upper Canada College, 1829–1892* by George Dickson M.A. and G. Mercer Adam (1893). At the 4th Earl's wedding in 1861 Kent presented himself at the reception, saluted one of the guests and disappeared "like a meteor". Kent later lived sometime on the Highclere Estate, and displayed odd swings of mood and action that were a concern and embarrassment to the 4th Earl. Kent lived the latter part of his life in Funchal, Madeira, where he died on 24 June 1905, aged 95. He contributed occasional pieces to the journal *Notes & Queries*.

[75] Parker, J.H. and Slatter, H., *The Oxford University Calendar for 1853* also includes Lord Dufferin, Lord Dungarvon, Viscount Sandon and the Marquis of Lothian as part of the list of BA graduates from Christ Church.

[76] Viscount Sandon (1831–1900) was the son of the Earl of Harrowby. Described in a note on political leaders (written in 1885) as a contemporary of the 4th Earl, "a statesman and kindred spirit and, in many respects, of similar qualities". He became the 3rd Earl of Harrowby in 1882. As MP for Liverpool he served as Disraeli's president of the Board of Trade 1878–1880. The 4th Earl cites Sandon as one of his lifelong intimates.

[77] Carnarvon, Earl [4th] *Recollections of the Druses of the Lebanon and Notes on Their Religion* (Reprinted 2004).

[78] Taken from Horace G. Hutchinson's *Portraits of the Eighties*. Ayer Publishing (1920).

[79] According to *Memoirs of Celebrated Men of the Nineteenth Century* (1842), on the death of her father (1824) the (then) unmarried Henrietta (the eldest daughter) succeeded "to the estates of the late Sir Francis Molyneux, and [took] the name and arms of Molyneux, in addition to those of her own noble family". These estates were at Teversall (where Henrietta had the mansion house completely renovated, in the 1860s and lived there sometime) and at Wellow by way of Henrietta's wealthy maternal grandfather, Sir William Molyneux, and her mother Juliana Molyneux. See also Gisbourne Molyneux's *Memoir of the Molineux Family* (1882).

[80] One of Henrietta's active patronages (with numerous other peeresses) was the Royal National Sea-Bathing Hospital at Margate "for the Scrofulous Poor of London and all parts of the Kingdom", established in 1796, with 250 beds.

[81] The Carnarvons occupied 43 Grosvenor Square and when this was sold, 3 Park Street, Westminster.

[82] *The Morning Post* of Thursday 12 May 1831 records a levee before the King at St James's Palace on the evening before.

[83] Sidney Herbert, 1st Baron Herbert of Lea PC (1810–1861), statesman and friend of Florence Nightingale. A Cabinet minister under Palmerston. As secretary of state for war he sent Florence Nightingale to the Crimean. A father of seven children, his eldest son George became 13th Earl of Pembroke; his next son Sidney was 14th Earl of Pembroke; another son, Michael, was a diplomat and for a short time US ambassador.

[84] See *The Morning Post*, 23 February 1854.

[85] *The Morning Post*, 6 March 1854.

[86] Extract from *A Great Man's Friendship: Letters of the Duke of Wellington to Mary, Marchioness of Salisbury 1850–1852*, edited by Winifred, Lady Burghclere. Winifred cites firsthand knowledge from Lady Mary Catherine Sackville-West (1824–1900), second wife of the 2nd Marquis of Salisbury; in 1870 she married the 14th Earl of Derby. The "Lord Stanhope" mentioned is Philip Stanhope (1805–1875), 5th Earl of Stanhope. The "literary breakfasts" are described in T.S.H. Escott's *Personal Forces of the Period*, Hurst and Blackett, London (1898).

[87] Reports appeared across the London and provincial press, with a good spread in *The Morning Post* of 13 May 1854, where this description can be found some other attendees.

[88] Ibid.

[89] *The Morning Chronicle*, 22 May 1854. The Ashburtons were part of the Baring (Bank) family.

[90] Evelyn's brother, George, was not anxious for an early marriage either. Despite a near-death accident in 1855 which left him with a serious fracture (reported in *Christian*

Weekly News, 24 April 1855), he was content to serve his Queen and country in the Royal Horse Guards Blue, allying himself closely with George, Duke of Cambridge (1819–1904), a grandson of King George III and commander-in-chief of the British Army, 1856–1895.90 In 1860, having retired from the Army, he entered Parliament as an MP (see *The Morning Post*, 2 December 1871).

[91] George Hamilton Gordon, 4th Earl Gordon (1784–1860). Prime minister 19 December 1852 until 30 January 1855.

[92] Gordon, Peter (ed), *The Political Diaries of the Fourth Earl of Carnarvon*, Camden Fifth Series, Volume 35 (2009).

[93] Field, Maunsell, B., M*emories of Many Men and of Some Women*, Harper & Brothers, New York (1874).

[94] Eardley-Wilmot, Captain S. (RN (retired)), *Life of Vice-Admiral Edmund, Lord Lyons*, London (1898).

[95] Ibid. p. 386:

> He [Lyons] left London for Paris on June 28, accompanied by his secretary, the Earl of Carnarvon, Count Strzlecki, Captain the Hon. F Egerton, R. N.and other friends who were anxious to visit the scene of the late war. After staying two days in Paris the party reached Marseilles on July 3, where the Caradoc awaited them. Here the Admiral embarked and once more resumed his command. The Carodoc left Marseilles on July 4, and touching at Malta arrived in the Bosphororus on the 11th. Here the Royal Albert was found at anchor, having just arrived from the Black Sea, but the Admiral being desirous of visiting the scene of the late war went on the Caradoc to Balaclava.

[96] The prime minister's son Lord (Edward) Stanley (1826–1893) (later 15th Earl of Derby) was colonial secretary until June 1858. He was replaced by Sir Edward Bulwer-Lytton (1803–1873) (later Lord Lytton). More a poet and novelist, he was less cut out for the role and depended heavily on Lord Carnarvon. This great opportunity accelerated Carnarvon's prospects in future government service. See Taylor Miles (ed), *Southampton Gateway to the British Empire*, I.B. Tauris, London (2007) pp. 20–1. The latter book has a complete chapter devoted to the 4th Earl of Carnarvon, "Highclere, Hampshire and Empire" by Bruce Knox, which is highly recommended.

[97] In 1859, as well as being named high steward of Oxford University, Lord Derby cited Carnarvon as being the calibre of a future party leader. Carnarvon was not ever one to trust Disraeli (albeit he was the next major political party leader). His loyalty in the Conservative party (after Lord Derby's death in 1869) lay firmly behind the likes of his old school friend, Lord Salisbury (Robert, 3rd Marquess (1830–1902) who succeeded his father in 1869) and in turn this snub infuriated Disraeli. Dizzy's revenge included backstabbing Henry (giving Queen Victoria a platform for airing her disappointment in Carnarvon over his posturings and increasing reputation for indecision) and nicknaming Carnarvon "Twitters", a name that stuck. In the end, several decades later, even Lord Salisbury had cause to be irked by Carnarvon's antics and he later snubbed him over his handling of the Irish Home Rule question. Carnarvon was briefly the viceroy/lord lieutenant of Ireland, under Salisbury from 1885–6. After some controversial dealings between Carnarvon and the republican Charles Stewart Parnell over Irish Home Rule, Carnarvon was criticised and silenced, and he later resigned. Salisbury did not offer him another government post.

[98] *The Morning Post*, 3 May 1860.

[99] *Evening Herald*, 7 November 1860.
[100] See *A Great Man's Friendship: Letters of the Duke of Wellington to Mary, Marchioness of Salisbury 1850–1852*, edited by Lady Winifred Burghclere. Winifred cites Lady Mary Catherine Sackville-West (1824–1900), 2nd wife of the 2nd Marquis of Salisbury; in 1870 she married 14th Earl of Derby.
[101] Carnarvon Papers, British Library, Add 61039.
[102] Ibid.
[103] *Evening Herald*, 6 September 1861 and *The Derby Mercury*, 11 September 1861.
[104] Ibid.
[105] Ibid.
[106] Henry Howard (1802–1875) brother of Henrietta, 3rd Countess of Carnarvon, who was owner of Greystoke Castle, Cumberland and an MP. He was also the father of Elizabeth, the second wife of the 4th Earl.
[107] Carnarvon Papers, British Library, Add 61039, Entry for 6 September 1861.
[108] *The Era*, 29 September 1861. Carnarvon Papers, British Library, Add 61039 indicate that they visited Ghent, Cologne, Antwerp, Baden, Geneva, Lucerne, and finally Paris where they stayed at the Hotel Clarndon. They saw Alan Herbert in Paris.
[109] *The Derby Mercury*, 6 November 1861.
[110] Carnarvon Papers, British Library, Add 61039. There were servants at Highclere in post, but until his marriage the 4th Earl had left such matters of hiring etc. to his mother and sisters.
[111] *Derby Mercury*, 20 November 1861.
[112] Ibid.
[113] Cox, J. Charles, *Hampshire*, Methun & Co (London).
[114] *The Morning Post*, 24 November 1840.
[115] Inside the house numerous there were numerous paintings of the great and good of previous generations and of interlocked families, including the first Lady Carnarvon and first Lord Porchester by Sir Joshua Reynolds and, also by Reynolds, the first Lord Porchester as Bacchus. A further painting was much prized, "Charles The First, on Horseback, the Duc D'Epernon, holding his Helmet; large as life, after Vandyck, by Old Stone." See Brayley, Edward Wedlake, *The Beauties of England and Wales or Delineations, Topographical etc.* (1805). Also, in the library at Highclere, pride of place was given to the table and chair which it was said that Napoleon used when he signed his abdication at Fontainebleau.
[116] See Girouard, Mark. *The Victorian Country House*, Oxford University Press (1971). An excellent overview of the social and economics of running a country house, as well as discussion of architecture. There is a section on Highclere Castle.
[117] The woods comprised beeches and limes, but surprising (at least in Victorian times) no oak trees, since an earlier Herbert believed that "trees were an excrescence provided by nature for payment of debts" and he did not favour planting oaks "as he did not propose that any spendthrift descendant should cut them down!" (Balch, Elizabeth, *Glimpses of Old English Houses*, 1890).
[118] Mogg, Edward, *Paterson's Roads, Being an Accurate Description of all the Cross Roads* (1831).
[119] In *The Letters of Disraeli to Lady Bradford and Lady Chesterfield (1873–1875)*, edited by the Marquis of Zetland (1929), vol. 1, p. 148, Disraeli sounded out Lady Chesterfield about Evelyn gleaning some information for him to pass on to Queen Victoria about Lord Ripon. Disraeli writes: "Lady Carnarvon could help us on this head."

[120] See Carnarvon Papers, British Library, Add 61039. Sir William Heathcote (1801–1881) was the Earl's tutor and guardian after his father's death, and represented a substitute father figure as well as adviser and mentor on Hampshire issues (as a former MP for the county).

[121] See *Daily News*, 1 January 1862 and *Evening Herald*, 31 December 1861.

[122] See *The Belfast News-letter*, 2 January 1862. Lord Dufferin was Frederick Hamilton-Temple-Blackwood (1826–1902), from a Scots-Ulster family, a Liberal politician and notable diplomat. He served in many notable roles including governor general of Canada (1872–1878) and viceroy and governor general of India (1884–1888).

[123] Family members and visitors dropping by included Earl and Countess Stanhope as well as calls from the Earl of Ducie, the Bishop of Oxford, Lady Emily Peel (wife of Sir Robert), and Sir William and Lady Heathcote again. A degree of family mourning was observed following the announcement of the death, in Florence, on 2 February 1862, of Carnarvon's great aunt, Hon. Mrs George Herbert. She was described as the only offspring and heiress of "Francis Head of Andrews Hall, Norfolk… By her death a numerous circle of relatives are placed in mourning."
Later, for the Easter holidays, Lord Stanley MP (later Earl of Derby) was one of the further parade of guests at Highclere. See also *Derby Mercury*, 26 February 1862, *The Belfast News-letter*, 28 February 1862 and *The Morning Post*, 1 March 1862. Also *The Era*, 16 February 1862 and *Daily News*, 16 April 1862.

[124] Carnarvon Papers, British Library, Add 61039.

[125] *The Morning Post*, 3 May 1862. The lease was taken for only a year at £800, a significant sum.

[126] *The Belfast News-letter*, 31 May 1862.

[127] See *Derby Mercury*, 4 June 1862: another "do" "being the French Ambassador and the Countess de Flahault's spectacle at Albert-gate House.."

[128] Emily Mary Lamb (1787–1869), a leading political hostess who had learned the ropes in social skills and for handling men in politics and at Court from her mother and her friends. She was Lady Cowper until 1837 and married Palmerston in 1839.

[129] See *The Times*, 23 June, 1862 and 11 May 1863.

[130] http://www.historyhome.co.uk/people/cowper.htm

[131] Carnarvon Papers, British Library, Add 61039.

[132] *The Belfast News-letter*, 17 July 1862.

[133] *Benjamin Disraeli Letters: 1860–1864* by Benjamin Disraeli (Earl of Beaconsfield), Mary S. Millar, M.G. Wiebe, Ann P. Robson (2009).

[134] George Thompson Gream MD King's College, Aberdeen, FRCP, Lond. Physician accoucheur to Alexandra, Princess of Wales (died 1888, aged 76). See *The British Medical Journal*, 28 July 1888 p. 209.

[135] A comment from Tony Leadbetter on a remark he once heard from Almina, which must have been said by the 5th Earl, talking about his mother.

[136] Carnarvon Papers, British Library, Add 61039.

[137] Carnarvon Papers, British Library, Add 60895.

[138] *The Gentleman's Magazine*, Volume 170, page 90 (1841): "Dec 10: in Grosvenor –sq, the Countess of Carnarvon, a daughter, who survived its birth a few hours only."

[139] *Evening Herald*, 8 October 1862.

[140] One guest was Sir Stafford Northcote, later Earl of Iddesleigh, who in the years that followed served in notable Cabinet posts with and after Carnarvon's tenures as Colonial Secretary Sir Stafford Northcote (1818–1887) was from an old Devon family. He served in Cabinet posts as president of the Board of Trade (1866–7), chancellor of

the exchequer (1874–80) and foreign secretary (1885–6). See *The Derby Mercury*, 5 November 1862 and *Guardian*, 26 November 1862. Andrew Lang's *Life, Letters and Diaries* of Northcote refers to him going on a yachting cruise to the Scilly Islands with Lord Carnarvon in 1872.

[141] Walter Bagehot (1826–1877), author of the English Constitution. After his visit of 1863 to Highclere he wrote that Carnarvon was "one of my sort" (quoted by Alastair Buchan in *The Spare Chancellor: The Life of Walter Bagehot*, 1959). The warm friendship, along intellectual lines, between Carnarvon and Bagehot is referred to almost all the biographies on Bagehot who was a visitor at Highclere and Pixton Park.

[142] Barrington, Mrs Russell *Life of Walter Bagehot*, Longmans, Green & Co (1914).

[143] Ibid.

[144] Ibid.

[145] Cited in *Concerning Society: The Playgoer and Society Illustrated*, Apr 1911; 4, 19; British Periodicals. Also cited by the writer Augustus J.C. Hare in his memoirs, *The Story of My Life*, volume IV, George Allen (1900).

[146] Based on remarks by Almina, 5th Countess, to her godson, Tony Leadbetter.

[147] See Carnarvon Papers, British Library, Add 60895.

[148] *The Belfast News-letter*, 5 and 11 December 1862.

[149] *Evening Star*, 10 December 1862.

[150] See Carnarvon Papers, British Library, Add 60895. Entry in the diary for 10 November 1862.

[151] There was earlier royal service by Elizabeth Wyndham (1752–1826), Dowager First Countess of Carnarvon (at 1813), when she became mistress of the robes to the ill-fated Caroline of Brunswick, then Princess of Wales.

[152] *The Derby Mercury* carried this news on 25 February 1863. *The New York Times* of 13 March 1863 records:

> The London News states that the household of the Princess of Wales has been determined upon, and that the principal parts will be filled as follows: Chamberlain –- Lord HARRIS; Ladies of the Bedchamber – the Countess of Morton, the Countess of Macclesfield, the Countess DE GREY and the Countess of Carnarvon...

[153] See *The Englishman*, 18 July 1863. NB: One noted visit by Lady Evelyn with the Princess was at Wimbledon on Monday 13 July 1863 where a shooting match was held between the two Houses of Parliament for the "Alexandra Prize", "a cup valued at £50, or money, named by the association in honour of her Royal Highness the Princess of Wales." The Prince was also present. Royals sat on chairs laid out inside a marquee, which had been carpeted. The Princess, who was dressed in mourning (such was still the Prince Albert effect), was with "Countess Spencer and the Duchess of Manchester and the Countess of Carnarvon and Captain Grey in waiting". Lord Elcho had directed that "two of his best telescopes" be provided to allow the Royal party to see things at close range.

[154] *Morning Post*, 29 October 1863.

[155] *Morning Post*, 31 October 1863 list the Marquis and Marchioness of Bath, the Earl Cowper, Lord Stanhope, MP, Countess Justina Herbert, Lord and Lady Harriet Ashley, Mr and Lady Dorothy Nevill, Mr Herman Merivale, and Lady Sophia Des Voeux, some of which company also regularly graced Bretby Park. See also Adeline

Louis Marie de Horsey, Countess of Cardigan and Lancastre, *My Recollections*, New York (1909).

[156] A constant visitor at Highclere. Author of several books edited by her son Ralph, who attended Eton College with Lordy.

[157] *The Englishman*, 21 May 1864.

[158] Eveline Portsmouth was an advocate of woman's suffrage and women's clubs The novelist, Thomas Hardy said of her " She is one of the few, very few women of her own rank for whom I would make a sacrifice: a woman too of talent, part of whose talent consists in concealing she has any." (From: Thomas Hardy : Wordsworth Editions (2007))

[159] *Evening Herald*, 27 May 1864.

[160] *The Englishman*, 9 July 1864.

[161] *The Englishman*, 30 July 1864.

[162] The line-up for one weekend included the Marquis and Marchioness of Salisbury, and Winchesters, the Countess of Portsmouth (Carnarvon's sister), the Merrivales, the Ashleys and regular guests Mr Melville and Lady Charlotte Portal. Lady Portal was born Lady Charlotte Mary Elliot, the first-born child of Gilbert, the 2nd Earl of Minto. All were key Society figures.

Another house party swept in a further collection of notables including the Marlboroughs, and Carnarvon's great friend, guardian and mentor Sir William Heathcote, as well as family members. *The Englishman* of 1 October 1864 says:

> The Earl and Countess of Carnarvon have been entertaining a succession of visitors at Highclere Castle, their seat near Newbury, their company including the Marquis and Marchioness of Winchester, the Marquis and Marchioness of Salisbury, the Countess of Portsmouth, Lord and Lady Harriet Ashley, Hon. F. Lygon, M.P., Hon. Mr. and Lady Louisa Howard, Hon. Win. Herbert, Sir Stafford Northcote, Mr. M. and Lady Charlotte Portal, the Right Hon. T.-H. Sotheron-Estcourt, M.P., and Mrs. Estcourt, Mr.and Mrs. Walter, Mr. Merriyale, Mr. Elliot, Mr. Murray, Mr. Fountain, &c.

A curious letter survives among the Carnarvon Papers from Charlotte, writing from Laverstoke Manor, Hants, dated 2 December 1878, Add 60864, suggesting some kind of estrangement between Carnarvon and Lady Portal. She writes (after congratulating the Earl on his forthcoming remarriage): "We have seen nothing of each other of late years, the ugly little cloud that rose between us never could ride out of us the happy part with its old kindnesses and friendly intercourse." Charlotte (who died in 1899) had a son Gerald (1858– 1894) a diplomat of note in Africa who died relatively young. He has "Herbert" as a middle name. Charlotte's husband Melville was sometime an MP and long-serving magistrate.

[163] *The Englishman*, 19 November 1864.

[164] *Evening Herald*, 22 November 1864.

[165] See Carnarvon Papers, British Library, Add 60896.

[166] The Earl's diary of this period (British Library, Add 60896) has three blank pages and then three (i.e. six sides) cut out probably done with a razor blade; the script continues part way through a sentence.

[167] Dr Pantaleoni was a controversial figure and exile, with a medical practice in Rome and Nice. His patients comprised mostly wealthy foreigners.

[168] See *Carnarvon Papers*, British Library, Add 60896.
[169] Ibid.
[170] The Earl's diaries held in the British Library are blank from 27 March 1865 until 6 February 1866.
[171] *Reading Mercury*, 18 February 1865.
[172] *Reading Mercury*, 18 March 1865.
[173] *Morning Post*, 28 April 1865.
[174] *Pall Mall Gazette*, 17 May 1865.
[175] *Morning Post*, 16 June 1865. The Count de Paris was Philippe d'Orleans (1838–1894), the pretender to the French throne. He lived in exile in Britain after the 1848 revolution in France.
[176] *Morning Post*, 19 June 1865.
[177] *Morning Post*, 27 June 1865.
[178] *Morning Post*, 24 July 1865.
[179] On 28 December 1865, several newspapers said: "Lord Carnarvon, in a letter to *The Times*, strongly urges the adoption of more severe restrictions both in the foreign and internal cattle trade."
[180] *Morning Post*, 4 September 1865.
[181] *Nottinghamshire Guardian*, 8 September 1865.
[182] *Morning Post*, 6 September 1865.
[183] *North Devon Journal*, 14 December 1865.
[184] *Morning Post*, 7 February 1866.
[185] See *Morning Post* for 24 February, 14 March, 16 March and 19 March 1866.
[186] Godwin, Henry, *The Worthies and Celebrities Connected with Newbury, Berks and its Neighbourhood* (1859) p. 64 records: "Sir Robert Peel said he [the 3rd Earl, at the time Lord Porchester and a member of Parliament] should be perfectly contented to rest the whole cause at issue upon the arguments contained in that single harangue."
[187] *The Derby Mercury*, 23 July 1873. In 1873, Lord Carnarvon gave evidence about the 6th Earl of Chesterfield to the Committee of Privileges of the House of Lords following the death of Evelyn's brother (and the light of the new claimant, a cousin of his wife having to prove his right to the Chesterfield titles). Carnarvon ended his statement: "I can give better evidence than that of his death because he died in my presence."
[188] The will and estate of Lordy's deceased grandfather and namesake George was unsurprising in content. Made in 1861, it confirmed the family arrangements in favour of his widow, Lady Anne, and his daughter, Evelyn, Countess of Carnarvon. The Chesterfield heir, Viscount Stanhope, was bequeathed all the rest of the property and lands. The Earl's estate was valued at under £70,000. (*Jackson's Oxford Journal*, 22 September 1866). Whilst this gave a prima facie picture of a healthy inheritance, the 6th Earl of Chesterfield had left some debts too, and his mode of living had only been secured by the family properties being "much encumbered…[and they were not expected] to produce a net rental at all in proportion with their reputed value" (*Nottinghamshire Guardian*, 29 December 1871).
[189] *The Standard*, 2 June 1866.
[190] Malmesbury, Earl of (James Howard Harris Malmesbury, 1897–1889), *Memoirs of an Ex Minister: An Autobiography*, Longmans, Green and Co. (1885).
[191] The well-informed racing correspondent of *The Standard* on 2 June 1866 also writes:

> Lord Chesterfield's career on the turf began in 1826, and he subsequently won every great race of the time. Thus in 1829 he was the winner of the Ascot Cup

with Zinganee; in 1830 he won the Derby – his first and only one – with Priam, a horse he purchased a short time before the race for 3000 guineas. Priam subsequently won him the Goodwood Cup two years in succession, 1831 and 1832, a trophy which he carried off again in 1836 and 1837 with Hornsea and Carew. Twice he was winner of the Oaks, with Industry in 1838, and Lady Evelyn in 1849; once of the St Leger with Don John in 1838. The Goodwood Stakes were won in 1835 by Glaucus, and the Cambridgeshire in 1862 by Bathilde. In 1843 he won the Liverpool Grand National Steeple-chase with Vanguard.

[192] There are memorials to George's antecedents and his own family in Gedling Church, Nottinghamshire. See *Nottinghamshire Guardian*, 5 January 1883, p. 2; Issue 1963, Local Notes and Queries No CLIV Gedling Church (Part II).
[193] *Morning Post*, 27 June 1866.
[194] Pal was the nickname for Dr Alan Herbert, the Earl's brother.
[195] See Carnarvon Papers, British Library, Add 61041.
[196] Ibid.
[197] Ibid.
[198] *The Watchman and Wesleyan Advertiser* of 4 July 1866 records sympathetically of Carnarvon's political track record to date:

> The Earl of Carnarvon's appointment to the Colonies can be attacked only by the grossest ignorance or the most unscrupulous malice. The career of the noble lord has shown far more than the average abilities which we are accustomed to expect in the most prominent of our public men, and there are few subjects that he has touched upon the last four or five years, whether within or without the walls of the House of Lords, of which he has not displayed a mastery, evincing not only considerable mental power, but the most painstaking application.

[199] *The Times*, 7 July 1866.
[200] Lysons, Daniel, M*agna Britannia*, Printed for T Cadell and W Davies, in the Strand. p. 240 et seq. (1817).
[201] *Reading Mercury*, 18 August 1866.
[202] *Belfast Newsletter*, 17 August 1866.
[203] *Reading Mercury*, 25 August 1866.
[204] *Daily News*, 30 October 1866.
[205] Mary Anne Evans (1792–1872), chosen by Dizzy since her roots were in Wales "where the girls are more loving than anywhere else..." See Baily, F.E., *Lady Beaconsfield and Her Times*, Hutchinson & Co, London (1935).
[206] See Samuel Carter Hall's *Retrospect of a Long Life 1815–1883* (1883) pp. 162–3. He cites Mrs Disraeli (later Viscountess Beaconsfield, in her own right) as follows:

> her mind was of a high order; and it may be regarded as certain that by her constant companionship – nay, by her frequent counsel and her wise advice – she aided largely in directing the after conduct of her statesman-husband so claims a share of the gratitude due to the illustrious man... It is enough to say of Lady Beaconsfield [as she was from 1868] that she was worthy to be the friend, companion, and counsellor of Lord Beaconsfield, as well as his wife.

[207] See Chapter 3 of *The Life and Secrets of Almina Carnarvon*, which cites Ralph Nevill's reminiscences of his mother, Lady Dorothy Nevill.
[208] *Reading Mercury*, 5 January 1867.
[209] *Derby Mercury*, 6 February 1867.
[210] See Carnarvon Papers, British Library, Add 60899, entry for 2 February 1867.
[211] Tony Leadbetter, Almina's godson (and a nurse for over 30 years) recalls mention by Almina of the 4th Earl's symptoms being brought on principally by his bad nerves, *not* his eating and drinking habits – to which gout is most commonly associated. Besides this the 3rd Earl suffered a frequent, unexplained paralysis which may have been inherited by his eldest son. As it bordered on a mental illness, some euphemism would have been favoured.
[212] An obituary writer (1890) comments on the Bill for the Confederation of British North American Provinces (as Canada was described) as "one of the most important measures that for many years it had been the duty of any Colonial Minister to submit to Parliament" (see *Derby Mercury*, 5 July 1890).
[213] See Carnarvon Papers, British Library, Add 61041.
[214] Lord Cranbourne (1830–1903; later, from 1868, 3rd Marquis of Salisbury) and General Peel also resigned on the same issue as Carnarvon. The news of the resignations broke on 3 March.
[215] The university chums of the 4th Earl – who were all together at Christ Church, Oxford were Lord Cranborne (Salisbury heir), Lord Sandon (Harrowby heir) and Dr George Portal (the 4th Earl's personal chaplain and rector of Highclere Church).
[216] Marindin, George Eden (ed.), *Letters of Frederic Lord Blanchford Under Secretary of State for the Colonies 1860–1871*, John Murray, London (1896).
[217] Ibid.
[218] Journal of John Wodehouse, Earl of Kimberley, entry for 4 March 1867.
[219] Journal of John Wodehouse, Earl of Kimberley, entry for 22 July 1867. NB: According to one obituary writer (1890) Carnarvon believed that the Reform Bill would transfer political power in five-sixths of the boroughs. He thought it was going too far in a democratic direction.
[220] See Carnarvon Papers, British Library, Add 60899, entries for 22 January and 2 February 1867.
[221] *Reading Mercury*, 4 May 1867.
[222] The Dowager Countess had been overseeing the latest enactment of much desired educational reforms in her lifetime, something she had achieved in Nottinghamshire, at least. In the parish of Hucknall-under-Huthwaite in Nottinghamshire, she provided sums for the building of schools. This included an acre of land and £400 towards the building fund. The foundation stone at Hucknall was laid on 2 September 1867 by the Countess, accompanied by her son, Auberon, and daughter, Lady Gwendoline. See reports in the *Nottinghamshire Guardian*, 23 August and 6 September 1867.
Having lavished some considerable expense in renovating her mansion house at Teversal in Nottinghamshire, Henrietta spent increasing time residing there. This tenure also in part led to Auberon (MP for Nottingham from 1870–74) securing an electoral base and the chance to develop and nurture his ideals at the start a long political and social career.
[223] *Western Times*, 5 April 1867.
[224] *Edinburgh Evening Courant*, 11 May 1867.
[225] *Reading Mercury*, 8 June, and *Morning Post*, 20 June 1867.
[226] *Bath Chronicle*, 4 July 1867.

[227] *Morning Post*, 31 July 1867.
[228] *Hampshire Advertiser*, 28 September 1867.
[229] *Hampshire Advertiser*, 25 January 1868.
[230] See Carnarvon Papers, British Library, Add 60900, entry for 23 April 1868.
[231] See Carnarvon Papers, British Library, Add 60900, entry for 13 April 1868.
[232] See *A Great Man's Friendship: Letters of the Duke of Wellington to Mary, Marchioness of Salisbury 1850–1852*, edited by Lady Winifred Burghclere (1927). Winifred cites Lady Mary Catherine Sackville-West (1824–1900), second wife of the 2nd Marquis of Salisbury; in 1870 she married the 14th Earl of Derby.
[233] *Morning Post*, 27 April 1868.
[234] Cyril Graham (1834–1895), attached to Lord Dufferin's mission to Syria 1860–1; private secretary to Carnarvon as colonial secretary 1866–67; governor of Grenada 1875–77.
[235] *Reading Mercury*, 17 August 1867.
[236] *The Belfast News-Letter*, 13 January 1869.
[237] *Reading Mercury*, 9 January 1869.
[238] *Morning Post*, 14 January 1869.
[239] *The Belfast News-Letter*, 17 February 1869.
[240] Campbell, John Douglas Sutherland, *Passages From the Past*, Volume II, Hutchinson, London (1907), pp. 349–50.
[241] Ibid.
[242] Ibid. "A pleasant little party, consisting of Sir Wm and Lady Heathcote, Lord Salisbury, the Mintos and Lord Hardinge."
[243] Richard Southwell Bourne, 6th Earl of Mayo (1822–1872), Irish aristocrat and politician, Viceroy of India, 1869–1872. Assassinated 8 February 1872. Lorne records:

> Lady C.tells a good story of Mayo and his gardener. It seems that Mayo, shortly after starting from India, bought a pair of emus and was very anxious that the birds should breed. He gave directions that he should be informed how they got on, and on his arrival at Bombay received this letter from his gardener: "My Lord – one of the emus you left with me has laid an egg. We are doing our best to hatch it, and, in your lordship's absence, we have taken the biggest goose we could find to put it under."

[244] *The Morning Post* of 21 June 1869 has the list of guests attending on Saturday 19 June.
[245] *Morning Post*, 28 July 1869.
[246] *Morning Post*, 30 July 1869.
[247] "Our list of visitors at present does not contain any great number of English. And none of any particular note, if I except the Earl of Carnarvon, the Countess Cowley, and a very few others." – *Morning Post*, 10 August 1869. In September the Earl used the platform of the Highclere Agricultural Association AGM to address the Irish Land question. Among the short stay guests at Highclere in October were the Hon. Gathorne Hardy, MP and his wife. Earls Cowley, Brownlow and Clan William followed a few weeks later.
[248] *Morning Post*, 20 December 1869.
[249] See *Reading Mercury* of 18 December 1869 for a list of visitors to Highclere Castle during two weeks in December 1869.
[250] *Derby Mercury*, 5 January 1870 and *Morning Post*, 5 January 1870.
[251] Ibid.

[252] See Carnarvon Papers, British Library, Add 60902. Edward Henry Stanley (1826–1893), eldest son of 14th Earl of Derby, who died in 1869. Lord Cairns was then caretaker leader in the Lords. In 1870 Stanley married the widow of the 2nd Marquess of Salisbury. The wife of the 3rd Marquess of Salisbury disliked Stanley.

[253] See Carnarvon Papers, British Library, Add 60902. Entry for Monday 28 February 1870:

> Went down to the House and took my seat according to promise on the front opposition Bench – with some rather curious feelings. Three years ago I deliberately resigned my seat on that bench... since then I have been in exile below the gangway, always an object of dislike sometimes of attack, with many opponents and few friends. And now I return at the earnest personal appeal of the new leader of the party whom I probably as much as any man helped to place there and apparently to the great satisfaction of the party. It is a curious piece of personal history and perhaps the end of the chapter is not yet. But I seek nothing, and if it comes as a matter of duty will refuse nothing.

[254] Charles Henry Gordon-Lennox, 6th Duke of Richmond (1818–1903). Carnarvon knew the Duke, having served with him on several Lords committees. In 1863 another member sitting on the Prison and Railways Committees (of which Carnarvon chaired) was John Wodehouse (Earl of Kimberly) who comments in his journal:

> Carnarvon does not manage his Committee successfully. His draft Report is written in an inaccurate slip-slop style, and he shows a want of "backbone" in defending it. The Duke of Richmond who is a hard, shrewd, persevering man of business worries C. as a dog worries a rat, always however with courtesy and good temper, which makes it more difficult to shake him off.

[255] *Morning Post*, 24 February 1870.
[256] *The Standard*, 11 March 1870.
[257] *Morning Post*, 19 March 1870.
[258] *Morning Post*, 25 March 1870.
[259] Edward Henry Charles Herbert (1837–1870). Edward's father was a brother of the 3rd Earl of Carnarvon.
[260] *Pall Mall Gazette*, 17 May 1870.
[261] Others victims of the tragedy were Frederick Grantham Vyner (1847–1870) whose body was also returned to England and buried at Gautby, Lincolnshire; Edward (Ned) Lloyd, an English lawyer living in Athens; and an Italian diplomat, Court Alberto de Boyl.
[262] Herbert was secretary of the British Legation at Athens. His remains were brought back to England, via Malta and Southampton, where Lord Carnarvon and his brother Auberon were waiting to accompany the body. It was taken to Burghclere Church to lie in state.
[263] *Pall Mall Gazette*, 17 May 1870.
[264] See FO 391/25, a file in National Archives, Kew: *Private Letters April to June 1870: Murder by Brigands of British Subjects in Greece.*
[265] See *Morning Post*, 9 August 1870. John Lothrop Motley (1814–1877) was an American historian and diplomat. Motley was the American ambassador to Britain 1868–1870. After his tenure as ambassador he settled in Britain.

[266] *Morning Post*, 19 September 1870.
[267] *Morning Post*, 29 and 31 October 1870.
[268] *The Times*, 21 November 1870.
[269] See Carnarvon Papers, British Library, Add 60903: Elsie (or it could have been the Earl himself) cut out the pages of the diary for the first three days of 1871. The time period corresponds with a large number of distinguished house guests (listed in *Hampshire Telegraph and Sussex Chronicle* for 11 January 1871) arriving and a New Year shooting party over beech woods, with the guns of Carnarvon, the Earl of Denbigh, Colonel the Hon. Sir Richard Charteris and Colonel Napier Stuart MP securing a very large bag of 449 pheasants, 10 hares and 36 rabbits.
[270] See Carnarvon Papers, British Library, Add 60903.
[271] *Reading Mercury*, Saturday 4 February 1871.
[272] The Earl wrote in his diary (Carnarvon Papers, British Library, Add 60903):

> Averst[Evelyn's doctor] is satisfied with the progress made but he says that he cannot feel as yet quite sure with regard to the top of the left lung. The right, he is confidant is organically sound but he is also apprehensive that there has been some... mischief done on the left side.

[273] James Smith Averst (1824–1885). A member of the Royal College of Surgeons. Associated with homeopathic and hydropathic methods. Between 1868 and 1884 he had a practice at 2 Belgrave Terrace, Torquay. NB: A William Edward Averst (1830–1904) was also a homeopathic doctor in London at this time.
[274] Aconite is aconitum napellus (the Common Monkshood). This was considered to be of therapeutic and toxicological importance in treating many conditions including colds, coughs, fever, infections, insomnia, pain and stress.
[275] See Carnarvon Papers, British Library, Add 60903, entry for 20 March 1871.
[276] The Siege of Paris lasting from 19 September 19 1870 to 28 January 1871, and the consequent capture of the city by Prussian forces led to French defeat in the Franco-Prussian War and the establishment of the German Empire as well as the Paris Commune.
[277] Sir Mountstuart Elphinstone Grant Duff, *Notes from a Diary*, Dutton (1898). Various volumes published.
[278] See Carnarvon Papers, British Library, Add 60903.
[279] These include reports in *Freeman's Journal*, 31 March (reception at Grosvenor Street on 28 March); *Morning Post*, 11 May (Lady Carnarvon's assembly and dinner party at Grosvenor Street, 10 May); *Morning Post*, 10 July (Lady Carnarvon received a fashionable circle); *Morning Post*, 15 June (Devonshire House Ball, 14 June); *Morning Post* 18 and 20 July attended functions at Grosvenor House and Lady Holland's; *Morning Post*, 1 July (Garden Party, Chiswick, 30 June).
[280] See Carnarvon Papers, British Library, Add 60903, diary entry 17 May 1871:

> Went down to Mr Beasley's, Pittsford Hall Joseph Noble Beasley, horse breeder, Northamptonshire, died 1904] to look at his mare for Evelyn tried her and on my return to London wrote to say I would pay the price of £157–10 shillings...

[281] An amusing sketch of Auberon from the *Birmingham Daily Post*, 25 February 1871, records:

He is a younger brother of Lord Carnarvon... he has gone through the usual course prescribed for cadets of noble families... that is to say, he had been to Oxford, and has served the customary two or three years in the army... he has selected the philosophical Radical creed... he is slightly built, wears his hair neatly parted in the middle, and carries an eye glass.

[282] Lady Cavendish (Lucy Caroline Lyttelton) records in her diary for 25 July 1871: "Florence [Cowper] engaged to Auberon Herbert (rather she than I!)." See www.ladycavendishdiary.com.

[283] *Western Times*, 15 August 1871.

[284] *Morning Post*, 5 August 1871.

[285] See Carnarvon Papers, British Library, Add 60903, diary Entry for 6 August 1871.

[286] See Carnarvon Papers, British Library, Add 60903, diary Entry for 22 August 1871.

[287] Almost certainly this was Friedrich Albin Hoffmann (1843–1924), author of the book *TB Diseases of the Bronchi, Lungs and Pleura* (1902).

[288] See Carnarvon Papers, British Library, Add 60903, diary entry for 28 August 1871. NB: Ischl is Bad Ischl, a spa town in Austria.

[289] See Carnarvon Papers, British Library, Add 60903, diary entry for 10 September 1871.

[290] See Carnarvon Papers, British Library, Add 60903, diary entry for 27 September 1871.

[291] Almost certainly Professor N. Friedrich of Heidelberg, who published several papers in medical journals on homeopathic treatments.

[292] See Carnarvon Papers, British Library, Add 60903, diary entry for 18 October 1871. Dr Mackenzie is Sir Morell Mackenzie (1837–1892), a British physician, one of the pioneers of laryngology in the UK.

[293] Almost certainly this was Dr Richard Payne Cotton (1820–1877), an expert on consumption.

[294] See Carnarvon Papers, British Library, Add 60903, diary entry for 18 October 1871.

[295] From the Earl's diary entry for 18 October 1871 it appears that Cotton found abnormalities in the upper part of Evelyn's right lung where tuberculosis deposits were embedded. He advised she spend January to Easter in the likes of Hastings, Bournemouth or Torquay. Medicinal supplements were prescribed in addition. The verdict was that there was no cause for present anxiety, but that she would need to be very careful. Coldish water, rubbing and a moderate exposure to a dry climate were also recommended.

[296] *Derby Mercury*, 3 December 1871.

[297] See Carnarvon Papers, British Library, Add 60903, diary entries from 15 November to 1 December, 1871:

> Nov 15, 1871: In the middle of the night woken by a telegram from Bretby begging me at once to come and bring E. with me... as Chesterfield (Stanhope) was in a very nervous and excited state. I got up and spent the whole night packing and at 0.30am we started a bitterly cold and long journey. At Reading I had another telegram saying he was better but we went on and on arriving here we found Dr Evans from Birmingham. It is a case of severe typhoid – caught apparently at the same time and made the same local influences which have affected the Prince of Wales. There is

much excitement and some delirium. The symptoms are described to me.

A clear case of typhoid not typhus, the spots (not a rash) are of typhoid character. Today is probably the 8th day. Strength not as yet failing but disinclination to food. He only takes milk. Pulse not very high, not generally above 100.

Nov 26, 1871: Stanhope refused his medicine until I came. I came about quarter of an hour and found him so delirious as to be mad. He sent everyone away to tell me of a conspiracy among the doctors to murder him. At last I got him to take the morphia and succeeded in this 4 times. About 3 pm he fell asleep. There has been in the night diahorrea [sic]

Nov 26, 1871: During the rest of the afternoon he continued drowsy but took food (milk) till about 11 o'clock. At about 1.30 Dr Murchison arrived and between 2–3 I was called to try to get Stanhope to take the medicine. Murchison and Evans had gone to bed. I tried to persuade him but he refused and as… was only in favour of trying persuasion nothing more could be done. Stanhope very delirious… though not so… violent as before.

Nov 27, 1871: Stanhope still very delirious and refusing all medicine but after a certain amount of force applied he took it. Then sleeping from 10 till late in the afternoon – one more struggle as to taking food settled quietly when I came in. Dr Murchison returned to town at 10am – his fee £94-10s.

Mr W. Peat came from the old Bank called to arrange with Lady Chesterfield as to cashing cheques to Stanhope's order. Agreed to take Lady Chesterfield's signature.

Nov 28, 1871: Last night again was quiet and good. In the middle of the day moved Stanhope to next room to remove a great catafalque of a bed and to substitute two smaller ones, accomplished satisfactorily. He remains quite, not to say lethargic taking little food but resisting as formerly. Strength keeps up a very partial consciousness. It is hard to say how much he knows or thinks. Sat up with Stanhope till 1.30. He had an excellent night and took ample nourishment.

Nov 29, 1871: This morning Stanhope sent for me. Recognised me and quite sensible of everything. He insisted on having his letter box opened and he then found his will in an open envelope, which he put into my hands. What his object was I do not know for he then became rather incoherent but I took it anyway and at the same time and asked Scott who was in the room to follow me. I sealed it up with my seal and one of the Chesterfields wrote on it that I had done this unread, made Scott put his initials and put it into my box for the present. On going to breakfast mentioned the fact to Orlando and Henry Forester. The day quiet, good deal of sleep.

Nov 30, 1871: A fatal day, in the morning all seemed secure and satisfactory except that the night had been rather sleepless though quiet. L… went to Burton at about 11–11.30 telling me he would be back by 7. During the day Stanhope took more than his usual amount of food and was quiet. About 5 or 5.30 Lady Chesterfield came to me to say that his hands were cold and his head hot. I certainly found this was so and put his feet on… hot water. Bye and bye the heat somewhat diminished, he took a little broth and slept – at 8 he certainly was. Louie and Dr Evans arrived and surmised it was a syncope. From 8.30 to 9 to 3 in the morning they gave 10–12 oz of brandy – 4 raw eggs, some ammonia and a good deal of beef tea but the pulse was really varied and at last the decline set steadily in.

At 1 or 2 am the case was hopeless and at 3.25 he died. He was conscious till nearly the end making great effort... to take the food and recognizing me and some others. About half an hour before his death Evelyn asked for a prayer to be read. There was no clergyman so I read the commendatory prayer and the Lord's prayer and I think he took it in. The desolation and anguish that followed I cannot think of but his departure was the quietest imaginable – not a movement or even a sigh. The breathing gradually died away and we sat for some minutes listening to see that it had finished. Lady Chesterfield took the shock better than I expected – Evelyn seemed turn to stone – unable to speak or cry or take comfort... The few remaining hours of the night were worse than when we had prayed.

[298] The Earl of Chesterfield's will was proved as being " under £80,000 personality" (i.e. personal estate). The Earl left sums to his uncles Henry and Orlando. To his mother (Lady Anne Chesterfield) he left a life interest arising from the rents and profits of his estates, which after her death were to held in trust for his sister (Evelyn, Countess of Carnarvon) for her life; and afterwards he bequeathed the same to his nephew, Lord Porchester.

[299] *The Wrexham Advertiser*, 9 December 1871.

[300] Lord John George Weld Forester (1801–1874), 2nd Baron Forester of Willey Park; Shropshire; George Cecil Weld Forester (1807–1886), 3rd Baron Forester; and Hon. Rev. Orlando Forester (1813–1894) (who was sometime rector of Gedling, an estate that Porchey inherited later from his mother), 4th Baron Forester. An ancestor of the Lord Forester held a grant from King Henry VIII conferring a right to wear a hat upon his head in royal presence. See also *Derby Mercury*, 14 October 1874.

[301] See *Derby Mercury*, 27 December 1871 and *Morning Post*, 12 January 1872.

[302] The Diary for early 1872 indicates meetings with his cousin Robert Herbert.

[303] See Carnarvon Papers, British Library, Add 60904.

[304] Ibid.

[305] *Bucks Herald*, 13 January 1872.

[306] *North Devon Journal*, 18 January 1872.

[307] See *Bucks Herald*, 20 January 1872. NB: Dr (Sir) George Burrowes or Burrows (1801–1887) of Cavendish Square, London, was at this time physician-extraordinary to Queen Victoria. He was an authority on disorders of cerebral circulation.

[308] See Carnarvon Papers, British Library, Add 60904.

[309] Ibid.

[310] *Morning Post*, 8 February 1872.

[311] See Carnarvon Papers, British Library, Add 60904.

[312] Ibid.

[313] Ibid.

[314] Ibid.

[315] *Morning Post*, 13 April 1872.

[316] Lord Derby adds in the entry for 16 April: "[Lord Carnarvon] tells me that he has just sold an estate in Wiltshire which gave him a return of £4,000 a year for £190,000: and has cleared off all his debts."

[317] *Hampshire Advertiser*, 12 June 1872.

[318] *Daily News*, 6 June 1872.
[319] The marriage of Lady Maud Herbert, second daughter of Lady Herbert of Lea and sister of the Earl of Pembroke, to Herbert Parry.
[320] *The Standard*, 3 July 1872.
[321] *The Graphic*, 6 July 1872. Carnarvon delivered the opening address in the Hall of the Middle Temple on Wednesday 3 July 1872.
[322] *Hampshire Advertiser*, 20 July 1872.
[323] *Hampshire Telegraph*, 21 August 1872.
[324] See the *Huddersfield Chronicle* and *Morning Post*, 24 August 1872. According to *The Morning Post* of 20 May 1872, the *Mercia* was bought from a Mr Sheridan.
[325] *Morning Post*, 7 September 1872.
[326] *The Graphic*, 14 September 1872.
[327] *Derby Mercury*, 18 September 1872.
[328] *Morning Post*, 26 September 1872.
[329] *Morning Post*, 19 October 1872.
[330] *Hampshire Advertiser*, 16 October, 1872.
[331] See *Hampshire Advertiser*, 6 November 1872 and *The Standard*, 19 November 1872.
[332] *Hampshire Advertiser*, 20 November 1872.
[333] *Hampshire Advertiser*, 11 December 1872
[334] See *Hampshire Advertiser*, 18 December 1872 .
[335] Knowsley was occupied by the Earl and Countess of Derby.
[336] *Hampshire Advertiser*, 18 December 1872.
[337] *Hampshire Advertiser*, 4 January 1873.
[338] *Morning Post*, 25 January 1873.
[339] *Morning Post*, 31 January 1873.
[340] See *Morning Post*, 21 February 1873. The *Hampshire Telegraph* of 22 February 1873 records:

> The Earl of Carnarvon's yacht has started for the Mediterranean; and his lordship, accompanied by Lord Henry Percy and Mr Corbett, will leave England in a few days for Gibraltar, and proceed from thence on a yachting cruise. The earl will return after the Easter holidays. The Countess of Carnarvon goes on a visit to Lady Chesterfield, Bretby Park.

[341] *The Standard*, 4 April 1873.
[342] *Hampshire Advertiser*, 23 April 1873. Another allegation made against Carnarvon was that he gave notice to labourers working on his Estates who did not go to Church regularly.
[343] See entry in the diaries (British Library, Add 60904) for 18 April 1872: " Sold... 66 Grosvenor St for £14,500."
[344] Ibid.
[345] *Morning Post*, 16 May 1873.
[346] *Morning Post*, 28 May 1873.
[347] *Morning Post*, 7 June, 1873.
[348] *Morning Post*, 16 June 1873. Guest lining up including Lord Derby, the Stanhopes, Lady Ailesbury, Lord and Lady Ashley, the Peels, Baron F. de Rothschild, and Mr and Lady Dorothy Nevill.
[349] *Hampshire Advertiser*, 2 July 1873.

[350] Ryerson, Rev. Egerton, *The Story of My Life*, edited by J. George Hodgins, William Briggs, Toronto (1884), pp. 580–1:

> The Earl of Dufferin enclosed flattering letters to the Earl of Carnarvon and the Dean of Westminster, both of whom have received me with great cordiality. The Earl of Carnarvon shook hands with me two or three times, and said how glad he was to see and shake hands with an old Canadian, who services to his country were spoken of as Lord Dufferin has spoken of mine. His Lordship told me he would give instructions, whenever I desired, to have every possible facility and aid given me in the Record Office in referring to any documents or papers there, relating to the history or affairs of the British Colonies.

[351] See Cooke, C. Kinloch, *A Memoir of Her Royal Highness Princess Mary Adelaide Duchess of Teck Based on her Private Diaries and Letters*, (Volume 1), John Murray (1900). The entry for Middleston, January 11, 1853: "... after luncheon, as it was a wet day, we made a tour of the house and wrote letters, Lord Chesterfield and Evelyn arrived." The Chesterfields were regularly in the company of Mary Adelaide.

[352] Princess Mary Adelaide of Cambridge, 1833–1897.

[353] See *Huddersfield Daily Chronicle*, 10 July 1873.

[354] See *The Sheffield & Rotherham Independent*, 18 July 1873. Evelyn supported this idea (sparked by the Marquis of Westminster and Princess Louise) at a meeting at Grosvenor House on 17 July. Among other ladies present was Mrs Gladstone and Lady Franklin.

[355] See Cole, Sir Henry, *Fifty Years of Public Work of Sir Henry Cole, KCB*, Volume 1, George Bell, London (1884), p. 370.

[356] *Hampshire Advertiser*, 23 July 1873.

[357] *Morning Post*, 30 August 1873.

[358] See *The Morning Post*, 22 August and 5 September 1873.

[359] See Girouard, Mark, *The Victorian Country House*, Oxford University Press (1971).

[360] This is echoed in what Almina told Tony Leadbettter about her impressions of Lordy's childhood.

[361] *Morning Post*, 18 September 1873.

[362] *Morning Post*, 20 September 1873.

[363] *Hampshire Advertiser*, 4 October 1873.

[364] *Hampshire Advertiser*, 15 October 1873.

[365] See *Derby Mercury*, 29 October, 1873. A report refers in this paper to Highclere guests including the Duke of Norfolk, the Earl and Countess Somers and Lord Lyons.

[366] *Derby Mercury*, 12 November 1873.

[367] One other guest, Lady Knightley, described Beust as a typical *homme du monde*, a man of the world or a sophisticate.

[368] *Morning Post*, 19 November 1873.

[369] Meredith White Townsend (1831–1911).

[370] *Morning Post*, 24 November 1873, has a list of more than forty guests. Augustus Hare (1834–1903) was a writer of biographies and travel books and was well known as raconteur and letter writer.

[371] Chevening House, Kent the seat of the Stanhope family.

[372] Hare, Augustus J.C., *The Story of My Life*, Volume IV, George Allen (1900).

[373] Ibid.

[374] Ibid.

[375] Ibid.

[376] Louisa Mary Bowater Knightley, baroness (1842–1913). She married Rainald Knightley, (1819–1895), who was MP for South Northampton from 1852–1892 and was the first and last Lord Knightley. Lady Knightley's Journals have been published.
[377] See *The Journals of Lady Knightley of Fawsley*, edited by Julia Cartwright, John Murray (1915).
[378] The list of guests in the *Morning Post* of 24 November 1873 records "Mrs and Miss Howard (of Greystoke)".
[379] See *The Journals of Lady Knightley of Fawsley*, edited by Julia Cartwright, John Murray (1915).
[380] *Morning Post*, 19 December 1873.
[381] *Reading Mercury*, 17 January 1874.
[382] *Hampshire Advertiser*, 21 January 1874.
[383] *London Daily News*, 20 February 1874.
[384] *Morning Post*, 24 February 1874.
[385] *Reading Mercury*, 14 March 1874.
[386] See *Belfast News-Letter*, 25 March 1874, and *Freeman's Journal*, 24 March 1874.
[387] See *Morning Post*, 18 March 1874, and *Reading Mercury*, 28 March 1874.
[388] Philip Henry Stanhope, 5th Earl Stanhope (1805-1875), politician and historian. His wife died in 1873. A regular face at Bretby and Highclere.
[389] Hare, Augustus J.C., *The Story of My Life*, Volume IV, George Allen (1900).
[390] *Hampshire Advertiser*, 26 August 1874.
[391] See *The Letters of Disraeli to Lady Bradford and Lady Chesterfield*, edited by the Marquis of Zetland (1929). Vol. 1 covers 1873–1875; Vol. 2 covers 1876–1881. There are several passing references to the Carnarvons.
[392] *Hampshire Advertiser*, 7 October 1874.
[393] *Morning Post*, 25 December 1874.
[394] In *The Letters of Disraeli to Lady Bradford and Lady Chesterfield*, edited by the Marquis of Zetland (1929), Vol. 1 there are several letters to Lady Chesterfield about Evelyn during her pregnancy; e.g. p. 180, 9 December 1874: "I hope to hear, also, that Lady Carnarvon continues better. Pray remember me to her most kindly."
[395] See Carnarvon Papers, British Library, Add 60924.
[396] See Carnarvon Papers, British Library, Add 60907.
[397] See *The Letters of Disraeli to Lady Bradford and Lady Chesterfield*, edited by the Marquis of Zetland (1929), Vol. 1 pp. 191–2.
[398] *Sheffield Daily Telegraph*, 23 January 1875.
[399] Hardinge, Sir Arthur (edited by Elizabeth, Countess of Carnarvon), *The Life of Henry Howard Molyneux Herbert 1831–1890* (1925). Three volumes.
[400] *Burks Herald*, 30 January, 1875.
[401] See Carnarvon Papers, British Library, Add 60907.
[402] Barrington, Mrs Russell, *Life of Walter Bagehot*, Longmans, Green & Co (1914).
[403] Ibid.
[404] Lord Derby's diaries.
[405] Ibid.
[406] In *The Letters of Disraeli to Lady Bradford and Lady Chesterfield*, edited by the Marquis of Zetland (1929), Disraeli writes to Evelyn's aunt, Lady Bradford, on 28 January 1875:

> I have also written to Carnarvon lest he should make any rash resolves, and letting him know that he might command retirement, even for months, and that I and his

colleagues would work his office for him – not so well as he could but with our best efforts.

[407] Hare, Augustus J.C., *The Story of My Life*, Volume IV, George Allen (1900).
[408] See *The Reminiscences of Lady Dorothy Nevill* (edited by her son, Ralph Nevill). (1906)
[409] *Freeman's Journal*, 13 February 1875.
[410] See *Derby Mercury*, 10 February 1875.
[411] A venerable edifice situated in Savoy Street, between the Strand and Waterloo Bridge, deemed in 1860 "with the exception of Westminster Abbey, the oldest ecclesiastical building in the city of Westminster" (*Birmingham Daily Post*, 18 September 1860).
[412] Lady Victoria Alexandrina Mary Cecil Herbert (1874-1952). The 4th Earl's diaries refers to the event at the Savoy Chapel taking place on 11 February 1875. Some other sources give a later date.
[413] The Queen was represented at the christening by Lady Ely, one of her ladies in waiting. A gold locket with a picture of the Queen was presented to the child.
[414] See Carnarvon Papers, British Library, Add 60907.
[415] The Earl's diary for 25 February 1875 (British Library Ref Add 60907) indicates he consulted one of his doctors, Sir William Gull, about "the pain in his heart". Gull dismissed it as being attributable to "any organic mischief" but due to the stress and strain he had been under.
[416] See Carnarvon Papers, British Library, diary entry for 16 March, 1875, ref: Add 60907.
[417] Winifred called the Wallops her " tribe of cousins".
[418] Winifred and "Baby" were at Eggesford already; Lordy and Margaret joined from Bretby. See also *Hampshire Telegraph and Sussex Chronicle*, 24 March 1875.
[419] Rev John Troutbeck, 1832–1891, priest in ordinary to Queen Victoria, minor canon of Westminster and chaplain to Lord Carnarvon.
[420] See Carnarvon Papers, British Library, diary entry for 11 March, 1875. Ref: Add 60907.
[421] Rolf Herbert (1872–1882). Rolf died aged ten.
[422] The 1875 diaries of the 4th Earl (held in the British Library under Ref: Add 60907) have numerous pages cut out with a sharp blade, probably a razor blade. The censor was likely Elizabeth (Elsie) Howard, the 4th Earl's second wife.
[423] See Carnarvon Papers, British Library, diary entry for 30 April, 1875. Ref: Add 60907.
[424] Report in *The Times* of 28 May 1875, lifted from *The Illustrated London News*.
[425] Ibid.
[426] See Carnarvon Papers, British Library, diary entry for 14 May 1875, ref: Add 60907.
[427] Frederick Percy Graves (1837–1903). There had only been one sitting for the picture during the previous winter at Bretby Park.
[428] The entry for 2 July 1875 in the 4th Earl's diary (British Library ref: Add 60907) indicates that the children were accompanied by Mrs Mayson and their nurses.
[429] See Carnarvon Papers, British Library, diary entry for 17 July 1875, ref: Add 60907.
[430] http://www.bbc.co.uk/history/british/victorians/boer_wars_01.shtml
[431] Lifted from Lord Derby's diaries published by Cambridge Journals.
[432] Ibid.

[433] News of the event, in a hotel room in Edinburgh, perturbed Highclere and Bretby's occupants, since her ladyship's demise was "caused by an overdose of laudanum". See *The Dundee Courier & Angus and Northern Warder*, 21 December 1875. The victim was the wife of George Philip Stanhope (1822–1883), the 8th Earl of Chesterfield, an Ulster squire of little note.

[434] The Cedar of Lebanon, barely alive and propped up by chains, was reduced to a stump in 1954 and blown down completely in a gale shortly afterwards.

[435] Carnarvon's correspondence with George, Duke of Cambridge, at National Archives, Kew Ref: PRO 30/6/14. The Duke was also (like Carnarvon) a prominent Freemason.

[436] *The Standard*, 20 April 1876.

[437] See *The Standard*, 14 June 1876.

[438] With more than an inclination towards the leisurely, sedate life, Lady Gwendolen Herbert was the companion-nurse of her mother, Henrietta, the Dowager Countess at their home at Pixton. Both women suffered from bad chests, so winters had to be spent in mild climes. During the winter of 1875–76 the two ladies took up residence in a hotel on the south coast at Bournemouth in order to be assured of more congenial weather than that prevailing in harder, harsher Devonshire countryside. Bournemouth was a fashionable society resort and in winter attracted some of Gwendolen and Henrietta's noble chums. Lady Gwendolen Herbert often lived at Highclere, although she had her own home at Putney. The 4th Earl's biographer records: "Since their Mother's death she had lived much with her brother, and to the younger generation she was as a second Mother". See Hardinge, *The Life of Henry-Howard-Molyneux Herbert* (1925)

[439] *The Observer*, 22 July 1894.

[440] Lady Gwendolen shared this home with a long-standing older female companion, Emily Anne Drury. Source: 1911 Census, taken 2 April 1911. The house comprised fourteen rooms and was managed with a cook and housemaid. Emily and Gwendolen were close friends for many decades. From Lord Carnarvon's diary for 31 July 1882: "down to Faircroft and saw G... I had a good deal to talk about with Emily." Emily Anne Drury died on 3 January 1936 "on the eve of her 98th birthday". See *The Times*, 6 Janaury 1936, and *London Gazette*, 17 March 1936.

[441] Remark by Lady Caroline Cavendish (née Lyttelton) (1841–1925) in her diary for 30 September 1878 (www.ladycavendishdiary.com).

[442] See Carnarvon Papers, British Library Add 61051. Letter dated 1 March 1878 (folio 46).

[443] This echoes a remark by Elsie (seen in Cumbria Archives' Howard Collection, Ref: DHW 3/26). It was made years later in respect of her step-daughter, Victoria (Vera) who was reared and influenced by Lady Gwendolen Herbert. In 1926, when Elsie was carving up her last estate, she recorded in a letter written to her brother Esme at Portofino on 1 May 1926: "it is to be remembered that [Vera's] money is almost certain to go to some of the girls of the family – she does not care for boys."

[444] This link was especially important after the death of the Dowager Henrietta. In Lady Burghclere's *Memoir of Alan Herbert* (p. 70) she records, "had it not been for Lady Gwendolen, Dr Herbert might insensibly have become detached from his family. But, thanks to her faithful correspondence and devotion, his long absences never estranged him from his own people and his father's house."

[445] *The Guardian*, 12 May 1896, and *The Observer*, 18 September 1897. Gwendolen was described as a "rigid vegetarian" (see *The North American Journal of Homeopathy*, Volume 53, 1905).

[446] *The Observer*, 19 June 1910.
[447] *The Observer*, 22 June 1902 and 28 June 1903.
[448] Some details of Lady Margaret's marriage on 10 September 1904 to George Duckworth (1868–1934) can be found in Chapter 4 of *The Life and Secrets of Almina Carnarvon*.
[449] In London Elsie often lived with Lady Victoria Herbert at 5 Stratford Place. According to the 1911 Census the address was an eighteen-roomed dwelling with seven servants.
[450] See National Archives, Kew, Ref: PRO30/6/14, folio 38. On 24 May 1876 Carnarvon wrote from Pixton Park, Dulverton, apologising to his Colonial Office boss, the Duke of Cambridge: "The great family anxiety with which I have been during the last few days beset... I am here watching the condition of my mother which is one of extreme dangers and of course quite unable to leave this..." The Carnarvon Papers at the British Library, Add 61044, folios 214–5, contain an account of the last illness of Henrietta, written by the 4th Earl.
[451] *Manchester Evening News*, 26 May, and *Western Times*, 30 May 1876.
[452] *Manchester Courier*, 23 May, and *Plymouth and Exeter Gazette*, 29 May 1876.
[453] See Carnarvon Papers, British Library, Add 61044.
[454] The Carnarvon Papers in the British Library, Add 61044 has letters to Henrietta from her "ever affectionate grandson" Lord Lymington (the Portsmouth heir) on Eton headed notepaper c1872.
[455] From *Alan Herbert 1836–1907: Letters and Memories by His Niece, Lady Burghclere*. The Author has seen a copy of this in the British Library, Shelf Mark 010855 b22.
[456] Ibid.
[457] *Reading Mercury*, 3 June 1876.
[458] *Derby Mercury*, 14 June 1876.
[459] Lord Dufferin wrote to the Earl from Canada:

> My Dear Carnarvon: I cannot tell you with what deep regret I have learned that you have had to submit a fresh misfortune. Though not so great as the last, it is in spite of the laws of nature one of the most terrible we have to endure. (Carnarvon Papers, British Library, letter dated 16 June 1876)

[460] Lady Catherine Wallop, later Gaskell (1856–1935), a "a lady of striking personality and presence" (*The Times* obituary of 22 August 1935), the eldest of the six Portsmouth daughters, author of novels *A Woman's Soul* and *Lady Anne's Fairy Tales* and several books on Shropshire where the Gaskell seat was at Wenlock Abbey.
[461] Charles George Milnes Gaskell (1842–1919) of Thornes House, Wakefield, Yorkshire and Wenlock Abbey, Shropshire; a lawyer and Liberal MP. Charles was an intimate friend of the American historian Henry Brooks Adams (1838–1918) when Adams' father was American ambassador in London. He was also a contemporary of Alfred de Rothschild and Bertie, Prince of Wales, at Trinity College, Cambridge. He is further described as "a very large and opulent iron master". See also *Trewman's Exeter Flying Post and Cornish Advertiser*, 15 November 1876.
[462] See Lewis, Samuel, *A Topographical Dictionary of England with Historical and Statistical Descriptions* (1833).
[463] In 1876 Lordy's Aunt, Lady Eveline Portsmouth began a seasonal festivity at Christmas by arranging concerts. Members of the Eggesford household and neighbours

comprised the audience. Junior members of the Wallop family (with their Herbert cousins) were involved as the performers. See *Western Times,* 8 January 1878.
[464] Carnarvon Papers, British Library, Add 60909, entries for 3 and 12 January 1877.
[465] Sibthropes, at Cambridge House School, 2 Belmont, Brighton is cited in the Carnarvon Papers.
[466] Derby's diary for 18 April 1877 records:

> Richmond [Duke of] spoke to me yesterday about Carnarvon, whose manner in cabinet & towards his colleagues is peculiar. He seldom speaks to any one except Salisbury, and looks miserable: whether from failing health & overwork, of which he complains, or from absence of sympathy on the Turkish business. I cannot call it disagreement, for he has generally acquiesced with little difficulty in what was settled. But he is much mixed up with Liddon & the high church party, to whom a Russian war on Turkey is a crusade.

[467] *Daily News*, 18 April 1877.
[468] See *Pall Mall Gazette*, 1 October 1877.
[469] Carnarvon Papers, British Library, letter from Dufferin to Carnarvon dated 16 June 1876.
[470] Carnarvon Papers, British Library, Add 60909 , 7 April 1877:

> Highclere: came down here and met Mr Troutbeck who had come for Porchey's Latin. Had a long talk with him about Porchey. He has thought of a tutor for him and from what he says he will do very well. He is to make enquiries…

[471] See *Guardian*, 23 May 1877. Hurstbourne was near Whitchurch, Andover, Hampshire. It was a mansion house at the disposal of the Portsmouth heir, Lord Lymington. It had a priceless library which was destroyed by fire in 1891 (see *San Antonio Daily Light*, 6 January 1891). Another description of it is of being "a charming place in the neighbourhood of the New Forest" (see *Black and White*, 1 September 1906).
[472] Carnarvon Papers, British Library, Add 60909, 26 May 1877.
[473] *Hampshire Advertiser*, 6 October 1877.
[474] *Hampshire Advertiser*, 26 December 1877.
[475] See Hardinge, *The Life of Henry-Howard-Molyneux Herbert* (1925).
[476] See Derby's diary for 16 January 1878.
[477] Various notes in Derby's diary on 23 January 1878.
[478] Papers Past, *Star*, 30 June 1890.
[479] Sir Spencer Walpole in *The History of Twenty Five Years* (Volume 4) (1908) says that Beaconsfield passed a "severe censure" on Carnarvon and comments that "this is the only record I know of where a Prime Minister has severely condemned one of his colleagues in Cabinet".
[480] See Carnarvon Papers, British Library Add 61050. Eveline Portsmouth was a great organizer in her brother's bleakest times and made decisions for him about the children although when there was time she asked for his agreement, in a letter. One such plan is outlined in a letter dated 2 September 1878…for Winifred and Mlle (her French mistress) to go to Highclere on 9 September to attend an inauguration,,, (this was the Falkland Memorial).

[481] The monolith, standing seventeen feet in height (with the total height of the granite memorial being thirty-three feet) and weighing forty tons, bears this inscription:

> In memory of those who, on the 20th September 1643 fell fighting in the army of King Charles I on the field of Newbury and especially of Lucius Cary, Viscount Falkland, who died here in the 32nd year of his age. This monument is set up by those to whom the majesty of the Crown and the liberty of their country are dear.

See also *Aberdeen Weekly Journal*, 10 September 1878.

[482] Carnarvon Papers, British Library, Add 61050 have references by Lady Eveline Portsmouth in a letter to Lord Carnarvon regarding the 12-year-old Lordy being linked up with a " Mr Rawson/ Rawston". He may be a chaperone, tutor or a Master at Sibthropes (Lordy's prep school at Brighton.)

1878 : "On Friday 19th Sept Lilias [Wallop] to go to you[meaning Lord Carnarvon] at Highclere and Porchey and Mr Rawson…Winifred and Mlle to return here and on Tuesday 17th Sept which is the day for the schoolboys return. [meaning Eveline's sons who were also at Sibthropes] Mr Rawson and the boys could all join Mr Sibthrope in Town if as I imagine he takes again a party down…" The Earl agreed to Eveline's plan, in a note on 7th Sept he writes " We will settle everything as to W and Porchey as you propose…."

NB Re: Rawson/ Rawston In Fiona Carnarvon book Carnarvon & Carter Highclere Enterprises (2007), page 7, there is a small photograph of " The 5th Earl (as Lord Porchester) aged 10 years with an Estate worker, Mr Rawston." Both are in smart clothes. This relationship seems an oddity, but on the count of the dates revealed here it lasted at least two years when Lordy was aged 10 –12 years old..

[483] Elsie, 4th Countess, was the eldest daughter of Henry Howard of Greystoke Castle, Cumberland, and granddaughter of Lord Henry Thomas Howard, brother of Bernard Edward Howard, 12th Duke of Norfolk.

[484] Carnarvon Papers, British Library, Add 61050, letter from Lord Carnarvon to Eveline dated 25 November 1878, folio 52.

[485] See Carnarvon Papers: Add 61058–9.

[486] See Carnarvon Papers, Add 61050. The Earl's sister, Eveline wrote to him " I had a very nice letter from Mrs Sibthrope yesterday – She spoke of Porchey as in wonderful health..doing very good average work but hardly yet in the swing of his work again – [it] read very genuinely and therefore to me very satisfactory. I hope dearest that we may meet before the dear boy's return or before you make any plans for him but at any rate I will write to you very fully about things which having (sic) occurred to me shortly"

[487] In Carnarvon Papers, British Library Add 61059 Lady Winifred writes to her " Dearest Papa on 28 December 1878 from Greystoke Castle, after The Earl and Elsie had left on their honeymoon saying " Porchey helped yesterday to build a snow hut they said it was quite warm inside."See ends the letter " Always your most loving child"

[488] Lady Eveline Portsmouth was unable to attend her brother's wedding at Greystoke on account of illness. She had concerns – with a new mother on the scene- about Lordy and his father drifting apart. She cautioned in a letter dated 1 January 1879 [Carnarvon Papers, British Library, Add 61050] about Lordy going to Eggesford after the wedding " I hope that dear P may be able to go out with you shooting for he can

take plenty of exercise here and it will be so desirable that he should find his companionship with you…"

[489] See Carnarvon Papers, diaries 1879, Add 60913, entry for 17 January 1879.

[490] See Carnarvon Papers, diaries 1879, Add 60913, entry for 4 February 1879.

[491] See *Daily News*, 25 January 1879.

[492] Carnarvon Papers, British Library, Add 61050, letter dated 10 January 1879, folios 77–9.

[493] Carnarvon Papers, Add 61050 " My dearest [to the Earl] about Gee – I know she is expecting to go to you and what I really think is the important and really necessary thing is that she should feel that you and yours acknowledge everything her own life and home so that there is a sense she is with you only for a time…This will really make her mind quite easy and not burdened with a sense of responsibility. She will be much more happy and bright in proposing herself and in coming at any moment – I think on reflection you will understand she clings to the thought of a life of her own – but with never prevent her readiness and employment in being of use to you and dear Elsie and the children." [a later reference appears in a letter dated 25 Feb 1879 saying that Elsie was using " wonderful tact when dealing with Gee].

[494] Carnarvon Papers, Add 61050 Letter dated 1 March 1879.

[495] Since there was subsequent outbreak of the disease at Lordy's prep school, he may have carried the virus with him back to Brighton.

Lady Eveline Portsmouth points out in a letter to Lord Carnarvon in the Carnarvon Papers, British Library Add 61050

" I told the Sibthorpes about the measles and I would almost advise your asking them specially to watch Porchey – They don't appear at all [forward looking] people…"

Winifred Burghclere makes reference in her 1923 biographical sketch to an outbreak of measles at Lordy's prep school at Brighton: "[Lordy] was at least fortunate in emerging alive from an epidemic of measles, which the boys treated by pouring jugs of cold water on each other when uncomfortably feverish."

[496] Burghclere, Lady Winifred, *Biographical Sketch of Lord Carnarvon* (1923).

[497] Most likely entry from Lordy's school is this from the Brighton Census of 1871:

1 and 2 Goldsmith Rd., Gordon House [a school] Brighton:
John A. SIBTHORPE, head, mar, 72, retired solicitor, b Guildford, Surrey
Frances M. SIBTHORPE, wife, mar, 72, b Taunton, Somerset
Emily K. SIBTHORPE, dau, 33, b Guildford, Surrey
William B. SIBTHORPE, son, 32, professor of
languages, b Guildford, Surrey
Phillip C. SIBTHORPE, son, 31, b Plymtree, Devon.

[498] See Carnarvon Papers, Add 61058, folio 193.

[499] See Carnarvon Papers, Add 61058. Eveline Portsmouth also refers in an enclosure letter to Lord Carnarvon in Add 61059 to " I send Mrs Sibthrope's [letter] as is has such a nice mention of Porchey…"

[500] See Carnarvon Papers, diaries 1879, Add 60913, entry for 7 May 1879.

[501] Freddy is Hon. Frederick Henry Arthur Wallop (1870–1953). Assistant private secretary to the president of the Board of Agriculture, trustee of the National Portrait

Gallery 1918–48. Freddy was an unmarried eccentric who was kind to children (see Joanna Smith's *Edwardian Children*). He shared home at Middle Wallop with his mother Lady Eveline, Dowager Countess of Portsmouth, until her death in 1906. He owned a good deal of art, especially fine pictures that were left to his nephew Alan Evans (died 1974, a contemporary-colleague of Society photographer, Cecil Beaton.) Alan's mother was the last-born Portsmouth daughter, Lady Henrietta Anna Wallop, later Mrs Evans (died 1932).

[502] Teddie is Rev Hon. Arthur George Edward Wallop (1867–1898). Died at Nassau in the Bahamas from the effects of fever at the age of thirty-one. After graduating with a BA he studied at Ely College and was ordained in 1894, and from 1894 to 1896 was vice principal of the Burgh Mission House, Lincolnshire. Later he was engaged in missionary work in Eleuthera, Bahamas.

[503] See Carnarvon Papers, diaries 1879, Add 60913, entry for 7 May 1879.

[504] See Carnarvon Papers, diaries 1879, Add 60914; the entry for 6 August 1879 reads: "Young Ash came to coach Porchey during the holidays. He is not a shy youth or one needing to be drawn out. But I hope he will do."

[505] See Carnarvon Papers, Add 61050. In a letter on No 10 Downing Street headed notepaper from Carnarvon to his sister Lady Eveline Portsmouth he writes " I am rather anxious as to Porchey: he does not throw off his cold and it has now lasted for a very long time, I am however now keeping him more to one room and I hope that some good will follow on this. But I am not quite satisfied as to him…"

[506] See Carnarvon Papers, diaries 1879, Add 60914, entry for 13 August 1879.

[507] A letter from Lady Portsmouth in the Carnarvon Papers 61050 addressed to " Dear People" at Highclere is generous in her praise for Elsie: "Everyone was charmed with Highclere with the pictures – with Milford with everything but above all with that lovely Lady Carnarvon. There was a great enthusiasm over you dear Elsie, your face, your ways, your hospitality. It makes me such a proud sister in law that I drink in with every word with happiness and feel [ing] of thankfulness when I think of my dear brother in such happy haven " Eveline adds a quote :

" For a sweeter Woman ne'er drew breath
Than my brother's wife Elizabeth"

[508] Carter, Ernest Frank, *An Historical Geography of the Railways of the British Isles* (1959).

[509] The Earl was on the board of the railway company and naturally encouraged the development of this branch line to and from Newbury as it provided the closest rail link to Highclere, for London and elsewhere.

[510] See Carnarvon Papers, diaries 1879, Add 60914, entry for 26 August 1879.

[511] See Carnarvon Papers, diaries 1879, Add 60914, entry for 23 September 1879.

[512] George Eden Marindin (1841–1939), fifth son of Rev. Samuel Marindin. A beloved and respected housemaster at Eton for more than 22 years. For obituary, see *The Times*, 24 February 1939.

Marindin wrote to Lord Carnarvon (Carnarvon Papers, British Library Add 61059) from Chesterton Bridgenorth Salop on 4 September 1879 :

"Dear Lord Carnarvon : I enclose a form which will best explain the only necessary preliminary- Porchester should arrive at Eton on Wednesday Sept 24. Anytime in the day afternoon or evening will do. He will be examined for his place early on the

Thursday morning. He need not of course bring anything but clothes and books. Eton will be my latest address meantime...."

[513] *Morning Post*, 15 December 1886. Said during an address to schoolchildren by Lord Carnarvon.
[514] See Carnarvon Papers, diaries 1879, Add 60914, entry for 28 September 1879.
[515] See Carnarvon Papers, Add 61050, letter dated 30 September 1879, folio 120.
[516] See Carnarvon Papers, diaries 1879, Add 60914, entries for 2–4 October 1879.
[517] Sir Robert Phillimore (1810–1885), lawyer, politician and author. Shared a close friendship with Carnarvon and Henry Parry Liddon (1829–1890), canon of St Paul's Cathedral, London.
[518] Information from Tony Leadbetter, as recounted to him by Almina Carnarvon.
[519] Public school terms in their cricket teams for the right to wear particular clothing (sweaters and scarves) showing they were part of the school/house squad and had played a number of matches.
[520] Exchange of emails between the author and Mrs P. Hatfield, Eton College archivist, 8–10 July 2012.
[521] See Carnarvon Papers, diaries 1879, Add 60914, entry for 2 November 1879. Several diary entries (and references in letters) refer to the developing relationship of "Elsie and the boy" (the "boy" being Lordy). The Earl mentions the state of things to brother Auberon, suggesting it had been a worry, to which Auberon responds, in a letter dated 24 April 1880, "so glad of good accounts of Elsie and the boy", to which is added by another's hand, "I am so glad Elsie and my nephew are going on well." See Carnarvon Papers, British Library, Add 61051, folios 144–45.
[522] Information from Tony Leadbetter, as recounted to him by Almina Carnarvon.
[523] John Fellows Wallop (1859–1925). From 1917 until his death, the 7th Earl of Portsmouth.
[524] John Wallop was known as "Jock". He was among the generation of boys (others included his own brothers) who were brought under the spell of the notorious pederast Oscar Browning. Jock was dubbed "a confirmed bachelor". See also *Washington Post*, 30 December 1905, and *New York Times*, 9 August 1908.
[525] Prince Victor Albert Jay Duleep Singh (1866–1918). Son of Maharajah Duleep Singh (1838–1893) of the Punjab, whose Indian state was annexed and he was brought to England in 1854. Victor's mother, Bamba Muller, was of European-Abasinian- white pedigree. Victor's father is regarded as the first Sikh settler in Britain.
[526] A sloppy derivation of Duleep.
[527] Victor's birth date was 10 July 1866. Lordy's was 26 June 1866.
[528] Private source. Please contact the author.
[529] Prince Frederick Victor Duleep Singh (1868–1926). Soldier and art collector.
[530] Private source. Please contact the author.
[531] Nevill, Ralph, *Floreat Etona: Anecdotes and Memories of Eton College*, Macmillan & Co., London (1911). Ralph Nevill (1865–1930) was a writer and diplomat. He was the son of Lady Dorothy Nevill, a regular face at Highclere. Ralph edited several volumes of his mother's diaries and memoirs which feature references to the Carnarvons. Ralph Nevill tended to walk mostly in all –male bastions of the diplomatic corps and in the London gentleman's clubs.
[532] Nevill, Ralph, *Floreat Etona: Anecdotes and Memories of Eton College*, Macmillan & Co., London (1911).
[533] Ibid. This tale is repeated by Nevill in his book *The Gay Victorians*. E Nash & Grayson (1930). " In the 'eighties there were a few boys of foreign birth at Eton. Prince

Demidoff, a Russian, and the Comte de Haro, a Spaniard, were however, popular, as were two or three Americans and the two sons of the Maharajah Duleep Singh. I remember that the eldest, Prince Victor, created quite a sensation shortly after his arrival by offering to bet the captain of the boats, who had spoken to him, a fiver on the Derby."

NB Prince Demidoff is Elim Demidoff (1868-1943) a well known sportsman, author and big game hunter. Comte de Haro is the Count de Haro, son of the Duke De Fraias.

[534] See Carnarvon Papers, diaries 1879, Add 60914, entry for 7 November 1879.

[535] See Carnarvon Papers, diaries 1879, Add 60914, entry for 25 December 1879.

[536] See Carnarvon Papers Add 61050: The Earl became obsessed with the welfare of Aubrey. When separated from the boy (during the tour of Australia of 1887) he writes in a letter : "Tell Aubrey from me that I trust to him his utmost to be a good boy and to do all that that he knows that I wish him to do. ...... I look to him day and night dear fellow and crave to see and talk to him – for I almost have to say it aloud ...I am wrapped up in his well being. I see his faults and dangers but I believe that his heart is in the right place and I look to him (not that I ever can see it) for much credit to himself and a little to me.."

[537] *Hull Packet*, 16 April 1880.

[538] Despite his afflictions Aubrey led an adventurous life. He was the inspiration for the character Sandy Arbuthnot in his friend John Buchan's novel *Greenmantle*. Aubrey died a few months after Lordy in 1923.

[539] Carnarvon refuted this claim publically and sent letters to editors of newspapers saying that his tenants were free to vote any way they wished.

[540] See *Pall Mall Gazette* of 8 June 1880.

[541] Aubrey Nigel Henry Molyneux Herbert was baptised at Highclere Church, with godparents named as the Earl's friend Sir Robert Phillimore, Elsie's brother Mr H.C. Howard, MP, and Lady Winifred. See *Bristol Mercury*, 19 May 1880.

[542] A letter dated 6 May 1880 is in the Carnarvon Papers, Add 61076, from Elsie to Sir William Heathcote and describes the trip to Wildbad; they were still there in July 1880.

[543] Sir James Paget (1814–1899), surgeon and pathologist. In 1881 he had a large consulting practice for society figures. He gave his name to a number of medical conditions of the bone and tumours including breast cancer.

[544] See Carnarvon Papers, diaries 1880, Add 60915, entry for 26 July 1880.

[545] See Carnarvon Papers, diaries 1880, Add 60915, entry for 3 August 1880.

[546] Ibid.

[547] See Carnarvon Papers, diaries 1880, Add 60915, entry for 4 August 1880.

[548] Robert William Frederick Harrison (1858–1945). Later a noted member of the Royal Society of London.

[549] Francis Parkman (1823–1893). Carnarvon recorded in his diary that he was "a good specimen of the literary and cultivated American". See Add 60915: entry for 28 August 1880.

[550] See Carnarvon Papers, diaries 1880, Add 60915, entry for 6 September 1880.

[551] See Morning Post, 28 July and York Herald, 1 August 1885.

[552] Dr Michael Comport Grabham, MD, LLd, FRCP (1840–1935), was a graduate of King's College, and St Thomas's Hospital, London. He took up residence in Madeira in the 1860s where he offered intensive medical and health treatments for local exiles and visitors from the UK. Several society figures feature among Grabham's cases. He also had experience of obstetrics. Obituary in *British Medical Journal*, 2 February 1935.

[553] See Carnarvon Papers, diaries 1880, Add 60915, entry for 22 September 1880.
[554] See Carnarvon Papers, diaries 1880, Add 60915, entry for 16 October 1880.
[555] The most moving of the farewells was between the 4th Earl and Sir Robert Phillimore. They met at Reading station on 25 October. Phillimore said: "If we never meet again I hope you will think of me." Carnarvon promised he would, but thought that his "own duration of days may not be so long...". See Diary, Add 60915, for 25 October 1880.
[556] After seeing the Earl off, Alan Herbert fell gravely ill at Highclere, suffering from jaundice and suspected typhoid fever. The episode is told in detail by Lady Winifred Burghclere in *Alan Herbert 1836–1907: Letters and Memories by His Niece, Lady Burghclere*. The author has seen a copy of this in the British Library, Shelf Mark 010855 b22.
[557] *Hampshire Advertiser*, 27 October 1880. The outward journey was via Gravesend, the Channel, Dartmouth (where the Portsmouths saw them), and then out on the Atlantic.
[558] The inference is that Kent had been exiled on Madeira, where he continued (even into ripe old age) to teach students. He was not the only Carnarvon servant living in Madeira. In the Earl's diary (British Library Add 60916) for 24 March 1881 there is a reference to a Mrs King:

> We paid a farewell visit to old Mrs King... Her memory is excellent and her recollection of both sides of the family very interesting. She remembers my great grandmother, the first Lady Carnarvon, my grandfather and his two daughters Lady Emily and Lady Harriet and she was at Camden House with my dear Mother... She also recollects well Lord H Howard... Longs... She was at Petworth when my grandmother was there...

[559] The 4th Earl went to Madeira with £400 in gold, in half-sovereigns (drawn from Drummonds Bank) to cover the family's expenses (including Grabham's fees). He gave this to the British Consul for safe-keeping. See Carnarvon Papers, diaries 1880, Add 60915, entry for 4 November 1880.
[560] See Carnarvon Papers, diaries 1880, Add 60915, entry for 4 November.
[561] See Carnarvon Papers, diaries 1880, Add 60915, entry for 5–7 November 1880.
[562] See Carnarvon Papers, diaries, Add 60915, entry for 10 November 1880.
[563] See Carnarvon Papers, diaries, Add 60915, entry for 27 November 1880.
[564] During the Carnarvon's five months on Madeira John Kent's loyalty was unflinching. The Earl visited Kent's own home near Funchal and pronounced it a place he would not have chosen for himself, but Kent seemed happy with it.
[565] *British Mail*, 1 January 1881.
[566] See Carnarvon Papers, diaries 1880, Add 60915, entry for 21 December 1880
[567] See Carnarvon Papers, diaries 1881, Add 60916, entry for 28 January 1881.
[568] See Carnarvon Papers, Add 60860. A letter dated 21 January 1881 from 5 Arlington Street, London, from Sir Robert Phillimore to Carnarvon refers to Porchester having a prosperous voyage (back from Maderia) and tells Carnarvon that Phillimore has "sent to Bruton Street a note asking Lordy to dine and sleep when he arrives, as I suppose he will not go down to Eton on the night of his arrival".
[569] Carnarvon Papers, Add 60860.
[570] Contracting muscles by applying an electric current.
[571] See Carnarvon Papers, diaries 1881, Add 60916, entries for 13–14 March 1881.

[572] James Anthony Froude (1818–1894), historian. As colonial secretary, Carnarvon had sent Froude to South Africa as his eyes and ears to promote federalism (along Canada lines). The mission failed.
[573] See Carnarvon Papers, diaries 1881, Add 60916, entries 9–10 February and 13–14 April, 1881.
[574] See Carnarvon Papers, diaries 1881, Add 60916, entry for 2 April 1881.
[575] Ibid.
[576] *North Devon Journal*, 31 March 1881.
[577] See Carnarvon Papers, diaries 1881, Add 60916, entry for 26 April 1881.
NB: Disraeli died on 19 April 1881, aged 77. On 26 April, he was buried at St Michael and All Angels Churchyard, Hughenden, Buckinghamshire. Alfred de Rothschild (with whom Disraeli had taken rooms at 1 Seamore Place, Mayfair) was involved in the funeral arrangements.
[578] Pages in the diary (Add 60916) are cut out for 3–10 May and 13–14 May. The Earl records on 11 May 1881, "I live in a strange gloom and dread…"
[579] A Georgian house reputedly designed by Repton in the late eighteenth century. Once owned by the Long family, collaterals of the Howards.
[580] See Carnarvon Papers, diaries 1881, Add 60916, entry for 15 May 1881.
[581] Carnarvon Papers, diaries 1881, Add 60916, entry for 31 May 1881.
[582] See Carnarvon Papers, diaries 1881, Add 60916, entry for 3 June 1881.
[583] See Carnarvon Papers, diaries 1881, Add 60916, entry for 4 June 1881:

> Lady Chesterfield, poor thing is less strong than she was though in many ways a wonderful person. Her lovely desolate life is very pathetic, but she seems to be really glad to see me here again and almost turns at times with a strange kind of affection to me. She is very solitary – for not one of her old friends is I think much comfort to her.

[584] *Morning Post*, 15 June 1881.
[585] *The Morning Post* of 1 July 1881 has a list of guests at this last dinner at Bruton Street. The list in the *Hampshire Advertiser* of 2 July includes Lady Gwendolen Herbert and Viscount Lymington (the Portsmouth heir).
[586] *Morning Post*, 14 July 1881.
[587] *Hampshire Telegraph*, 20 July 1881.
[588] The *Morning Post* of 22 July 1881 has a long list of attendees.
[589] *York Herald*, 2 August 1881.
[590] *Morning Post*, 22–23 August 1881, and *Hampshire Advertiser*, 24 August 1881.
[591] *Morning Post*, 8 September 1881.
[592] Burghclere, Lady Winifred, *Biographical Sketch of Lord Carnarvon* (1923).
[593] *Hampshire Advertiser*, 10 September 1881.
[594] See "Truth", Volume 10, 1881; also *Morning Post*, 16 September 1881.
[595] *Morning Post*, 24 September 1881.
[596] On 6 October 1881, wedding of Robert Mowbray Howard (1854–1928) to Louisa G. Sneyd (who died in 1910). Robert later remarried.
[597] *Hampshire Advertiser*, 19 October 1881.
[598] *Morning Post*, 13 December, 1881.
[599] *Hampshire Advertiser*, 4 January 1882.
[600] See Carnarvon Papers, diaries 1882, Add 60918, entry for 9 January 1882.

[601] From Tony Leadbetter recollections of what Almina told him – from Lordy's own lips.
[602] See Carnarvon Papers, diaries 1882, Add 60918, entry for 13 January 1882.
[603] From Tony Leadbetter's recollections of what Almina told him.
[604] *Morning Post*, 26 January 1882.
[605] Burghclere, Lady Winifred, *Biographical Sketch of Lord Carnarvon* (1923).
[606] *Morning Post*, 2 March 1882.
[607] *Hampshire Advertiser*, 8 March, 1882.
[608] *Hampshire Advertiser*, 29 March 1882.
[609] *Hampshire Advertiser*, 21 March 1885.
[610] *The Morning Post*, 18 April 1867.
[611] Elsie's brother, the diplomat Esme Howard, records in his memoirs *Theatre of Life*: "I never remember [Lord Carnarvon shooting or hunting] after his marriage with my sister, in 1878."
[612] See Carnarvon Papers, diaries 1882, Add 60918, entry for 8 April 1882.
[613] See Carnarvon Papers, diaries 1882, Add 60918, entries for 9–11 April 1882.
[614] *The Standard*, 22 April 1882. Carnarvon records the child's grave health in his diary for 11 April 1882.
[615] *Hampshire Advertiser*, 7 June 1882.
[616] *Morning Post*, 10 May 1882.
[617] *Reading Mercury*, 3 June 1882.
[618] William Henry Fremantle (1831–1916), Anglican priest, devotee of Dr Jowett at Balliol College, Oxford. Later dean of Ripon. The Earl records of Fremantle: "we were boys and great friends at Eton. He is still very much the same I think as I remember him though the attraction which I remember feeling has considerably diminished..." (see Diary Add 60919 entry for 14 June 1882)
[619] See Carnarvon Papers, diaries 1882, Add 60919, entries for 17 and 24 June, 23 and 31 July 1882. Gwendolen was living with a companion at Faircroft, Putney. The health of his cousin Robert Herbert was also playing on the Earl's mind.
[620] An architect named Beeston (possibly Frederick Robert Beeston, sometime a partner in firm of Beeston Son & Brereton) was commissioned to carry out the renovations at Porto Fino. See Carnarvon diaries for 1882–3.
[621] See Carnarvon Papers, diaries 1882, Add 60919, entry for 16 August 1882.
[622] The Australian property and land transactions were handed by W.W. Billyard, who headed a firm of lawyers in Sydney. The Earl's cousin, Robert Herbert, was a key player with him regarding purchase of vast stretches of land at Eucla in Western Australia. That land was later sold at some considerable loss to the family. See *The Political Diaries of the Fourth Earl of Carnarvon*, edited by Peter Gordon, p. 70.
[623] *The Standard*, 25 August 1882.
[624] Carnarvon Papers, diaries 1882, Add 60919, entry for 3 September 1882.
[625] Carnarvon Papers, diaries 1882, Add 60919, entry for 8 September 1882.
[626] Carnarvon Papers, diaries 1882, Add 60919, entry for 27 October 1882.
[627] Ibid.
[628] Carnarvon Papers, diaries 1882, Add 60919, entry for 15 December 1882 reads: "Beech and Lymington and Jekyll were here for a day's shooting with Porchey. I could not go out myself, for though better I was not yet really well."
[629] *Hampshire Advertiser*, 25 October 1882.
[630] *Hampshire Advertiser*, 30 December 1882.
[631] Carnarvon Papers, diaries 1882, Add 60919, entry for 27 December 1882.

[632] Mervyn Herbert (1882–1929). Diplomat and sportsman.
[633] Carnarvon Papers, diaries 1882, Add 60919, entry for 29 December 1882.
[634] Ibid.
[635] Carnarvon Papers, diaries 1882, Add 60919, entry for 27 December 1882.
[636] Carnarvon Papers, diaries 1883, Add 60920, entry for 16 January 1883.
[637] Carnarvon Papers, diaries 1883, Add 60920, entry for 17 January 1883.
[638] *The Hampshire Telegraph* of 3 February gives full details. The child's godparents were Lady Abercromby and Lady Rachel Howard and Mr Howard of Greystoke and Sir Robert Herbert.
[639] Carnarvon Papers, diaries 1883, Add 60920, entry for 4 February 1883.
[640] *Pall Mall Gazette*, 7 February 1883.
[641] *Morning Post*, 5 April 1883.
[642] Lordy is cited in Harrison, Hilda Mary. *Voyager in time and space : the life of John Couch Adams: Cambridge astronomer*. The Book Guild (1994) as being present when Adams visited Eggesford, Chulmleigh in March 1883 " in connection with the Newton Papers". Lordy's uncle Isaac Newton Wallop donated the scientific papers of his family collateral, the scientist Isaac Newton, to Cambridge University. These papers were eventually sold by the Wallop family by Sotheby's in 1936.
[643] Carnarvon Papers, diaries 1883, Add 60920, entry for 4 April 1883.
[644] Carnarvon Papers, diaries 1883, Add 60920, entry for 6 April 1883.
[645] Carnarvon Papers, diaries 1883, Add 60921, entry for 7 August 1883.
[646] Carnarvon Papers, diaries 1884. Add 60922, entry for 2 January 1884.
[647] Burghclere, Lady Winifred, *Biographical Sketch of Lord Carnarvon* (1923).
[648] Mandell Creighton (1843–1901), a high churchman, historian and scholar (he was known to Lord Carnarvon, who was high steward of Oxford University, from 1859, at Oxford as a well-placed don and rising star. Creighton ultimately became the Bishop of London.
[649] See Carnarvon Papers, diaries 1883, Add 60920, entry for 27 June 1883:

> Mr Creighton called. I talked over Porchey's future with him and finally it was decided that P should pay a visit in the beginning of August and then after the holidays go to him for good... I liked him – he has a pleasant smile and is clearly a man of ability...

[650] Louise Creighton (1850–1936). Of French descent and a notable woman's rights organiser.
[651] This curious array of boys assembled together included notables (before they had made a name for themselves) like Sir Edward Grey (famed foreign secretary in World War I) and Sir George Sitwell (the father the famous literary Sitwells).
[652] See Lord Carmichael of Skirling, *Mary Helen Elizabeth [Nugent] Baroness Carmichael*, Hodder and Stoughton (1929).
[653] See James Thayne Covert's *A Victorian Marriage: Mandell and Louise Creighton* (2001) and also by Covert, *Memoir of a Victorian Woman: Reflections of Louise Creighton 1850–1936*, John Wiley & Sons (1994).
[654] Newton Wallop (1856–1917). From 1891 the 6th Earl of Portsmouth. Married a rich heiress; they had no children. When Newton Wallop was at Eton College he was one of the boys under the influence of the Oscar Browning. He later went to Balliol College, Oxford.

[655] Stopford Wentworth William Brooke was born in Kensington, London, 1859. Stopford died in 1938 aged seventy-eight. He married Helen T. Ellis in 1903, who died in 1928.
[656] See Covert, *Memoir of a Victorian Woman: Reflections of Louise Creighton 1850–1936*, John Wiley & Sons (1994).
[657] Obituary on the 4th Earl in *Saturday Review of Politics, Literature, Science and Art*, volume 70 (1890).
[658] *Hampshire Advertiser*, 25 August and 8 September 1883.
[659] John Douglas Sutherland Campbell (1845–1914); from 1900, 9th Duke of Argyll. An old friend of Lord Carnarvon and visitor to Highclere in 1869. Best known by his courtesy title of the Marquis of Lorne, he married Queen Victoria's daughter, Louise.
[660] *The Star*, 8 September 1883.
[661] *Leeds Mercury*, 10 September 1883.
[662] *The Star*, 20 September 1883.
[663] *Charity Records and Philanthropic News*, 1 May 1884.
[664] See Hardinge, *The Life of Henry-Howard-Molyneux Herbert* (1925).
[665] Carnarvon Papers, diaries 1883, Add 60921, entry for 10 October 1883.
[666] Carnarvon Papers, diaries 1883, Add 60921, entry for 13 October 1883.
[667] Ibid.
[668] Benjamin Jowett (1811–1893), scholar and master of Balliol College, Oxford.
[669] *Nottinghamshire Gazette*, 19 October 1883.
[670] *Derby Mercury*, 24 October 1883.
[671] Carnarvon Papers, diaries 1883, Add 60921, entry for 2 November 1883.
[672] Carnarvon Papers, correspondence file, Add 61059.
[673] Ibid.
[674] Carnarvon Papers, diaries 1883, Add 60921, entry for 21 December 1883.
[675] Victor Duleep Singh was determined to encourage Lordy to pursue an army quest. This was Victor's plan to ensure their pairing continued after Eton. Victor went to Sandhurst in 1887, so it seems unlikely the steer was coming from Victor in 1884.
[676] See *The Times*, 18 January 1891: Creighton "defly rolling cigarettes which he shared with his pupils…".
[677] *Morning Post*, 31 December 1883. Among the members of the Howard family present were Lady Mabel Howard, Lady Rachel Howard, Mr Stafford Howard, Miss Maud Howard and Mr Mowbray Howard.
[678] *Preston Guardian*, 22 December 1883, and *Derby Mercury*, 2 January 1884.
[679] See Hardinge, *The Life of Henry-Howard-Molyneux Herbert* (1925).
[680] In Andrew Lang's *Life, Letters and Diaries of Sir Stafford Northcote First Earl of Iddesleigh* (1891) he records "in 1872 Sir Stafford went on a yachting cruise with Lord Carnarvon among the Scilly Islands".
[681] *North Devon Journal*, 24 January 1884.
[682] See Carnarvon Papers, British Library, Add 61051, folios 151–2. A letter from Auberon to Lord Carnarvon dated January 1884 from Ashley Arnewood Farm, Lymington.
[683] Joseph Garnet, Viscount Wolseley (1833–1913). Notable British soldier reaching rank of field marshall.
[684] Wolseley's papers in Hove Central Library reveal that the Earl wrote to him on 16 January 1884 after calling Wolseley (W.) in London on 13 January. The summary of the letter (from the Hove catalogue GB 0510 Wolseley) reads: "Has decided to send Porchester to Capt. James for instruction, the deciding factor being that Lord Bath had

a son there. Later will talk over with W. the important question of cavalry or inf. And the regt [for P]." "Capt. James" was Captain Walter James who ran a famous crammer called Jimmies on the Cromwell Road, London. One of its most famous recruits was Winston Churchill.

[685] Adverts in newspapers were headed with "Capt James, late RE and Col. Lynch… 19 Lexham gardens W. Prepare for all Civil Service and army Examinations, aided by a staff of 43 tutors".

[686] See Yardley, Michael, *Sandhurst*, Virgin Books (1987). This explains that where boys required help with army entrance "deficiencies could be made up for at specialist crammers", the most famous of which was Jimmies. Winston Churchill was one recruit at Jimmies – and as this was c. 1884 his time may have coincided with Lordy's.

[687] Carnarvon Papers, diaries 1884, Add 60922, entry for 14 January 1884.

[688] Jane Emma Hannah Macan, Dowager Lady Antrim (1825-1892), widow of the 5th Earl of Antrim. Elsie's brother Henry (Harry) Howard, MP of Greystoke, was married to Lady Mabel McDonnell, one of Lady Antrim's daughters. The arrangement for Lordy's accommodation was therefore almost certainly Elsie's idea.

[689] Carnarvon Papers, diaries 1884, Add 60922, entry for 15 January 1884.

[690] Capt. Hon. Sir Schomberg Kerr McDonnell (1861–1915). Between 1888 and 1902 he was private secretary to Lord Salisbury. McDonnell was killed in action in the Great War.

[691] Carnarvon Papers, diaries 1884, Add 60922, entry for 20 January 1884.

[692] *Hampshire Advertiser*, 1 March 1884.

[693] *Hampshire Advertiser*, 7 May, has a list of attendees. See also *Derby Mercury*, 7 May 1884. *Hampshire Advertiser*, 21 May, also has another list of guests.

[694] *Hampshire Advertiser*, 21 June 1884, has a list of guests for one of these events.

[695] Quote is by Thomas Edward Kebbel (1827–1917), author and journalist, from his book *Lord Beaconsfield and Other Tory memories*, M. Kennerley (1907).

[696] Cited by Adonis, Andrew, *Making Aristocracy Work*, Clarenden Press (1993).

[697] *Centaur*, 26 January 1884.

[698] *North Devon Journal*, 10 April 1884.

[699] Carnarvon Papers: British Library, diaries 1884, Add 60922, entry for 13 April 1884.

[700] Almost certainly this refers to Rev. Dr N.G. Wilkins, MA LLD, English chaplin to the English and American expats of Hanover, Germany.

[701] *Derby Mercury*, 25 June 1884.

[702] Quote is by Thomas Edward Kebbel (1827–1917), author and journalist, from his book *Lord Beaconsfield and Other Tory memories*, M. Kennerley (1907).

[703] An advertisement appears in *The Times* of 21 December 1883: "HANOVER: Rev N G Wilkins, MA, LLD, Cambridge, English Chaplin at Hanover prepares for resident and a few non resident pupils for military and other Examinations…"

[704] Carnarvon Papers: British Library, diaries 1884, Add 60922, entry for 25 June 1884.

[705] The entry in Carnarvon's diaries merits inclusion. Add 60923, 5 July 1884:

In the evening Lorne and Princess Louise dined with us, a small party. She was agreeable and I think things were placid. I was very glad to have some opportunity of... and not forgetful of all their kindnesses last year in Quebec.

Lorne was a homosexual (See A.L. Rowse's *Homosexuals in History*). He was for many years a member of the Royal Household at Windsor. He largely lived apart from his wife, Louise, although she nursed him in his last illness. Lorne died in 1914; Louise survived until 1939.

[706] *Hampshire Advertiser*, 9 July 1884.

[707] See Taylor, Richard H. (ed.), *The Personal Notebooks of Thomas Hardy*, The Macmillan Press (1978). The entries for 16 May and 14 June 1887 indicate Hardy attended parties "at Lady Caernarvon's"... [hic].

[708] See Carnarvon Papers, British Library, diaries 1884, Add 60923, entry for 14 July 1884.

[709] See Carnarvon Papers, British Library, diaries 1884, Add 60923, entry for 25 July 1884.

[710] See Carnarvon Papers, British Library, diaries 1884, Add 60923, entry for 30 August 1884.

[711] See Carnarvon Papers, British Library, diaries 1884, Add 60923, entry for 11 October 1884.

[712] *Hampshire Advertiser*, 11 October 1884.

[713] See Carnarvon Papers, British Library, diaries 1884, Add 60923, entry for 5 November 1884.

[714] See *Morning Post*, 12 December 1884.

[715] See Carnarvon Papers, British Library, diaries 1884, Add 60923, entries for 8 and 10 December 1884.

[716] See Carnarvon Papers, British Library, diaries 1884, Add 60923, entry for 17 December 1884.

[717] See Carnarvon Papers, British Library, diaries 1884, Add 60923, entry for 23 December 1884.

[718] Ibid.

[719] See Carnarvon Papers, British Library, diaries 1884, Add 60923, entry for 31 December 1884.

[720] Ibid.

[721] See Carnarvon Papers, British Library, diaries 1885 Add 60924.

[722] *Morning Post*, 6 and 12 January 1885.

[723] *The Times* of 15 January 1887 includes "Prince Victor Duleep Singh" as an old boy at Jimmies in an advert listing the institution's successes for 1885–86.

[724] Carnarvon Papers, British Library, diaries 1885, Add 60924. The diary entry for 2 June records:

> Poor Mr Kent is in a sad way. It is a most mournful and even terrible spectacle of the results of a man doing to and for himself alone – divorcing himself from all distinct religion and keeping himself under no moral discipline or control. It is most painful.

[725] *Hampshire Advertiser*, 8 April 1885.

[726] Lady Eveline Camilla Wallop (1858–1894) was a gifted writer of short stories and Suffolk folk-lore. She married a much older man, Sir William Brampton Gurdon KCMG CB MP, of Assington Hall, Suffolk, 1840–1910, who was for many years private secretary to Gladstone. In Camilla's obituary in *The Ipswich Journal* of 15 September 1894, Lady Gurdon is described as being "of a retiring disposition", but she well supported her husband as an MP, to the extent of appearing on platforms with him, to some controversy that ladies should take an interest in politics. She died of "an internal disorder" and left no children. Esme Howard (Elsie Carnarvon's brother) refers to her

being a source of wisdom in his biography *Theatre of Life 1863–1905*, Hodder and Stoughton (1935).

[727] Lady Camilla is on the list of attendees for a dinner and receptions held by Elsie at Portman Square on Saturday 25 April 1885. See *The Standard*, 27 April 1885.

[728] Lord Carnarvon became lord lieutenant of Ireland under Lord Salisbury's term as prime minister, and after the fall of Gladstone's government. On 17 June 1885 Carnarvon was pressed by Lord Salisbury to accept the post and he agreed to take it on as a special mission. The Earl was sworn in as lord lieutenant at Dublin Castle. A brief summary of this period is as follows:
7 July 1885: Carnarvon is sworn in at Dublin Castle and makes state entry into Dublin
16 July 1885: Serious banking failure in Ireland
1 Aug 1885: Visits Lord Salisbury (prime minister) at Hatfield
4 Aug 1885: Returns to Ireland
7 Aug 1885: Knights the Mayor of Derry
17–22 August 1885: Visits the West Coast Galway, Aran, Chifden, Westport, Achill Island, Sligo and Bellmullet
4 Sept 1885: Opens Marine Promenade at Bray
7–17 Sept 1885: Tour of the North, Belfast, Belvoir Park, Antrim, Londonderry, Barnscroft, Lurgan, Lisburn and Armagh Cathedral
23 November 1885: Visits Windsor
25 November 1885: Returns to Dublin
16 January 1886: In Edinburgh
23 January 1886: State dinner, Dublin
25 January 1886: Levee at Dublin
26 January 1886: Drawing room
28 January 1886: Departure from Ireland

[729] *The Era*, 1 August 1885.

[730] See Carnarvon Papers, British Library, Diaries 1885, Add 60924. When asked by Salisbury to serve in Ireland (with a seat in Cabinet) Carnarvon consulted his old friend Lord Sandon " Sandon was really kindness itself. If he had ben my brother he could not have done or said more..", Robert Herbert and James McCraw (the latter was financial adviser, secretary and land agent to the 4th and 5th Earls.)

[731] Murders in Phoenix Park, Dublin, on 6 May 1882 of Lord Frederick Cavendish (chief secretary for Ireland) and Thomas Henry Burke (a senior Irish civil servant).

[732] *Derby Mercury*, 29 July 1885.

[733] Tributes spoke of the Countess as Lady Anne Forester and referred to her sister Isabella, who were in their youth great beauties of the age. Lady Chesterfield was "a dazzling brunette", whilst her sister – who married Hon. George Anson – was "as fair and sunny as the dawn of an Eastern day". (See *Otago Witness*, 17 October 1885, reproduced tribute from *The Daily Telegraph*).

[734] See *The Life & Letters of Lady Dorothy Nevill* (edited by her son, Ralph Nevill).

[735] *Reading Mercury*, 10 October 1885.

[736] It was stated that Lordy's underlying wealth was from 13,000 acres in Nottinghamshire, worth £24,000 a year in rents. His father's interests in Somersetshire and Hampshire comprised 22,000 acres but with a rent roll of only £13,000.

[737] Announced in the *Derby Mercury* and Nottinghamshire papers.

[738] See *Hampshire Advertiser*, 26 September 1885. By early 1887 Lady Winifred had moved into Bretby Park with her first husband, Alfred Byng.

[739] In a letter to Elsie dated 30 July 1885 in the Carnarvon Papers, Add 61059: " talked a deal to P and have done a fair amount of business……."

[740] *The Observer*, 4 October 1885, declares: "The Earl and Countess of Carnarvon, accompanied by Lord Porchester (Lordy), and attended by Captain Byng, aide-de-camp, left Dublin yesterday morning, via Kingstown and Holyhead, for London."

[741] Esme Howard (1863–1939), notable diplomat and British ambassador to USA (1924–1930), Baron Howard of Penrith (1930).

[742] Howard, Lord [of Penrith], *Theatre of Life*, Hodder and Stoughton, London (1935).

[743] See *The Times*, 30 November 1885. The two new knights of St Patrick invested by Lord Carnarvon were Viscount Wolseley and the Marquis of Headfort; the latter was a Irish landowner.

[744] It is recorded that the Earl also received deputations from his bedside One report remarks "During the period which he [Lord Carnarvon] was Viceroy of Ireland he astonished the officials by the informality of his modes of governing. one occasion be was suffering from a severe cold that necessitated his remaining in bed for several days. Instead of postponing business possible to deferred, Lord Carnarvon insisted on receiving deputations, and giving his awards in his bedroom." See *Cheltenham Looker* of 3 January 1903.

[745] Carnarvon Diaries, Add 60926, Entry for 1 January 1886.

[746] *Western Mail*, 11 January 1886.

[747] Robert Herbert was hard hit financially by land deals in Australia. These purchases (where he had also advised Carnarvon to invest) , had initially been seen as lucrative, but soon backfired. Carnarvon was able to absorb the losses, Herbert was not. A letter in the Carnarvon Papers, Add 61059 dated 3 Feb 1886 from 3 Grosvenor Place, London relating to Robert Herbert from W H SMITH says:

" Mr Woods tells me that he was with Mr Herbert for two hours on Sunday trying to induce him to face his position and place himself in the hands of an honest man if business to get his affairs arranged but he failed.. Mr Woods has not given up all hope and promises to communicate with me if there is any hope of effecting an arrangement to please the poor man in a position of peace ……"

[748] Charles Stewart Parnell (1846–1891), MP, Irish nationalist leader and land reformer.

[749] Even although Lord Salisbury returned to power later in 1886, Carnarvon was never offered another post in Cabinet. This was seen by Carnarvon as a snub, and reflected Salisbury's own dislike of any attempt to hasten devolution in Ireland. Just before Carnarvon died (in 1890) he and Salisbury, the two great old friends, were eventually reconciled.

[750] *Morning Post*, 29 January 1886.

[751] Ibid.

[752] Carnarvon Diaries, Add 60926, entry for 4 February 1886.

[753] *Hampshire Advertiser*, 14 February 1886.

[754] Carnarvon Diaries, Add 60926, entry for 27 February 1886.

[755] Carnarvon Diaries, Add 60926, entry for 11 April 1886.

[756] *The Morning Post*, 1 May 1886.

A moving letter dated 9 April 1886 is in The Carnarvon Papers , British Library Add 61050 from Eveline to his brother, Lord Carnarvon.

" My dearest C : I have come up here to find dear Dolly very changed – very weak – Diarrhea has come on not severely but enough to add to the symptoms that the end cannot be far off. Auberon very broken – Dolly very calm and facing death as I think she always faced life very patiently and resignedly. She says she has a deep peace and speaks with a complete composure. I think she hardly knows how near the close may be and still imagines a few weeks with A and her children around her in some house near London. I do not think she will leave this unless a great improvement came which is most improbable. I think days may number it but A poor fellow is very anxious not to be in the way. And to get to get the boys to satisfy this lingering fancy of a little home life like the fact he must misdoubt its [probability…possibilities] . It would be all too sad were it not that she is full of peace and he poor dear bearing up with a touching gentleness and resignation but sometimes it seems too much for him."

[757] *Morning Post*, 3 May 1886.
[758] See *Hampshire Advertiser*, 15 May 1886.
[759] See *Morning Post*, 7 June 1886. The exhibition was at South Kensington. At the Highclere event (for which special trains were laid on between Newbury and Paddington) there were representatives from Australia, Trinidad, India, Hong Kong and Natal. A list of visitors is included with a detailed report of the day's activities and speeches in the *Morning Post* of 27 June 1886.
[760] See *Waikato Times*, 19 June 1886. This gathering included Sir Samuel Davenport of South Australia. One colonial (on an earlier visit to Highclere by the South African Boer leader, Paul Kruger) was said to have remarked that "the beer in Highclere cellars was a credit to the house". See *Feilding Star*, 20 March 1907, paraphrasing from T.H.S. Escott's book *Society in the Country House*.
[761] http://en.wikipedia.org/wiki/Primrose_League
[762] *Morning Post*, 16 June 1886.
[763] *Jackson's Oxford Journal*, 17 July 1886.
[764] See Carnarvon Papers, British Library, Add 61059, for two letters dated 6 May and 10 December 1886 from Rev. V.H. Stanton (Lordy's tutor at Cambridge) to Lord Carnarvon.
[765] Rev. Vincent Henry Stanton (1846–1924), sometime senior dean at Trinity College, Cambridge, and later Ely professor of divinity.
[766] See Burghclere, Lady Winifred, *Biographical Sketch of Lord Carnarvon* (1923). Before he was aged ten Lordy was given lessons in French and German, which stood him in good stead for later life; especially French, which was widely spoken in Egypt. He was also forced to study Latin and Greek.
[767] See Carnarvon Papers, British Library Add 61059 (letter of 8 May 1886 from Lordy's tutor to his father:

> He [Lordy] is continuing to attend Mr Prior's lectures in Mathematics and I have arranged also that he should read privately in Mathematics with Mr Gerdard a former scholar of the College very competent to preparation for the Previous Exams and also a nice man and anxious to exercise a good influence where he can.

[768] See Carnarvon Papers, British Library, Add 61059. Lordy's tutor had concerns about the switch from College rooms to lodging (with a man called Alexander) and set this out in a letter to Lord Carnarvon on 10 December 1886.
[769] *Reading Mercury*, 31 July 1886.

[770] See Carnarvon Papers, British Library, Add 61059, letter from Rev. Stanton to Lord Carnarvon, dated 8 May 1886.
[771] Ibid.
[772] *The New York tribune* of 19 August, 1886 under "Home News" lists with " Prominent Arrivals": " Albemarle Hotel: Lord Porchester, of England."
[773] *Freeman's Journal*, 19 August 1886.
[774] *Hampshire Advertiser*, 9 October 1886.
[775] *The Observer*, 14 November 1886.
[776] According to Ralph Nevill in *The Gay Victorians,* Brighton was a centre for " especially high gambling" during race weeks " where several well-known characters afforded racing men every opportunity to lose."
[777] *Hampshire Advertiser*, 17 November and 4 December 1886.
[778] See *The Times*, 21 December 1886.
[779] Burghclere, Lady Winifred, *Biographical Sketch of Lord Carnarvon* (1923).
[780] Letter of 10 December 1886 from V H Stanton to Lord Carnarvon in Carnarvon Papers, Add 61059 : "My Lord : Lord Porchester has been to me to say that he wishes to give up his rooms in College and to go into lodgings. No doubt he could in various ways be made more comfortable in lodgings. I have sent for the man, Alexander by name, who keeps the house which he most wishes to lodge to hear from him what vacant rooms he has and to have a general talk with him. I have known him before. He has been a butler in gentleman's families and therefore knows how to make his house comfortable. I think too that he wishes to take care that all the regulations for licenced lodgings shall be kept and that he is a thoroughly respectable man. The men at present lodging in the house and continuing next term are so far as I know them reasonably quiet and sensible, I see no reason for refusing leave to Lord Porchester to move from College to these lodgings. But I thought it right as I told Lord Porchester, that you should know before the matter is settled. As it is too late now, probably, to let the rooms in College to another occupant for next term , Lord Porchester may have to pay for them. This will not sound much as doubt. I shall of course try to assign them to someone else if he gives them up. I have nothing special to report with regard to his general conduct, he assures me he has been working well and going regularly to his private tutor as I have not heard from the latter I have no doubt this is so. I was obliged to excuse him from College lectures, owing to his suffering for some time in the mornings from bleeding in the mouth. I hope he will get through the exam which he is now going through. Believe me my Lord… V H Stanton "
[781] Ibid.
[782] Sir William Jenner (1815–1898), society doctor and consultant, expert on fevers. In 1887 Jenner was also president of the Royal College of Physicians.
[783] See Carnarvon Papers, British Library, Add 60928, entry for 2 January 1887.
[784] Ibid, entry for 9 January 1887.
[785] Names listed included some of Porchester's Eton contemporaries: Hon. John Walter Edward Montague-Douglas-Scott, son of Lord and Lady Montagu of Beaulieu, June 10; Lord Porchester, son of the Earl of Carnarvon, June 26; Hon. Francis Denzil Edward Baring, son of Lord and Lady Ashburton, July 20.
[786] The novelist, Thomas Hardy records of seeing Winifred on a visit by him to Highclere just before the wedding. " Lady Winifred told me she was going to be married on the 10th January at the Savoy Chapel, with other details of the wedding. She was serious and thoughtful – I fancied a little careworn. She said she was not going to let her honeymoon interfere with her reading and means to carry a parcel of books.

Spoke to her betrothed as " He" – as a workman speaks of his employer – never mentioning his name." During this visit Hardy was working on the final stages of his book The Woodlanders. He asked Elsie Carnarvon about the trees at Highclere, suggesting it might have been an influence to the text. Winifred appealed to Hardy to call his heroine of the book, "Winifred". He records " wants me to call my heroine "Winifred" but it is too late to alter it. [One of the main characters of the book is Grace Melbury.] see Thomas Hardy: Wordsworth Editions (2007).

[787] A noticeable feature of attendees was a link back to the Howard clan of Winifred's late grandmother Henrietta. There was a later marital link between the Howards and Byngs. Henrietta's sister, Isabella Katherine Howard (1806–1891), the Dowager Countess of Suffolk, was also present as a guest.

[788] *Liverpool Mercury*, 11 January 1887.

[789] *Hampshire Advertiser*, 29 January 1887.

[790] Ibid.

[791] George Stevens Byng, 2nd Earl of Strafford (1806–1886). Alfred Byng was from his father's second marriage.

[792] *Morning Post*, 11 January 1887.

[793] *Hampshire Advertiser*, Saturday 22 January 1887, records: "HIGHCLERE: Viscount Porchester, who has quite recovered from his recent indisposition, left Portman-square, London, on Thursday, to join the Earl and Countess of Carnarvon and family at Porto Fino, near Genoa."

[794] See Carnarvon Papers, British Library, Add 60928, entry for 26 January 1887.

[795] Burghclere, Lady Winifred, *Biographical Sketch of Lord Carnarvon* (1923).

[796] See Carnarvon Papers, British Library, Add 60928, entry for 3 April 1887.

[797] See Carnarvon Papers, British Library, Add 60928. The entry for 5 April 1887 includes the following: "I had a conversation today with P on 1. Chesterfield annuity 2. his… election legally – whether under will or settlement – when he comes of age."

[798] *Nottinghamshire Guardian*, 15 April 1887.

[799] See Carnarvon Papers, British Library, Add 60928, entry for 22 April 1887.

[800] *Daily News*, 28 April 1887.

[801] Sir William Jenner (1815–1898), fever/typhus specialist, had lifelong associations with University College, London, and University College Hospital. Attended Queen Victoria and her family at Windsor and Balmoral.

[802] See Carnarvon Papers, British Library, Add 60928. The entry for 19 May 1887 records: "An unsatisfactory letter from Mr Stanton as to P. It is clear that the best thing is for him to leave Cambridge at once."

[803] See Carnarvon Papers, Add 61059.

[804] *Hampshire Advertiser* of 4 June 1887 records: "Highclere: The Earl and Countess of Carnarvon have arrived at their Hampshire seat, Highclere Castle, from town. Lord Porchester, who comes of age on the 26th instant has gone to Paris."

[805] Victor was presented at the Queen's levee held at St James's Palace on Saturday 20 May 1887. He was presented by Lord Henniker, his father the Maharaja's close friend (at least from the early days: Lord Henniker was John Major Henniker-Major, 1842–1902, 5th Baron.)

[806] *Pall Mall Gazette*, 14 June 1887.

[807] See *Belfast-Newsletter*, 14 June 1887, for full coverage of the speeches at the gathering.

[808] *Freeman's Journal and Daily Commercial Advertiser*, 15 June 1887.

[809] The Queen blamed Carnarvon personally for major blunders in colonial policy over Russia (Twitters was less anti-Russian than any of his Cabinet colleagues) and South Africa (where to great opposition he favoured a federation of states, a carve-up which had worked in Canada).

[810] See Barnes, Leonard, *Empire or Democracy: A Study of the Colonial Question*, Victor Gollancz, London (1939).

[811] Cited by Peter Gordon (ed.) in *The Political Diaries of the Fourth Earl of Carnarvon, 1857–1890*, Cambridge University Press (2009).

[812] *Hampshire Advertiser*, 15 June 1887.

[813] *Berrow's Worcester Journal*, 18 June 1887.

[814] See *Derby Mercury*, 13 July 1887, quoting from *The World*. This report also cites another reason for the default, that Lord Carnarvon "has been much out of health for more than a year past".

[815] Carnarvon Papers, British Library, Add 60928, entry for 26 June 1887.

[816] Carnarvon Papers, British Library, Add 60929, entry for 19 August 1887.

[817] Carnarvon Papers, British Library, Add 60929, entry for 25 August 1887.

[818] Majority celebrations were a good way for a titled family to reach out to those dependent on an estate. It was a useful opportunity for the family, estate workers and tenants to show their loyalty to the heir in waiting, as well as their attachment to the existing lord etc. The Hon. John Scott Douglas Montagu (later Lord Montagu of Beaulieu) enjoyed a large gathering at Palace House, Beaulieu, in August, laid on by his parents (see *Hampshire Advertiser*, 13 August 1887: "Great Festivities at Beaulieu"). Hon. Francis Baring (later 5th Lord Ashburton) had his grand celebrations in September 1887 (see *Hampshire Advertiser*, 17 September 1887, "Festivities at Lord Ashburton's Mansion near Alresford").

[819] *The Reading Mercury* of 18 June, 1887 reports:

> COMING OF AGE OF LORD PORCHESTER: It will be seen in the report of the Town Council meeting that an address was unanimously adopted for presentation to Lord Porchester on attaining his majority. It was also the intention of the Mayor and the inhabitants of Newbury, to give a public dinner to Lord Carnarvon and Lord Porchester on the occasion, but while personally appreciating the kind feeling which promoted the proposal, it is thought desirable, on account of the Queen's Jubilee and other circumstances to postpone the gathering for the present.

[820] *The Reading Mercury*, 23 July 1887.

[821] *Hampshire Advertiser*, 30 July 1887.

[822] See Campbell, Christy. *The Maharajah's Box,* Harper Collins (2001). Victor was enrolled at Sandhurst. He was heavily indebted to bookmakers, Messrs Goodson, Fry and O'Connor. 1887 marked a low point in his financial affairs, which ran into the years that followed. A Chapter in Campbell's book entitled " Victor" focuses on the clamour by Courtiers behind the scene to paper over the cracks in the money matters of the debt ridden Prince. This included him being sent into "snowbound obscurity" to Canada, where he continued to cause concern over his personal actions and behaviour.

[823] *Hampshire Advertiser*, 20 July 1887.

[824] The *Pall Mall Gazette* of 27 August 1887 records:

> Lord Carnarvon's Departure for the Colonies: Yesterday the Earl and Countess of Carnarvon embarked on board the *Rimutaka*, for the Cape, en route to Australia. On

reaching the Cape the Earl will take a prominent part in one or two public ceremonials, and after a short stay there Lord and Lady Carnarvon will resume their voyage. They intend spending some months in the Australian Colonies. Lord Carnarvon, whose health has been indifferent since last winter, hopes to derive benefit from the sea voyage.

[825] Lordy was elected to the Royal Yacht Club, Cowes, on 13 August 1887.

[826] Aphrodite: The Greek Goddess of beauty and love – perhaps some subliminal reference by Lordy to his mother, Lady Evelyn Stanhope.

[827] The Maharani Bamba Duleep Singh, born Bamba Muller, died in London on 18 September 1887.

[828] Among his companions were Hon. A Macdonald/McDonnell and Mr Sutherland (see *Hampshire Advertiser*, 1 October 1887). Curiously there is no mention of Victor, but see Epilogue.

[829] Described in *The Life and Secrets of Almina Carnarvon*, Chapter 2.

[830] See Burghclere, Lady Winifred, *Biographical Sketch of Lord Carnarvon* (1923).

[831] This event is covered by Captain (later Rear Admiral Sir William Robert) Kennedy (1838-1916) in his book *Hurrah for the life of a Sailor!* Kessington Publishing. (2008). And features in Winifred Burghclere's sketch of Lordy from 1923.

In the Carnarvon Papers, British Library, Add 61059, folios 123-5, is a long letter from Kennedy to Lord Carnarvon dated 21 August 1888 from Rio de Janeiro, saying that this is" to give you the latest accounts of your son that I am writing. I left him and Sutherland quite well abroad the Aphrodite….. a week ago,,, They are I believe going to follow ..route to England… I believe Lord Porchester is a very poor correspondent he gave me to understand as much and he read me an extract from a letter he had received from you relative to his trip up the Panama [Canal] which is the immediate cause of my writing to you now." There then follows a description of several parts of Aphrodite's voyage.

[832] *Baily's Magazine of Sports and Pastimes*, Volume 71, from the year 1899.

[833] Ibid.

[834] Sir Andrew Clark (1826–1893), physician and pathologist, authority on constipation.

[835] Sir James Sawyer (1844–1919), Birmingham-based physician and leading medical author.

[836] *Western Times*, 17 November 1887.

[837] *The Derby Mercury* of 16 November 1887 has this further detail:

> [Byng] died at Bretby Hall, Burton on Trent after a brief illness.. He was taken ill and Dr Hooper of Burton [on Trent] was called in, and seeing the serious nature of the malady summoned Sir Andrew Clark and Sir James Sawyer. So alarming were the symptoms... that it was found necessary for Captain Byng to undergo an operation…

[838] *Reading Mercury*, 12 November 1887.

[839] James McCraw – Agent and financial adviser to the Carnarvon Estates. In a long letter dated 29 December 1887 , to her father (Carnarvon Papers Add 61059, folios 115-6) Winifred writes "Mr McCraw has been kindness itself…I am afraid I have given him a great deal of trouble , poor man but he is so very nice about it all..".

[840] *Reading Mercury*, 19 November 1887. Winifred writes in a letter to her father (Carnarvon Papers, Add 61059) "Porchey telegraphed from Barbados and I suppose we can expect a letter from him shortly…"

[841] See Carnarvon Papers, British Library, Add 60929. Lord Carnarvon had a run-in with Byng earlier in the year. In a curious entry in the diary for 12 August 1887, he records: "A vicious scene with Byng – which I only note because it may hopefully work… remembering the date. It has not altogether surprised me..." Byng's faults are unspecified; the issue may have been matrimonial or financial. The Earl's scathing comment begs the question of whether the marriage between Byng and Winifred had been consummated. In the Earl's diaries for 1890, on the prospect of Winifred remarrying, he describes her as "still only a child", strongly suggesting the latter conclusion was the cause of the "vicious scene with Byng".

[842] *Aberdeen Weekly Journal*, 16 February 1888.

[843] *Standard*, 6 April 1888.

[844] *Pall Mall Gazette*, 2 May 1888.

[845] *Jackson's Oxford Journal*, 5 May 1888.

[846] *Western Daily Press*, 26 April 1888.

[847] See Atkinson, C.W., *History of the Royal Dragoons 1661–1934*, Regiment (1934).

[848] According to the *Reading Mercury* of Saturday 24 December 1887, on the previous Saturday Prince Victor Dhuleep Singh (with Prince Adolphus of Teck, and Prince Christian Victor, the Duc d'Orleans) was among those cadets inspected at Royal Military College, Sandhurst, by the Duke of Cambridge. See also *Essex Standard*, 7 April 1888.

[849] Lordy was on the First Committee of the International Club "founded for the association of gentlemen and no question of nationality or politics shall ever affect the qualification for membership". See *The Times*, 6 March 1888.

[850] Ralph Nevill reveals some insight into West End life in London in several of his books. See *Light come. Light go* Macmillan & Co (1909) and *Mayfair and Montmarte* Methuen (1921).

[851] According to Christy Campbell in *The Maharajah's Box*, Harper Collins (2001) on Victor's mother's death in 1887 " £500 a year had been held back to pay [Victor's] debts for champagne and delicacies.".

[852] Play began at nine o'clock in the evening in several gambling clubs and went on all night. See Ralph Nevill's *The Gay Victorians*. E Nash and Grayson. (1930).

[853] See *Bury and Norwich Post*, 2 April 1889.

[854] Ibid.

[855] *Birmingham Daily Post*, 2 June 1888.

[856] *Penny Illustrated Paper*, 2 June 1888.

[857] *Morning Post*, 9 June 1888.

[858] *Morning Post*, 22 June 1888.

[859] *Bury and Norwich Post*, 17 July 1888.

[860] *York Herald*, 27 August 1888.

[861] *Morning Post*, 3 September 1888.

[862] See Carnarvon Papers, British Library, Add 60931. September – November 1888.

[863] *Worcestershire Chronicle*, 1 September 1888.

[864] See Burghclere, Lady Winifred, *Biographical Sketch of Lord Carnarvon* (1923).

[865] *Morning Post*, 1 November 1888.

[866] Carnarvon Papers, British Library, Add 60931, entry for 12 November 1888.

[867] Carnarvon Papers, British Library, Add 60931, entry for 17 November 1888.

[868] *Morning Post*, 4 and 7 December 1888.
[869] Carnarvon Papers, British Library, Add 60931, entry for 28 December 1888.
[870] Carnarvon Papers, British Library, Add 60931, entry for 30 December 1888.
[871] Almost certainly Dr Carl Breiting, an English-speaking physician attending on foreigners in Genoa and district. He was also in residence at the Protestant Hospital, Salita, San Rocchino. His name features in guides and travel books on northern Italy and the Riviera.
[872] Carnarvon Papers, British Library, Add 60932, entry for 3 January 1889.
[873] Carnarvon Papers. British Library, Add 60932 Entry for 5 January 1889. At this time the Earl had problems with his Australian investments involving the land agent Billyard. He writes on 5 January 1889: "I have a troublesome business on my hands with the Billyard case. I hope I am acting rightly but it is hard to tell at this distance from the place in question."
[874] Carnarvon Papers, British Library, Add 60932, entry for 21 January 1889.
[875] Carnarvon Papers, British Library, Add 60932, entry for 4 February 1889.
[876] *The Hampshire Advertiser*, 27 February 1889.
[877] Edward Charles Robson Roose (1848–1905), society doctor. He was the author of a book *Gout, and its Relations to Diseases of the Liver and Kidneys*, London, Lewis (1885).
[878] Carnarvon Papers, British Library, Add 60932. Based on an unreadable entry for 19 February 1889: "talk with Roose… His opinion is that organically there is complete… everywhere..." [The entry stops there].
[879] See the Carnarvon Papers, British Library, Add 61060, folios 229–30. This correspondence suggests that the Earl was not finally told that he had "a disease to which there could be only one ending…." until a few weeks before he died and the doctor who broke this news, E.B. Turner, recorded "no case have I ever been more impressed by the calm, steadfast courage, the resolution and perfect faith...".
[880] *Morning Post*, 27 February 1889.
[881] Carnarvon Papers, British Library, Add 60932, entry for 9 March 1889.
[882] Carnarvon Papers, British Library, Add 60932, entry for 5 April 1889. The Earl saw Salisbury on 9 April and they exchange a few words only about Portal's death. The Earl and Elsie went down to Highclere (from London) for the funeral.
[883] Dr Joseph Mortimer Granville (1833–1900), inventor and doctor. He invented the electric vibrator to relieve muscle aches and pains.
[884] Carnarvon Papers. British Library, Add 60932, entry for 14 April 1889.
[885] Carnarvon Papers. British Library, Add 60932, entry for 5 May 1889.
[886] Carnarvon Papers. British Library, Add 60932.
[887] Carnarvon Papers, British Library, Add 60932, entry for 19–20 May 1889.
[888] *Gout in its Clinical Aspects* by J. Mortimer Granville, MD, London, J and A Churchill (1885).
[889] J. Mortimer Granville was a regular writer in *The Times*. One article of 17 April 1884, "Hope as a Remedy Against Disease", was a much talked about premise.
[890] *Morning Post*, 31 May 1889. The *Hampshire Advertiser* announced: "1 June Highclere: Lord Porchester has returned to England after an absence of several months in Africa."
[891] *Bury and Norwich Post*, 7 May 1889.
[892] See *Essex Standard*, 28 September 1889. Victor's father, the Maharaja, had remarried and was living in Paris in disgrace following his earlier acts against the Crown, including an attempt to return to India to incite the people in his native Punjab

against the British. The Maharaja had been turned back in Aden and fled to Russia seeking help, which was snubbed. During that time Victor's mother had returned to England, with Victor and his other siblings. Victor (who was shielded by his mother on many counts, and kept away from his father) took no part in his father's anti-British campaign.

[893] See Cross, William, *The Life and Secrets of Almina Carnarvon*, Chapter 2.

[894] Ibid.

[895] Tony Leadbetter, Almina's godson, remarked on this. It's based on what Almina saw for herself in later years when Carnarvon suffered similar attacks when he "lost consciousness and was delirious". Almina had no doubts that this was "the pox".

[896] Quinsy is a complication of tonsillitis. It is a collection of pus that develops between the back of one of your tonsils and the wall of your throat. This is known as an abscess. An abscess can develop when an infection spreads from a swollen tonsil to the surrounding area.

[897] Almina told Tony Leadbetter that Carnarvon's health was frequently affected by an infection he contracted whilst abroad, before they were married. She was in no doubt it was a venereal disease.

[898] Edward Charles Robson Roose (1848–1905), society doctor of considerable note. Famously treated Lord Randolph Churchill for syphilis. He was also concurrently treating the Earl.

[899] See Lee, Celia and John, *The Churchills: A Family Portrait*, Palgrave MacMillan (2010).

[900] See Carnarvon Papers, British Library, Add 60933, entry for 16 July 1889.

[901] Lordy suffered several life-threatening recurrences arising from his Egyptian malady, notably in 1892 and 1918. The fuller details are given in *The Life and Secrets of Almina Carnarvon*. Reference is also made in *Secrets* to Lordy having skin distortions of the face, also consistent with venereal disease.

[902] See Carnarvon Papers, British Library, Add 60933, entry for 29 July 1889.

[903] Ibid.

[904] See Carnarvon Papers, British Library, Add 60933, entry for 29 September and 3 October 1889.

[905] *Hampshire Advertiser*, 19 October 1889.

[906] *Hampshire Advertiser*, 5 October, and *Derby Mercury*, 23 October 1889.

[907] John Walter Edward Scott-Montagu of Beaulieu (1866–1929), 2nd Marquess from 1906. Motor car pioneer.

[908] *Preston Chronicle*, 16 November 1889.

[909] See Carnarvon Papers, British Library, Add 60933, entry for 6 November 1889.

[910] An example of this in the leader to the *Pall Mall Gazette* of 30 June 1890, following the 4th Earl's death. In 1889 the Earl had made mention to the paper's " special correspondent" who was *en route* to South Africa that Lordy was staying out there. Carnarvon offered to write to Lordy to have him make himself available to the journalist. On arrival by the latter at his hotel a card was brought to him bearing Lordy's name. Victor and Lordy duly put themselves at the man's disposal arranging (through Lordy's father's influence as ex-Colonial Secretary) for attendance at an important Government House reception, involving the installation of the Governor and High Commissioner, Sir Henry Loch. The motive in part by Lord Carnarvon was to find out from the journalist (or return to Britain) how he found his son in circumstances, company, health and behaviour.

[911] See Carnarvon Papers, British Library, Add 60933, entry for 30 December 1889.

[912] *South Australian Register* of 25 February 1890 reports from Port Darwin that the (ship) *Chingtu* sailed for Hong Kong on Sunday 23 February and "Lord Porchester is a through passenger to China".
[913] *The Argus* (Melbourne) records on 4 February 1890 that "Lord Porchester and valet were travelling overland to Sydney passing through Albury...".
[914] See *Hampshire Advertiser*, 1 February and 15 March 1890.
[915] John Adrian Louis Hope (1860–1908), later Marquess of Linlithgow and from 1900 the first governor general of the whole of Australia. His wife was Hersey Alice Evelighde-Moleyns, daughter of the 4th Baron Ventry.
[916] *Australian Town and Country Journal*, 15 February 1890.
[917] Sydney Burdekin (1839–1899), pastoralist, landlord and politician.
[918] *The Australian Town and Country Journal* reported: "Lordy was entertained at luncheon in Sydney's Town Hall by the Mayor, on February 6. Among those present on that occasion were Sir John Robertson, Messrs. Halliday, R.D. White, and Walker... and several prominent citizens."
[919] See Cross, William, *The Life and Secrets of Almina Carnarvon* (2011).
[920] See Carnarvon Papers, British Library, Add 60934, entry for 7 February 1890.
[921] Herbert Colstoun Gardner, 1846–1921, a Cambridge graduate, actor and playwright, MP for the Saffron Walden Division of Essex, sometime Cabinet minister, later became 1st Lord Burghclere.
[922] Carnarvon Papers, British Library, Add 60934, diary entry for 31 January 1890. A Dr Graville was treating him.
[923] Carnarvon Papers, British Library, Add 60934, diary entry for 1 January 1890.
[924] Edward Beadon Turner, physician and surgeon, died 1931, aged 76. His obituary is in *The Times* of 1 July 1931.
[925] There is a letter from Turner to Elsie Carnarvon in the Carnarvon Papers, British Library, Add 61060, folios 229–30.
[926] The Earl did not know of the romance between Lady Winifred and Gardner. He records in his dairy for 7 February 1890 (British Library ref: Add 60934)

> This evening after dinner, received letter from Winifred and one from Herbert Gardner telling us they were engaged and entreating my consent. Elsie had in some measure forecast it with her usual quickness and instinct. To me it came as perfectly unexpected news. We decided to postpone our departure for Italy for a short time and I set in motion all the means... to obtain some more knowledge of him. It may mean, as I hope and trust it does, her happiness and I am quite sure that it is of great importance for her to marry – for she is still really a child and her present position is a difficult one.

[927] Carnarvon Papers, British Library, Add 60934, diary entry for 4 March 1890.
[928] 5 March 1890: Left England for Port Fino; 21 April 1890: Returns to England via Milan, Wiesbaden, Cologne, Brussels and Dover; 28 April 1890: Arrives in England (Dover).
[929] Carnarvon Papers, British Library, Add 60934, diary entry for 8 March 1890.
[930] Carnarvon Papers, British Library, Add 60934, diary entry for 21 April 1890.
[931] *The Times* of 15 May 1890 reports: "Lord Porchester, eldest son of Lord Carnarvon is expected to return to England today."

[932] The *Morning Post* of 9 April 1824 records Lord Porchester (late 3rd Earl) was presented by his father, the 2nd Earl of Carnarvon. The 3rd Earl's son was barely nineteen in 1849 when he inherited the title.

[933] *Hampshire Advertiser*, 18 June 1890. The 4th Earl final illness (and in great pain) predated this event, with newspaper bulletins about his " neuralgic gout" appearing from early June 1890 onwards.

[934] The last bulletin posted by Lord Carnarvon's doctor, E M Turner, FRCS, was at noon on 28 June 1890 " Lord Carnarvon is free from pain, but sinking". He died at 5.30 that evening. Turner later wrote to Elsie (in 1921, when she was finalising the Earl's biography) "For himself he was content to leave all things in the hands of his God – His pluck at all times, and his quiet patient endurance of sickness and suffering during many weary days might well have been an example and lesson to mankind. – no murmers – no complaints…" [See Carnarvon Papers, Add 61059.]

[935] Victor had only just escaped at bankruptcy order being made against him, reported in *The Times* of 21 June 1890.

[936] *Essex Standard*, 19 July 1890.

[937] From the *Nottingham Evening Post*, 4 July 1890:

> The lady members of the family rode in carriages, but the great majority of the mourners and friends proceeded on foot. Among those present were the widowed Countess of Carnarvon, Lord Porchester (now Earl of Carnarvon), Lady Gwendolen Herbert, the late earl's sister; Lady Margaret Herbert and Lady Victoria Herbert daughters; the Hon. Aubrey Herbert and the Hon. Mervyn Herbert, the earl's youthful sons; Mr. Herbert Gardner, M.P., son-in-law; the Earl and Countess of Portsmouth, Lord and Lady Lymington, Lady Mabel Howard, Mrs. Howard, Miss Howard, the Hon. Alan Herbert, of Paris, brother to the late earl; Mr. Stafford Howard, Mr. H. Howard, Mr. Mowbray Howard, Mr. William Herbert, Mr. Alan Herbert, Mrs. Jeune, Sir Brampton and Lady C. Gurdon, the Hon. G. B. Wallop, the Hon. F. Wallop, General Lord Wolseley, the Duke of Norfolk, General Sir Redvers Buller, the Earl of Bradford, the Earl of Chesterfield, the Earl of Suffolk, Lord Newport, Lord Moreton and Lord Knutsford.

[938] *Pall Mall Gazette* and *Morning Post*, 4 July 1890.

[939] *The Star*, 4 September 1890.

[940] Victor had been involved on his father's behalf with making apology to Queen Victoria for acts of disloyalty to the Crown. It had been widely reported in the Press that correspondence had passed between the secretary of state for India and the Maharajah with the latter expressing regret for past conduct. The Queen acknowledged the apology.

[941] *Essex Standard*, 13 September 1890. The Derby Telegraph of 10 September adds " Lord Carnarvon has been staying at Dulverton during the last week at the Carnarvon Arms Hotel, where Prince Victor Dhuleep Singh is his guest, and they have been shooting partridges every day."

[942] *The Standard*, 12 September 1890.

[943] Raymond George Portal, MA, 1827–1889. A high-ranking Freemason with the 4th Earl of Carnarvon. Portal was appointed to Burghclere in 1871.

[944] *The Observer* of 21 September 1890 says " Lord Carnarvon has left England for the Continent ."

[945] *Hampshire Advertiser*, 15 October 1890. *The Observer* of 19 October 1890 indicates that Lordy was at Greystoke staying with Elsie's family. Once the reading of the will was over he was planning to go to Bretby and then Highclere to hold shooting parties.

[946] Summary of the WILL OF THE LATE LORD CARNARVON. "Probate of the will (dated 14th June, 1884, with codicils made 14th June, 1884. 2nd December, 1886, 19th October, 1889, 7th February, 1890, and 5th June, 1890, of the late Right Honourable Henry Howard Molyneux, fourth Earl of Carnarvon, Constable of Carnarvon Castle, D.C.L., of Highclere, Hants, who died on June 28 last, aged 59 years, at his house Portman-square; and was Under-secretary for the Colonies in 1858-9, Colonial Secretary in 1866, and from 1874 to 1878 Lord Lieutenant of Ireland, from 1885 to 1887, Grand Master of Freemasons, President of the Society of Antiquaries, and High Steward of the University of Oxford, has been granted to the executors, the Right Hon. Henry John, Earl of Ducie; Sir Robert George Wyndham Molyneux Herbert, KCB, of the Colonial Office, Whitehall ; and Mr. Edward Stafford Howard, of Thornbury Castle| Gloucester, by whom the value of the testator's personal estate has been sworn £313,259 -0s-9d. was the testator's desire that his funeral might be simple, and he desired to express the opinion that the provision which he had made for his eldest son, in addition to his interest under other settlements, will, with reasonable care and prudence, fully and completely maintain the earldom and the position attaching to it. He devises all his real estate in the counties of Southampton, Somerset, Devon, Middlesex, Wilts, and Berks, and elsewhere in England (not otherwise disposed of by him) to the use of every son of his in order of birth for life, with remainder to his son's first and other sons successively in the order of their seniority in tail male, and his copyhold and leasehold estate England, including his leasehold in Portman-square, are to be held to the same uses. Lord Carnarvon bequeaths the machinery, implements, stores, and live and dead stock, at the Bretby Collieries Farm, Derby, and the stock on the Collieries Farm, to his own son, Lord Porchester and he leaves the property lately acquired for him in George Street, Sydney in trust, to accumulate the income thereof, until Lord Porchester is 35 years of age. and then pay the income to him for life, and subject to his life interest to hold the trust estate in trust for his children. The diamonds left to Lord Carnarvon by his aunt, Lady Harriette Stapleton, and the plate and pictures at Highclere, are to devolve as heirlooms. He bequeaths to Lady Carnarvon £2,000, certain furniture, his books, letters, and manuscripts (with respect which she knows his intentions), and the income for life of his real and personal estate in Sydney and elsewhere in New South Wales, and in Toronto and elsewhere in Canada. The manors and manor house of Kneeton, Hucknall, and Bridgeford in the counties of Notts and Derby, comprised in Lady Carnarvon's marriage settlements, are left to her use for life, in satisfaction of her jointure, with remainder to the testator's son Aubrey, his first and other sons, and with remainder the testator's son Mervyn. The New South Wales real and personal estate is also settled subject to Lady Carnarvon's life interest, favour of the testator's son Aubrey, with remainder to his son Mervyn, and the estate in Canada is settled in favour of his' son Mervyn, with remainder to his son Aubrey. There are legacies of £1,000 each to Lord Carnarvon's sister Lady Portsmouth, to his brothers the Hon. Alan Percy Herbert and the Hon. Auberon Herbert, and to Sir Robert George Wyndham Herbert; £500 to his brother-in-law, Mr. Edward Stafford Howard, £50 to his brother-in-law, Mr. Esme Howard ; £50 to his nephew, the Hon. John Wallop; £25 to his nephew, Lord Lymington; £ 200 to Mr. James Mc Craw ; one year's wages to each servant of five years' service, and other legacies and annuities. The testator bequeaths to his sister, Lady Gwendoline Herbert. £800 a year for her life, and he

devises and bequeaths all his residuary real and personal estate in trust to pay the income thereof to Lady Carnarvon for her life, with power of appointment to her in favour of all or any of his children."

[947] *Essex Standard*, 15 November 1890.

[948] *Daily News*, 20 October 1890.

[949] Houghton and Gun v. Prince Victor Duleep Singh was the action against Victor in Westminster County Court at this time. The debt was for only £16 for stationery owed from 1888. Victor was described in the action as someone:

> who lived in a most sumptuous manner at a fashionable hotel, and that he had several male servants whose maintenance he paid for at the hotel upon a liberal scale. He was a member of two of the leading clubs, kept a private hansom cab, and held the office of lieutenant in the Army. He was looked upon as a leading member in society, and was, by repute, a rich man…(from *The Times*).

[950] See Cross, William, *The Life and Secrets of Almina Carnarvon* (2011).

[951] These letters are among the Carnarvon Papers, British Library Ref 61054. A small sample follows:

> My Dear Else I wish I could write to you as I feel for you or that I could kiss your dear face so that you might know it. I am very sad for you but words will not come and I cannot say it… I wish I might have seen him once again to say goodbye… I always saw in him the type of an honourable, true and high minded gentleman… I hope very soon to be in England. Esme [Howard; Elsie's brother]

> My darling, Darling Elsie: I feel I must write for I could not speak today. One feels that words are poor things to express what one feels. Mabel [Howard relation of Elsie]

> My darling Aunt Elsie I write you one short line to tell you how very, very sorry I feel for you. I cannot tell you how much I have thought about you. Dear, dear Aunt Elsie your very loving [niece] Clair Herbert. [Daughter of Auberon Herbert, the Earl's brother. NB Clair Herbert died on 8 January 1893, aged 18.]

> Dear Lady Carnarvon… no one I'm sure can ever have been brought into contact with Lord Carnarvon without coming to entertain for him a warm feeling of regard of his unwavering kindness to myself, his readiness to advise in difficulties where his tact and experience were of the utmost value… Little did I think at our last interview when he so kindly received me in spite of the pain from which he was even then suffering, that I should never see him again. Believe me. Yours very faithfully George A Macmillan, Solihull Rectory B'ham.

> Madam: You will I hope forgive me for intruding upon your sorrow, with the expression of my grief at the sad death of the Earl of Carnarvon… I had a very

strong regard for him and received from him much kindness. We are so very, very sorry. Yours faithfully Charles Evans, Brizlincock House Burton on Trent.

My Lady… on hearing the melancholy new from Mrs Campbell of his Lordship's death I cannot refrain from expressing on my own behalf and on behalf of my sons James and George – tenants on the estate sincere condolences to you in your great sorrow...

[952] *Hampshire Advertiser*, 15 November 1890. Elsie bought Pixton Park from Lordy in 1901. However, Almina insisted that the bulk of the furniture at Pixton be transferred to Highclere before the sale, which meant Elsie had to replace the entire contents of the house, to much greater expense than she wished.

[953] Ibid.

[954] This annual shooting party (and its associated house party) each November attracted the major "guns" of the era and many members of the gentry. In December 1895 the Carnarvon cohorts at Highclere were chosen by Bertie, the Prince of Wales (later King Edward VII) to shoot and stay over. See Chapter 3 of *The Life and Secrets of Almina Carnarvon*.

[955] Described in *The Life and Secrets of Almina Carnarvon*, Chapter 2. Lordy spent the winter of 1891/2 in Egypt. He returned to England in March 1892. See *The Observer* 3 April 1892. A serious (near-fatal) attack of ill health followed. See *Secrets*.

[956] Lordy was at Monte Carlo- with Victor- in January 1891 shooting pigeons in the Monaco Grand Prix, an international competition. (See *The Observer* 25 January 1891). He also spent time in Italy in the Spring through to Easter of 1891. He was in Naples on 22 March 1891 (see *The Observer* of that date and 5 April 1891). There was also a trip in the summer of 1893 to Sweden. (See *The Observer* 20 August 1893). Winifred sums up this widespread " love of travel" in her biographical sketch of 1923. "He would suddenly dash off to Paris or Constantinople, Sweden, Italy or Berlin for long or short periods, returning home equally unexpectedly, having collected pictures and books and any number of acquaintances and friends..,"

[957] Elsie arranged for Lordy's younger sisters ladies Margaret and Victoria to visit Highclere to see their brother. Winifred (Lordy's heir) occasionally acted on her brother's behalf as hostess at Highclere.

[958] *The Hampshire Advertiser* of 18 November 1891 lists that period's attendees at Highclere including the Duke and Duchess of Wellington, Earl and Countess de Grey, Lady Dorothy Nevill, Lord and Lady Carrington, Sir William and Lady Harcourt, Herbert Gardner MP and Lordy's sister Winifred (who acted as hostess), with Sir Philip Currie, Sir Donald Mackenzie Wallace, Mr F.W. Myers and Mr Smalley.

[959] *The World*, 11 November 1893, reported: "Lord Carnarvon has lent Bretby, his place in Derbyshire... to his friend Prince Victor Dhuleep Singh, the eldest son of the late Maharajah, who has gone to stay there for a few weeks." This had been preceded with a waltz around Europe with Victor.

[960] A legal action against Victor in 1896 by a notorious moneylender named Alfred Moore, reported in *The Times* of 11 June 1896, refers to the period September 1892 to August 1894 when Victor "was always away, yachting or shooting".

[961] Richard Henry Fry, died 1902, aged 66. Victor was obliged to raise money from pawnbrokers on the Singh family jewels to cover his borrowings and betting losses. See Singh v. Attenborough, reported in *The Times* of 14 July 1896. For more information on this era of gentleman's gaming and the bookmaker Richard (Dicky) Fry, see also

Huggins, Mike and Mangan, J.A. *Disreputable Pleasures: Less Virtuous Victorians at Play*, Routledge (2004).

[962] Remarks made by Tony Leadbetter in interviews 2009–11. In the years prior to the Oscar Wilde scandals of the mid 1890s there was considerable fallout from a number of other major Society horrors, including the 1888 Whitechapel murders of prostitutes, and the Cleveland Street case (from 1889): a male brothel, also in Whitechapel, for homosexual aristocrats. It is a curious aside, that at this time among those who (unsuccessfully) protested in favour of the laws on homosexual conduct being repealed was the Irish playwright George Bernard Shaw. Editors snubbed Shaw's representations. Shaw turned to engage in further appeal with the "champions of individual rights". This included Lordy's uncle Auberon Herbert whose philosophy of "Anarchy" dictated the abolition of all laws.

[963] Victor was at Monte Carlo with Lordy in February 1894 pigeon shooting (they also enjoyed competing in this sport at the Gun Club, Notting Hill (see *The Observer* 4 June 1893). They were together at Aix-les-Baines in September 1894, shooting at Highclere in October 1894 and Pixton Park in December 1894. (See *Nottingham Evening Post*, 18 September and 19 October 1894 and *Bath Chronicle* 13 December 1894.)

[964] *York Herald* of 1 August 1894 records:

> Although promoted to a troop in the Royal Dragoons, Prince Victor Dhuleep Singh does not intend to resume military duty for the present. The Prince lately accepted a commission in the Suffolk Hussars (the Duke of York's Yeomanry Regiment), and has shown his interest in his work by going to the Aldershot Cavalry School and obtaining a certificate of proficiency after a mouth's course under the energetic Commandant, Captain Brown, 14th Hussars.

[965] Victor married Lady Anne Coventry (1874-1956) (daughter of the 9th Earl of Coventry), in 1898. Anne was the sister of Lord Deerhurst (the Coventry heir). She knew Lordy and Victor from time spent in their company when her brother was at Cambridge at the same time as Lordy and Victor. Deerhurst opposed his sister's marriage to Victor, see *The Life and Secrets of Almina Carnarvon*.

[966] Victor Duleep Singh was declared bankrupt in London on 4 September 1902. This was "attributed to Stock Market speculation and gambling". See *The Times* 4-5 September 1902]. He later pursued a claim (on behalf of his deceased father, whose estate was also bankrupt) for sums owed (estimated at £600,000) by the British and Indian governments. This action (handled by his trustee in bankruptcy, in 1904–6 Salaman v. Secretary of State for India, in Council) failed.

[967] *The Observer* of 21 October 1894 records "*A marriage will shortly take place between the Earl of Carnarvon and Almina, only daughter of the late Frederick Wombwell and niece of Sir George Wombwell, bart.*" Lordy was quick to point out that the marriage "*will not take place until May or June*" [1895] as he planned " a yachting cruise [with Victor] at the end of 1894. (See *Nottingham Evening Post*, 31 October 1894).

[968] Marie Felicie Boyer (c1846-1913), from 1868 Marie Wombwell. Almina's mother lived for many years at 20, Bruton Street, Berkeley Square. In the 1911 Census (the first Census return to be signed by householders) Marie (Wombwell) is described as a Widow aged 59 (this is understated) born Paris, France, living on private means, with 8 servants and 16 rooms.

[969] *Hampshire Advertiser*, 23 January 1895.

[970] Full details of what was termed "the half-million pound fund" are in *The Life and Secrets of Almina Carnarvon*.
[971] Ibid.
[972] See Ellis, Roger, *Who's Who in Victorian Britain*, Shepheard-Williams (1997), p. 344.
[973] Malmesbury was a Cabinet minister at the same time at the 4th Earl of Carnarvon. See Malmesbury, Earl of (James Howard Harris Malmesbury (1897–1889) *Memoirs of an Ex Minister: An Autobiography*, Longmans, Green and Co (1885).
[974] According to Rev E. Hugh Rycroft, Rector of Highclere, in a paper on Highclere in the *Winchester Diocesan Chronicle*, Vol xii, No 8 (August 1904):

> Highclere was an Episcopal residence; the old church was part of, or else close to the residence, and in an ancient yew "Grampus" took up his abode, from which he emerged at odd intervals to annoy the peaceful inhabitants. However, by the aid of bell, hook, and candle, he was despatched to the Red Sea for a thousand years. The date of his banishment is unknown, so that each morning we wake up fancying that the day of his return may have come at last.

There is no explanation as to whom or what "Grampus" was supposed to be. [Quoted in Notes and Queries, 6 November 1926.]
[975] Lang, Andrew, *Life, Letters and Diaries of Sir Stafford Northcote, First Earl of Iddesleigh*, William Blackwood (1891).
[976] One newspaper report from 1893 declares " Highclere possesses its authenticated ghost, which required no fewer than twelve assembled divines to effectively lay, [exorcise], just a century since." See *Nottinghamshire Guardian*, 18 November 1893.
[977] Attributed to F.W.H Myers in *On Recognised Apparitions Occurring More Than a Year After Death*. The reference to Lady Carnarvon is to Lady Elizabeth Alicia Maria Wyndham, the first Countess, who died in 1826.
[978] See *Memoir of Alan Herbert* by Lady Burghclere. British Library: Ref 010855 b22. This incident had a shattering effect on Lordy. Several Carnarvon ghost stories have been published – In his amusing *Ghost Book: A Collection of True Stories* Lord Halifax repeats Lordy's sister Winifred Burghclere's tale of the appearance of deceased Henrietta Howard (the Third Carnarvon Countess) during the illness of her son Alan Herbert at Highclere. Alan was suffering from typhoid fever. His sister Lady Gwendolen and some other nursing ladies cared for him. After many days of anxiety Winifred says:

> the day came when he [Alan] could dismiss his nurses. Before they departed, however, the housekeeper suggested that she should show them over the Castle. One room after another was visited. At last they reached Lady Carnarvon's sitting room, and here the nurse came to a pause before a picture of the Dowager Countess exclaiming "Why that is the old lady who came into the doctor's room when he was so ill." Inquiries elicited the explanation that at the most anxious moment, as she was watching by the patient's bedside, she suddenly became aware of an old lady, gazing fondly down on the sick man. The nurse concluded that it was some member of the family with whom she was unacquainted, and thought no more of the incident, except that she remarked that it was from this hour that he began to mend…

[979] The story of Victor seeing the Maharaja's head is to be found in *Lectures on Psychical Research* by C.D. Broad and it is briefly referred to by Peter Bance in his compendium of the entire Duleep Singh Dynasty, *Sovereign, Squire and Rebel: Maharajah Duleep Singh and the Heirs of a Lost Kingdom*, Coronet Books, London (2009).

[980] See Lady Burghclere's biographical sketch of Lordy from 1923.

[981] See *Maureen's Story, A 32-Year Love Affair with Highclere Castle*, ISBN 0-9552004-0-7. Maureen Cummins worked as housekeeper at Highclere for the 6th and 7th Earls of Carnarvon.

[982] *Ermine Tales: More Memoirs of the Earl of Carnarvon*, Weidenfeld and Nicolson, London (1980) is a collection of tall stories, jokes and chuckles.

[983] *Ermine Tales* exploits the 6th Earl's mischief and must be challenged as a serious example. This describes a séance after the end of the Great War, as the 6th Earl had returned from service in Mesopotamia. Howard Carter is mentioned as being present. The latter was not in Britain for *three years* prior to the middle of 1919.

Taking a closer, critical look at the participants of this séance, it's more an entertainment sideshow than a serious enterprise.

A Carnarvon family friend, Lady Helen Cunliffe-Owen, was present. On the last day of 1918 she married the tobacco millionaire (of British American Tobacco fame) Sir Hugo Cunliffe-Owen (thirty years her senior).

Lady Helen was put into a trance by a photographer-medium called Louis Steele (he was actually an electrical engineer in civilian life). An attempt at levitation followed, one that caused the flowers on the table to "rise several feet into the air". Lordy's daughter Evelyn (who was a seventeen-year-old in 1918) apparently spent two weeks in a nursing home recovering from the shock of it all.

Helen Cunliffe Owen had some acting ability. She was an American moll named Helen Mazie Oliver who was known in Chicago cabarets, eventually appearing on Broadway and having minor roles in silent movies. Sir Hugo (who had a huge house at Weir Bank, Bray, Berkshire) picked her up in a bar!

Sadly, Helen died in 1934 after a spell in Alfred House, Almina Carnarvon's nursing home in Portland Place. She left four children behind. Helen had also tried to broker a deal between Almina and Dorothy Dennistoun, to prevent the case of Dennistoun v. Dennistoun going to court in 1925.

T.G.H. James asks in his excellent biography of Howard Carter about [the medium] "Louis John Steele" who in 1920 was doing some kind of work in Portsmouth Dockyard. The source is a letter to Carter addressed as "My Dear Old Carter" in the Metropolitan New York. Steele (possibly a relative of a New Zealand artist of the same name; hence the 6th Earl's use of the word "domiciled", see *Ermine Tales*) was a photographer and old chum of Carnarvon and Carter. He worked as an engineer (with a few patents to his name).

[984] Rowse, A.L., *Homosexuals in History. A Study of Ambivalence in Society, Literature and the Arts*, Dorset Press (1977).

[985] In Lordy's youth one of his mother's admirers was the art critic (and homosexual) Lord Ronald Gower (1845-1916), youngest son of the 2nd Duke of Sutherland, whose mother was a member of the Howard family. He was an occasional visitor at Highclere. He also visited Dr Alan Herbert in Paris " at his rooms in the Rue Chaveau Lagarde" (see Gower's *My reminiscencies*. J Murray (1885). Gower's labyrinth spanned a wide part of the homosexual community. He was a friend of Oscar Wilde and it was said by John Addington Symonds (1840-1893) (who features in Rowse's *Homosexuals in History* and described as " conscious of himself as a same –sex loving man) as " he knows everybody " from cabbies, corporals and carabinieri". Symonds was a regular visitor at Eggesford House where Lordy's aunt Lady Portsmouth gathered a collection of the Victorian literati together including Thomas Hardy, Robert Browning, Henry James and George Eliot. A long letter from the repressed homosexual, American writer, Henry James (1843-1916) (whilst staying at Eggesford) to his father is quoted in McWilliam, Candia. *What To Look for in Winter*. Jonathan Cape (2010). In the late Professor Gordon Haight's biography of George Eliot [Clarenden Press (1968)] he remarks " Lady Portsmouth's house [at Eggesford] was also filled with figures whose sexuality was multi layered including John Addington Symonds".

[986] Sir Robert George Wyndham Herbert (1831–1905). Cousin of 4th Earl of Carnarvon. Premier of Queensland, Australia (1860–1865). Hebert was (from 1871) a permanent under-secretary of state at the Colonial Office in London, a position he held for over 30 years.

[987] Sir John Bramston (1832–1921). Colonial administrator and civil servant at the Colonial Office for over 20 years.

[988] Herbert and Bramston met at Balliol College, Oxford. They shared rooms at university and in London. In 1859 they both went out to Australia together. When Herbert was premier of Queensland, Bramston was his attorney-general. The two of them lived together at a farm-steading called *Herston*, a combination of their names. Herbert never married. He provides insight into the idyllic life they shared in one letter to his sister and explains why he could not consider marriage: "it does not seem to me reasonable to tell a man who is happy and content, to marry a woman who may turn out a great disappointment."

[989] *The Times*, 16 September 1921.

[990] Several of the sons of Lady Eveline Herbert and Isaac Newton Wallop (5th Earl of Portsmouth) sought service in Australia and elsewhere.
http://www.cracroftspeerage.co.uk/online/content/index567.htm

[991] Oscar Browning (1837–1923). A disciple of another Eton master, William Johnson Cory (1823–1982). Both men left Eton under a cloud connected with their close relations with pupils. Browning was dismissed in 1875. His personal papers including letters relating to the Wallop boys are in King College, Cambridge. [Nine letters from the Wallop family to Browning and 29 letters from John Fellowes Wallop (1859–1925, later 7th Earl of Portsmouth) to Browning.]

[992] Field, Osgood Julian: *Uncensored Recollections* (1925) p.247: "When I first knew Lord Porchester as he was then, he was fine handsome youth, but Victor Duleep Singh let him into wild ways."

[993] The author has recorded elsewhere:

> Porchey was awkward, shy and clumsy with women. Victor delighted in leading his weaker, inexperienced, friend astray, indeed even into indulging in "wild ways". The preferred course was for visiting common prostitutes, who were

available (and tolerated) on the Continent and in Egypt, although the host of diseases these women carried put young men in danger of being blighted for life. Whilst at Cambridge, both men formed all male – but more social associations – their contemporaries included the notorious "Prince Eddy", Duke of Clarence and Lord Francis Hope – of the Hope diamond fame – but there is no evidence either Victor or George was deflected into seeking carnal pleasures in the company of these sometimes darker fellows.

http://ladyalminacarnarvon.wordpress.com/2011/10/14/the-friendship-between-prince-victor-duleep-singh-and-the-carnarvons-of-highclere-castle/

[994] "…on taking up yachting he [Lordy] made it a rule that no ladies and no black shoes [since he had established the fashion for wearing brown leather boots/ shoes] were to be allowed on board." See *Huddersfield Chronicle*, 25 October 1894.

[995] See Bance, Peter, *Sovereign, Squire and Rebel: Maharajah Duleep Singh and the Heirs of a Lost Kingdom*, Coronet Books, London (2009).

[996] Leadbetter Collection. Lady Evelyn Leonora Almina Herbert (1901–1980) married (Sir) Brograve Beauchamp (1897–1976).

[997] Lordy was a partner in a photographic firm in Dover Street, London. See also *The Life and Secrets of Almina Carnarvon*. In 1916 he became president of the Camera Club (based at 17 John Street, London) where he "infused still greater keenness into the members" including staging an exhibition of his own work.

[998] See *The Life and Secrets of Almina Carnarvon*.

[999] Tony Leadbetter – Almina's godson – felt there was a strong inference of an affair between Carnarvon and Carter from what Almina told him, but she was coy about spelling it out.

[1000] The most authoritative narrative about the building of Castle Carter, situated " at the entrance to the rocky wadi leading to the Valley of the Kings" which was lived in from 1911 is by T G H James in his book *Howard Carter :The Path to Tutankhamun*. James had research done on the detail relating to the use of Bretby stones/ bricks. See also Fiona Carnarvon's *Carnarvon & Carter*. Highclere Enterprises. NB Carter left the house and its contents to the Metropolitan Museum, New York. It is now a museum. (2007) which also states that Lordy and Carter visited Europe together " in August 1912" visiting " Florence, Paris and Turin." It should be noted that Carnarvon did NOT secure a concession to dig in the Valley of the Kings until 1914.

[1001] See Roberts, Paul William, *River in the Desert*: *A Modern Traveller in Ancient Egypt*, Tauris Parke Paperbacks (2006). Roberts found an old guide in the Valley of the Kings named Khadry who knew Howard Carter. "I urged... him onto Carter's personality: Was the man really celibate… Khadry grinned toothlessly, slapping his knee, then answering in a roundabout fashion that implied both boys and the occasional 'dancing girl' enhanced Carter's domestic life from time to time."

[1002] Source withheld. Please contact the author.

[1003] Mervyn Robert Howard Molyneux Herbert (1882–1929). Private source (e-mail). Please contact the author for background details.

[1004] Walter Bryan Emery (1903–1971). Egyptologist. Worked with Carter at the tomb of Tutankhamun.

[1005] Taylor, G R. *Sex in History*, Thames Hudson, London (1953).

[1006] John Godl in a review of the life and writings of T.E. Lawrence (of Arabia fame), 22 August 2009.

[1007] The rumour of a romance growing between Carter and Lady Evelyn Herbert caused one fall out. Lordy's financial "deal" with *The Times* granting them exclusive rights over the reporting of the tomb and its contents was another. Carter honestly believed that the introduction of large amounts of money to the discovery was fatal to the principles of scientific work. But Lordy (and Almina) had invested large sums over many years. Carter's journal and diaries – at the Griffith Institute, Oxford (now available online) often comprise just a few words or sentiments. The entry for 5 April 1923 is "Poor Ld C died during the early hours of the morning" and 12 April 1923 refer again to "Poor Ld C's remains"; perhaps the use of the word "poor" repeated simply captures Carter's sorrow and even grief.

[1008] One portrait of Carter describes him as a modern-day hermit, set apart from his fellow Egyptologists.

[1009] Robinson, Edward, *Lord Carnarvon*, The Metropolitan Museum of Art Bulletin Vol. 18, No 5 (May 1923).

[1010] *The Reading Mercury* of 16 February 1901 records: "The Earl and Countess of Carnarvon have left England and gone to Paris en route to Cairo where they propose staying for about two months." The trip took in excursions to other parts of the Middle East and Turkey.

[1011] Jeremiah Lynch (1849–1917). Politician, businessman and traveller. Lynch was a Member of the Royal Geographical Society, London.

[1012] In 1890, while in Egypt, Lynch procured a mummy, which he presented to the Bohemian Club (a private gentleman's club, founded in 1872, still in existence today). The female mummy was a member of the regal family from the 24th dynasty and was discovered at Girgeh on the Nile just prior to the arrival there by Mr Lynch with the US Consul-General Schuyler on their way to Thebes. Two other mummies that Lynch brought to USA, those of high priests, found their way into the Golden Gate Park Memorial Museum. But these were all destroyed in the San Francisco fire of April 1906.

Lynch replaced the Bohemian Club's Mummy in 1914 with "The Lady Isis". She was a royal princess, a worshipper of the great goddess Isis, from the palace of a Pasha. Because of the restrictions imposed on exports by the Cairo Museum, Lynch had to obtain permission from Lord Kitchener (consul general of Egypt), a mutual friend of Lordy and Lynch.

[1013] Lynch was author of *Egyptian Sketches* (1891), "a work that the book reviewers promptly termed a classic. It was commented upon by the Athenaeum Club and the London Spectator for its vivid portrayal of true Egyptian life and scenery." He also wrote a sketch called "The Lady of Isis" with illustrations of the mummy. Lynch also had knowledge of Egyptian hieroglyphics.

[1014] Tony Leadbetter referring to Almina's recollection of her daughter Lady Evelyn's comments.

[1015] All the reports qualify themselves using language of this kind, indicating that no one knew the cause of Lordy's. The Carnarvon family called the tune from the start of Lordy's illness. It was referred to as "a mosquito bite on the face". Lady Evelyn controlled statements from the start until her mother arrived in Cairo. Other reports refer to the bite being from a spider – several infer that this was the shape assumed by the gods reeking revenge on Lordy for breaching the tomb of the pharaohs. Lordy's initial symptoms were "lassitude, headache, breathlessness and enlarged glands".

[1016] A more detailed, medical analysis of Lordy's death (by a Canadian, Ann M. Cox) is to be found in *The Lancet*, Vol. 361, 7 June 2003.

[1017] A theory (from 1975) of Dr George Dean of Dublin: "We may never know for certain, but the evidence strongly suggests that Lord Carnarvon's death was due to inhalation of dust... from dried bat droppings in the passage leading to King Tutankhamun's tomb."

[1018] One of these was Dr Frank Cole Madden, FRCS (1873-1929), a cancer expert (in dietary diseases and parasitic worms). Cole Madden is also the author of a book *Syphilis in Egypt*. He committed suicide. Another attendant was Dr William Fletcher-Barrett, MB, BS London, a Cairo physician. Fletcher-Barrett died in France in 1935. He signed Carnarvon's death certificate which is full of errors of fact relating to the Earl's name, his date of birth and the duration of his last illness.

[1019] The author, with Tony Leadbetter, made a nostalgic trip to the village of Bicknoller, Somerset, on 18 April 2012. Almina lived here at Orchard Grove from 1943–1949. Several villages (and their present-day relations) spoke about Almina. Two sources revealed "Almina always said that Lord Carnarvon died from throat cancer". Tony Leadbetter comments " Almina said that Carnarvon was a heavy cigar and cigarette smoker – when he usually used a "holder" – and he had a collection of tobacco pipes from Germany".

[1020] Private source, please contact the Author for more details.

[1021] Email exchange with the author in July 2012.

[1022] As far back as 1886 – when he was aged 20 – evidence in the Carnarvon Papers, British Library, Add 61059, reveals a serious medical issue. Lordy's tutor (V.H. Stanton) at Trinity College, Cambridge, wrote to the 4th Earl on 10 December 1886: "I was obliged to excuse him [Lordy] from College lectures, owing to his suffering for some time in the mornings from bleeding in the mouth. "

[1023] Interviews with Tony Leadbetter 2009–12.

[1024] As well as four doctors and nurses attending on the dying Earl, Almina kept night vigils at Lordy's bedside (relieved by Lady Evelyn).

[1025] This informant is unknown. Among the possible "friends" to go to South America (in 1888) with Lordy and Victor (who were still alive in 1923) was Hon. Alexander McDonnell (1857–1945), chief clerk of the House of Lords. He was a son of the 5th Earl of Antrim and elder brother of Hon. Schomberg Kerr McDonnell (1861–1915) who was sometimes Lordy's tutor. Alexander McDonnell was an occasional gun at shooting parties with Lordy and the Singh brothers at Bretby, Bingham and Highclere. See *Reading Mercury* 7 October 1893. Another gentleman with Lordy in South America is less easy to identify, he is only recorded as being a " Mr Sutherland". One other possible candidate who was greatly upset by Lordy's death was Frederick Robinson, (1852-1923), 2nd Marquess of Ripon, best known in his peak years as "Earl de Grey". Alongside the Singh brothers he was a regular gun with Lordy, and dubbed the best shot in England. He attended Lordy's memorial service in London on 30 April 1923. There is also a Herbert family tie, Lady Ripon (his wife, who died in 1918) was a sister of the 13th Earl of Pembroke. Earl de Grey died on 23 September 1923.

[1026] *Nottingham Evening Post*, 9 April 1923.

[1027] Hugh Hampton Young, MD (1870–1945). Head of urology at the Johns Hopkins Institute, Baltimore, Maryland, USA. He was a pioneering surgeon in the treatment of prostate cancer, and inventor of "the Young Punch" used in prostatectomy procedures.

[1028] Interviews and correspondence with Tony Leadbetter 2009-12.

[1029] Young, H., *Hugh Young, a Surgeon's Autobiography*, Harcourt, Brace& Co. (1940).

[1030] Private source. Refer to the author for further details.

[1031] Mercury was a common (and successful) treatment for syphilis. See Blom, Ida, *Medicine, Morality and Political Culture: Legislation on Venereal Disease in Five Northern Eurpean Countries, c1870–c1995*, Nordic Academic Press (2012). According to Peter Clarke in *Mr Churchill's Profession* (Bloomsbury Books, 2012) Dr Robson Roose (Lordy's doctor at the time in the 1888–9 when the malady was diagnosed), with another Society doctor, prescribed mercury treatment for Lord Randolph Churchill, a well-known victim of syphilis.

[1032] See also Cross, William, *Lady Carnarvon's Nursing Homes: Nursing the Privileged in Wartime and Peace* (2011) This contains an illustrated (mini) biography of Elsie's War and later years.

[1033] Some further details about George and Margaret can be found in Bell, Vanessa. *Sketches In Pen and Ink*, edited by Lia Giachero, Random House (1998).

[1034] Following Victor's bankruptcy and associated social stigma, the Duleep Singhs made Paris their home. See also *The Life and Secrets of Almina Carnarvon*.

[1035] These matters are fully described in *The Life and Secrets of Almina Carnarvon*. A fourth edition of the title will appear in the autumn of 2012.

[1036] Friedman, Dennis, *Inheritance, A Psychological History of the Royal Family*, Sidgwick & Jackson (1993).

[1037] The British Library Copyright Department stresses (without accepting their advice constitutes a legal opinion).. " Despite the long copyright duration of unpublished works there are exceptions in UK law that allow publicly accessible copies of unpublished works which are older than 100 years and where the author has been dead for 50 years, to be made available and even subsequently published. However it is generally advised that if the copyright resides with an extant titled family that they should be contacted prior to publication." The author has contacted the 4th Earl's great grandson to no response.

[1038] The Society of Authors written guidelines on the other hand state "if an author died before 1st August 1989, works not published during his/her lifetime remain in copyright until 50 years from the end of the year of first posthumous publication or until 1st January 2040, whichever is the sooner." Source material / extracts from the diaries was published 1923 by Lady Winifred Burghclere and in 1925 by Elsie, the 4th Countess.

The Author : William Cross, FSA Scot

About the Author: William Cross (Will) spent 28 years as a Civil Servant in London. He took early retirement in July 2005 to concentrate on writing and research. His roots are Scottish, although he now lives in Wales. He is the author of many articles and booklets on Scottish history and genealogy topics. A Fellow of the Society of Antiquaries of Scotland since 1984, he is an authority on the Morgan women of Tredegar House, the one time seat of the Lords Tredegar. Will is also a member of the Society of Authors. He has written three books on the life and times of Almina, Countess of Carnarvon and is co-author of *A Beautiful Nuisance : The Life and Death of Hon. Gwyneth Ericka Morgan.* [Copyright to William Cross, FSA Scot (2012) and Alfred Jones Ph.D(Introduction) (2012).] Contact William Cross at williecross@aol.com

Titles From William Cross, FSA Scot

The Life and Secrets of Almina Carnarvon : A Candid Biography of Almina, 5th Countess of Carnarvon. 3rd Edition . ISBN 9781905914081

Lady Carnarvon's Nursing Homes: Nursing the Privileged in Wartime and Peace. ISBN 9781905914036

The Dustbin Case : Dennistoun versus Dennistoun ISBN 9781905914043

Lordy! Tutankhamun's Patron As A Young Man. ISBN 9781905914050

Titles From Book Midden Publishing

A Beautiful Nuisance by Monty Dart and William Cross. ISBN 9781905914104

Daphne's Story : The Long Journey from the Red Brick Building by Daphne Condon. ISBN 9781905914128

Steaming Light : by Bernard Pearson. ISBN 9781905914135

The Dancing Countess of Carnarvon: Tilly Losch & Her Husbands. By William Cross ISBN 9781905914098   [To be published 2013]

The Court Martial of Evan, Viscount Tredegar by Monty Dart and William Cross. ISBN 9781905914142 [To be published 10 December 2012]

Contact William Cross by e-mail williecross@aol.com

.....In his last illness Lord Carnarvon put up a brave fight but sank rapidly shortly after midnight. His wife, Almina, his daughter Lady Evelyn Herbert, and his heir, Henry, Lord Porchester, were summoned hastily. Physicians earnestly tried to save " Lordy" by administering artificial respiration but he drifted into unconsciousness..... He was 56 years old....

The death certificate records that he died at 1.45 am. But what (or who) killed Carnarvon?

Almina ignored the accounts of bites and curses; no historian or commentator ever noted her input on the Egyptian years until long after her death....but she was none the less fascinated by the published material on her husband and Carter. She was blase about some, but overtly hostile to others remarking..that the narratives were often inaccurate. She declared "it was nothing like that....no, nothing like that at all"......

Now, at long last the truth can be revealed in this book. " Lordy!"